Minster Churches
in the Dorset Landscape

Teresa Anne Hall

BAR British Series 304
2000

This title published by

Archaeopress
Publishers of British Archaeological Reports
PO Box 920
Oxford
OX2 7YH
England
www.archaeopress.com

BAR 304

Minster Churches in the Dorset Landscape

Printed in England by The Basingstoke Press

ISBN 1 84171 075 X

All BAR titles are available from:

Hadrian Books Ltd
122 Banbury Road
Oxford
OX2 7BP
England

The current BAR catalogue with details of all titles in print, prices and means of payment is available free from Hadrian Books

For my parents

Synopsis

This study was presented for the degree of M. Phil in the department of English Local History at Leicester University in May 1997. This thesis examines the minster churches of Dorset in relation to their immediate and intermediate environs within the context of the recent minster debate. It begins with the identification of high-status churches through the use of a table of weighted characteriestics. These high-status churches divide into three types: primary minsters, monastically or episcopally owned churches and Alfredian foundations. The *parochiae* of the minsters are compared with the units of royal demesne and the hundreds leading to the conclusion that both were based on the original royal estates. Many of the minster settlements have river names (a strong determining characteristic) resulting from the royal demesne consisting of large geographically-based units with river names. The boundaries of the *parochia*, where discernible, followed influential landscape features (rivers and watersheds) to a greater extent than the subsequently formed parish boundaries which delineate the estate units that the royal estates broke down into in the late 9th / 10th centuries. Examination of the previously suggested relationship between minsters and villas in Dorset (which led to claims that the Saxon church in Dorset merely filled in an existing British system) found no direct link between the two: more roman remains were found in association with minor churches than with minsters.

The morphology of the settlements of the high-status churches was investigated revealing areas of rectilinear planning centred on the minsters around which medieval suburbs had grown leading to the conclusion that the dominant form of enclosure around the primary minsters of Dorset was rectilinear. The factor of very sparse evidence for continuity of British Christianity together with the uniform rectilinear planning of the minsters along 'Roman' lines in new locations is seen as pointing to a suppression of the British church probably as a result of the victory of the Roman faction at the synod of Whitby and the reinforcement of that stance by archbishop Theodore and his Wessex pupil Aldhelm, first bishop of Selwood.

Acknowledgements

My foremost thanks must go to my family, Michael, Peter and Katy, for their encouragement and forbearance during the production of this work. I am entirely indebted to my supervisor, Dr Harold Fox, for his unstinting guidance and patience. I also owe a debt of gratitude to my examiners, Christopher Taylor and Professor Charles Phythian Adams for their helpful comments. Many of my Dorset friends have provided useful discussion, principally Peter Woodward, June and Richard Warmington, Ann Sims, David Reeves and the late Norman Field, along with my fellow students in the Department of English Local History at Leicester, Dr Graham Jones and Dr Michael Thompson. My new friends in Somerset have also offered helpful advice and much encouragement, especially Professor Mick Aston, Dr Michael Costen, Nick Corcos and Sue Fitton. I am grateful to those who have read various drafts, in particular, Dr John Blair, James Bond and Dr Paul Hindle. Professor Dilke kindly supplied information on the agrimensor Hyginus Gromaticus. The work has been much facilitated by access to the library at Downside Abbey, for which I wish to thank Dom Daniel Rees and Mrs Bridget de Salis. Those in the Dorset Library Service, particularly the staff at Wimborne Library, were indispensable in accessing papers. The staff of the Dorset County Museum were exceedingly helpful, particularly the former curator Roger Peers. Claire Pinder, keeper of the Dorset Sites and Monuments Record supplied much archaeological information, and the staff of the Dorset Record Office spent many hours making available the relevant maps.

CONTENTS

LIST OF FIGURES

LIST OF TABLES

LIST OF PLATES

ABBRIEVIATIONS

Alfred	S Keynes and M Lapidge, 1983, *Alfred the Great: Asser's Life of King Alfred and Other Contemporary Sources*
Arch J	*Archaeological Journal*
ASC	M J Swanton, trans and ed., 1996, *The Anglo-Saxon Chronicle*
BAR	British Archaeological Reports
CAD	*A Descriptive Catalogue of Ancient Deeds in the Public Record Office*
CDF	*Calendar of Documents Preserved in France Illustrative of the History of Great Britain and Ireland* I
CLR	*Calendar of Liberate Rolls Preserved in the Public Record Office Henry III AD 1245-1251*
CPL	*Calendar of Papal Letters*
CPR	*Calendar of Patent Rolls Preserved in the Public Record Office*
DB	F Thorn and C Thorn, eds, 1983, *Domesday Book: Dorset*
DGPA	William of Malmesbury, *De Gestis Pontificum Anglorum*, Rolls Series 52 (1870)
DPN	*Dorset Place*-Names, A D Mills, 1977-89, *The Place-Names of Dorset* 1-3, English Place-Name Society
DRO	Dorset County Record Office
Dorset Records	E A Fry and G S Fry, eds, 1896, *Dorset Records: Full Abstracts of the Feet of Fines Relating to the County of Dorset, remaining in the Public Record Office, London, from their commencement in the Reign of Richard I*
DS,	*Devonshire Studies*
HER	*Economic History Review*
EME	*Early Medieval Europe*
Hutchins	J Hutchins, 3rd edn, 1861-70, *History and Antiquities of Dorset* 1-4
IPM	*Calendar of Inquitistions Post Mortem and Other Analogous Documents Preserved in the Public Record Office*
JBAA	*Journal of the British Archaeological Association*
JEPNS	*Journal of the British Place-Name Society*
JHG	*Journal of Historical Geography*
Leland	J Leland, 1774, *De Rebus Britannicus Collectanea* 4
LHA	*Lincolnshire History and Archaeology*
MA	*Medieval Archaeology*
Monasticon	J Caley, H Ellis and B Bandinel, eds, 1817-30, *Monasticon Anglicanum: A New Edition* 1-6,
Nonarum	G Vanderzee, 1807, *Nonarum Inquisitiones in Curia Scaccarii. Temp. Regis Edwardi III* Record Commission
Osmund	W R Jones, 1883, *Vetus Registrum Sarisberiense alias dictum Registrum S Osmundi Episcopi*
OUCA	Oxford University Committee for Archaeology
PDNHAS	*Proceedings of the Dorset Natural History and Archaeological Society*
RCHM	Royal Commission on Historical Monuments
RJC	T C B Timmins, ed., 1984, *The Register of John Chandler 1407-17*
RSG	C T Flowers and M C B Dawes, eds, 1934, *Registrum Simonis de Gandavo Diocesis Saresbiriensis AD 1297- 1315*
S	P H Sawyer, ed, 1968, *Anglo-Saxon Charters: An annotated List and Bibliography.*
Sarum	W R Jones and W D Macray, 1891, *Charters and Documents Illustrating the History of the Cathedral, City and Diocese of Salisbury in the Twelfth and Thirteenth Centuries*
SMR,	Sites and Monuments Record for Dorset
Taxatio	J Caley, 1834, *Taxatio Ecclesiastica Angliae et Walliae, Auctoritate P Nicholai IV*, circa *AD 1291* Record Commission
TRE	*Tempore Regis Edwardi*
TBGAS	*Transactions of the Bristol and Gloucestershire Archaeological Society*
TDA	*Transactions of the Devonshire Association*
TSSAHS	*Transactions of the South Staffordshire Archaeological and Historical Society*
VCH	*The Victoria History of the Counties of England*

CHAPTER ONE: INTRODUCTION

Introduction to the 'minster model'

Over the last twenty years or so huge steps forward have been made in the comprehension of the organization of Saxon Christianity. It has been proposed that from about the end of the seventh century a system of mother-churches or minsters was established providing parochial care for the countryside within well-defined adjoining territories which corresponded closely with areas of estate and judicial administration. This model, which has its roots in the work of Page, has been extended by localized research, in the first instance by Kemp around Berkeley, and by Hase for Hampshire (Page 1915; Kemp 1968; Hase 1975). The most recent work has been synthesized by Blair, the chief proponent of the theory (Blair 1985; 1988a; Blair and Sharpe 1992). The aim of this thesis is to study the minster churches of Dorset in their local context against this model. Initially this involves the identification of the minsters and their areas of influence, the *parochiae*. The relation of the minsters to the surrounding landscape in both their immediate and intermediate environs will be examined in an attempt to elucidate the date and circumstance of their foundation, and their subsequent influence on the development of Dorset.

In essence, the minster model, as it has come to be defined, proposes the Saxon foundation of churches staffed by different types of communities of religious. The terminology describing these churches in the literature current at the time of their foundation was not sophisticated enough, or it was not considered important enough, to differentiate between the various types of foundations, and they were all referred to as *monasteria* in Latin or *mynsters* in the vernacular. As the term 'monastery' conjures up pictures of enclosed orders to our modern minds, it has been seen as prudent to use the term 'minster' to describe these early churches as it has less modern connotations (Foot 1992, 225). Minsters are sometimes referred to as mother-churches, but this term covers a wider range of churches as any church with a dependent chapel can be described thus. Minster churches appear to have been founded as part of royal policy in some areas, and were often central to royal or episcopal estates (Hase 1988, 48). The staff of the early minster communities are thought to have served large surrounding areas which have been termed *parochiae* and probably consisted of the royal or episcopal estates.[1] The evidence for these *parochiae* derives from their survival, though often in a depleted form, into the middle ages and beyond in some cases, and from clues suggesting the former dependency of other churches and chapels on the minsters. As the large royal estates served by the minsters split up, manorial church foundations took place on the new independent land units. The minster churches exercised rights, evolving from the necessity to guard their income, over these 'daughter' churches including such practices as a monopoly on burial at the minster site, thus hampering the passage of newly founded churches to independence. Strong minster churches often retained their daughter churches as chapels until after the Reformation.

The minster model has been brought into question recently by Rollason and Cambridge, who believe that many of the minsters referred to in contemporary literature were essentially enclosed monasteries with no pastoral dealings with the surrounding countryside. They see the characteristics of minster churches as possibly arising from a reorganization of the church in the post-Viking period, brought about by Carolingian influence. Rollason and Cambridge argue against the formation of local parishes as they now exist through the disintegration of the *parochiae* system, attributing parish formation to reforms linked with the introduction of compulsory tithe payments. Their statement that the fragmentation of minster *parochiae* would have been unlikely to have taken place in this country because of the strength of the Crown does not fit the facts. Numerous local studies have shown the breaking-up of minster *parochiae* into smaller parishes with manorial churches often as the result of the disintegration of royal estates. As will be shown below, Dorset has several examples of *parochiae* where fragmentation was only partial and the minsters retained very large parishes with subject chapels. This is not suggestive of the 'imposition of a hierarchical system' (Cambridge and Rollason 1995, at 101). Most of the objections of Cambridge and Rollason have been addressed by Blair in his reply to their paper (Blair 1995).

Within the county of Dorset, two main works have begun the investigation of minsters and their *parochiae*; Keen in his paper on Anglo-Saxon towns, and Hinton in 'Minsters and royal estates in south-east Dorset' (Keen 1984, 203-247; Hinton 1987, 50-4). The remit of Keen's article necessitated the restriction of his coverage, albeit extremely thorough, to those minsters situated in the Saxon towns of the county. Hinton's work was restricted to the south-eastern part of the county where he showed that a similar coverage existed to that proposed by Hase for Hampshire. The minsters of Dorset have also been addressed as part of larger regional studies mainly by Pearce in 1978, and by Hase in 1995 (Hase 1994, 47-81; Pearce 1978, 98-100). In the south-western counties, in particular, it has been suggested that the minster system overlies an earlier structure of British Christian churches (Hase 1994, 50-2). The evidence for this is seen to take the form of churches on villa sites, sub-Roman inscribed stones, churches with British dedications, and churchyards with a sub-circular form suggesting earlier British use. Pearce gave examples of minsters on villa sites in Dorset and also pursued the theme of estate continuity set rolling by Finberg with his investigation of Withington.[2] In a recent review of the early church in Wessex, Hase stated that 'the Middle-Saxon church in the west of the region must have been based almost entirely on a sub-Roman foundation' (Hase 1994, 51). This sweeping statement needs to be examined as the proposed correlation between minsters and villas in Dorset is not as clear cut as has been previously suggested.

The topography of minster sites has been reviewed by Blair, who suggested that the accepted view of different forms of enclosure being associated with Celtic and English foundations is largely imagined, and that 'remarkably few real distinctions can be sustained'. Blair examined the location of minsters, detecting a preference for waterside sites, often in the bends or at the confluence of rivers (Plate 1), and sites on promontories or on low hills, not only in Ireland, Scotland and Wales, but also in England and on the continent. Where evidence exists, minsters can be shown to have consisted of groups of churches laid out along an east-west axis (Blair 1992, 226-266).

Very little work has been done on the layout of minster settlements in Dorset. Keen comments incidentally on some of the minster settlements, mostly those associated with burhs. He notes that these display differing degrees of rectilinear planning attributable to the burh foundations, but that where previous settlement already existed it may have been incorporated into the burh plan as for example at Wareham, where the area around the church of Lady St Mary does not display the same degree of planning as other parts of the burh. Barker proposes that Sherborne itself, along with several other Dorset towns, was laid out as a large sub-circular enclosure surrounding a British Christian community (Barker 1982, 101-4). The Sherborne enclosure has come under much criticism from Keen as the British site of *Lanprobi*, with which Barker equates it, has been located elsewhere in the vicinity (Keen 1984, 209-19). Penn, who surveyed the towns of Dorset from an historical point of view for their archaeological potential, noted that the towns dominated by large ecclesiastical institutions showed similar street patterns (Penn 1980, 6). Finally, Taylor included a chapter on the landscape of the towns of Dorset in his book in the *Making of the English Landscape* series. He noted that many of the county's market towns grew around minster settlements, and whilst now often little more than villages they were important centres in their day (Taylor 1970, 173-201). In addition to the above-mentioned works which look at groups of settlements, comment has been made on individual settlements such as Wimborne Minster by various writers and these will be noted in the appropriate places.

Wessex - The Political Background
Until the late seventh century the West Saxons were known by the name *Gewisse* (Yorke 1995, 34). Bede tells us that they consisted of Jutes and Saxons and their point of entry into the British Isles had been the Southampton area (*Bede*, 56). Yorke, however, having taken into consideration the archaeological evidence as well as the sparse literary sources has suggested that the heartland of the *Gewisse* was the area around Dorchester-on-Thames (Yorke 1995, 34-6). Because of pressure from Mercia, initial expansion from this area took place into Hampshire, and then south-westwards into Wiltshire and north Somerset. Throughout these early stages the *Gewisse* were pagan and it was not until the mission of bishop Birinus in 634 that the first steps were taken to convert them to Christianity. Cynegils was baptized in 635 with the Northumbrian king, Oswald, as his patron, and he immediately donated Dorchester-on-Thames to Birinus for his episcopal seat. The baptisms of the later kings, Cenwalh (646) and Caedwalla (688), are mentioned in the *ASC* but it is only with the succession of Ine that Christianity appears to have become much more established (*ASC*, 26,40).[3] The lack of pagan cemeteries in Dorset implies that Christianity was the accepted religion when Dorset was conquered.

The consolidation of Christianity in Wessex may have been accelerated by the arrival of Theodore in 668. One of his first acts was to install new bishops (Leuthere in Wessex) and to instigate annual synods (Bischoff and Lapidge 1994, 134-5). Roman (as opposed to Celtic) Christianity had begun its rise to ascendancy with the Synod of Whitby in 664 at which the Celts were defeated over matters such as the date of Easter and the form of tonsure (see below pp 82-3). In addition to the strengthening of the framework of the English church, Theodore enforced the Roman teaching.[4] Following the synod of Hertford, Aldhelm, a pupil at the Canterbury school of Theodore and Hadrian and later to become first bishop of Sherborne, was commissioned to write to the British about their erroneous observance of Easter (Lapidge and Herren 1979, 140-3, 155-60). The introduction of Ine's law code states that the laws were formulated with the help of two bishops indicating the important role that Christianity had assumed in West Saxon affairs. It was against this background that the Saxon infiltration of Dorset took place, probably in the third quarter of the seventh century following the defeat of the British at Penselwood in 658. The foundation of the minster churches may well have occurred towards the end of the seventh and in the beginning of the eighth centuries.

Method
The minsters will be identified using a system of weighted characteristics which will isolate churches of high-status within the county. These churches will then be analyzed as a group. Whilst in some cases the identification of the minsters is fairly straight-forward, and likewise the identification of many churches of lesser status is also simple, there are a group of churches with intermediate status whose origins are by no means clear. The collation of evidence for these different groups may well enlighten their origins. The *parochiae* of the high-status churches will be examined, along with their relationship to the landscape, the ancient royal demesne, and the later systems of hundreds. In the final chapter the immediate environs of the minsters, *i.e.* the form of the settlement in which they stand, will be analyzed for any signs that might elucidate their origins. Throughout the study the analysis of place-names will be used where appropriate.

A map of the parishes of Dorset as they existed at the time of the tithe survey is attached in Appendix 1. For each of the high-status churches examined (Chapter 2 and Appendix 2) a map has been produced showing the possible extent of the *parochia*. The boundaries are based mainly on evidence from the tithe maps. All of the *parochiae* maps are on the same scale. Because of suggested links with geographical areas such as river basins, rivers or streams rising beyond the limits of the maps are indicated with a double arrow, and a single arrow indicates direction of flow away from the *parochia*. In Chapter 4, where the plans of the minster settlements are analyzed, three different maps are used for each settlement. The first shows the plan of the settlement in the earliest form that can be reconstructed with any accuracy with the churchyard shaded diagonally; the second is a sketch plan of the settlement indicating phases of growth etc.; and the third is a contour map showing the settlement in its immediate environs. All corresponding maps are drawn on the same scale for ease of comparison.

Terminology

The term minster will be used for all churches staffed by groups of religious, founded between the Saxon conquest of Dorset and the middle of the ninth century when the system may have been disrupted by Viking incursions and the measures taken by Alfred to deter them. As noted above, the terms minster and mother-church are sometimes seen as being interchangeable. However, whilst most minsters are likely to have been mother-churches, mother-churches were not necessarily minsters. The term *parochia* is used to refer to the area of influence of the minster churches whilst 'parish' refers to the areas attached to churches at the time of the tithe survey. Various types of chapel developed within the *parochiae* and these will be categorized below p 5. The terminology associated with the analysis of the plans of the minster sites will be defined in Chapter 4.

---

[1]The term *parochiae* originally applied the extent of a bishop's jurisdiction but it has been brought into use to describe the area served by a minster in order to distinguish it from the parish system of today.

[2]Most of the sites proposed have been put forward by Pearce, but as will be shown below pp 21-4 they do not form the neat group she suggests (Pearce 1978, 98-100; Pearce 1982, 117-138; Finberg 1955).

[3] See, for instance, his laws (Whitelock 1995, 398-407).

[4]The first canon of the Synod of Hertford (672/3) was an affirmation of the Roman teaching on the date of Easter (*Bede*, 187-192, 214-17).

CHAPTER TWO:
THE IDENTIFICATION OF MINSTER CHURCHES

Within the county of Dorset, few minster identifications can be made through the written record alone. Because of this lack of literary evidence other sources have to be utilized in order to attempt to identify the key churches of pre-Alfedian Dorset. There are many characteristics arising from the nature of minsters and their *modus operandi* that can point to minster status, some of which are more significant than others. These are identified and examined in this chapter and weighted to produce a system for use as a tool in minster church recognition within the county.[1] The churches thus singled out as possible minsters are then examined and additional characteristics identified.

Evidence from post-Conquest sources, sometimes as late as the Reformation, is employed in this method of identification. Until recently it has been seen as reliable because of the 'innate conservatism of ecclesiastical authority' (Blair 1991, 91). Doubts have been raised by Cambridge and Rollason (1995) on the date of some of the characteristics that are seen to epitomize minsters which cast suspicion on this statement. In defence of their reliability Blair notes that there is a high correlation between churches recorded as pre-Viking minsters and those that exist in the middle ages with minster characteristics (Blair 1995, 199-201). The specificity of the characteristics to minster churches when met *en masse* makes them a valid tool in minster recognition. However, the two main questions raised in the minster debate will be borne in mind in the examination of the Dorset evidence: firstly, whether the earlier foundations had parochial functions; and secondly, can any differences be drawn between foundations of the later Saxon period and their functions and those that existed in the pre-Viking period? The main problem in examining the evidence is that successive layers of foundation mask the earlier state of affairs. This is particularly true of the monastic reform of the tenth century: it is difficult if not impossible to discern earlier arrangements in such cases as Cerne, Milton Abbas, and Abbotsbury. In addition, if the whole system was re-arranged by Alfred some three-quarters of a century before Dunstan's monastic reform, as suggested by Rollason and Cambridge, the original minster system may be obscured indeed. It is probable, however, that any rearrangement by Alfred in Wessex was connected with his defensive measures and may be related to the foundation of the burhs.

The Characteristics of Minster Status

The indications of minster status can be divided into three types; literary, economic, and physical. The most conclusive evidence for the presence of a minster church is obviously the mention of a minster or monastery in early sources; the literary evidence. As already noted, this is sparse for Dorset and clues to minster status must be gleaned from the economic standing of the churches as well as from their physical characteristics. It has to be stressed from the outset that the possession of a single characteristic may have little significance: it is only when many characteristics occur together that higher status is implied.

Literary evidence

A literary reference to a *mynster* or *monasterium* before 950 almost certainly indicates a minster church. After this date the Benedictine reform of the tenth century was initiated and monasteries referred to from 950 onwards cannot be discounted as new creations. Early sources mentioning minsters include such texts as *Bede* and the *Anglo-Saxon Chronicle*, *vitae*, charters and wills. A small group of Dorset minsters are known through literary sources: Wimborne Minster, Sherborne, Beaminster and Wareham. The next most significant literary reference is to a group of priests or canons before 1150. Church reforms in the twelfth century led to the introduction of stricter rules for groups of clerks so that after about 1150 new canonical foundations were established and later literary mentions may represent new foundations. Canons are mentioned at Wareham before 1150 (Levien 1872, 246) and a further two such groups of priests occur in Dorset at Canford and Powerstock, though both slightly after 1150 (below pp 90, 95). A literary reference of lesser import is the occurrence of the word *church* or *minster* in place-names before 950. Two places, Sturminster Marshall and Whitchurch Canonicorum, both of which are mentioned in Alfred's will, fall into this category. There is also a reference in a ninth-century charter to a *monasteriunculo* dedicated to St Michael at Halstock (O'Donovan 1988, 6) but this diminutive of the Latin word for monastery probably implied something less than a minster church, possibly a hermitage or cell. A further type of significant literary reference is to a royal burial. From the seventh to the tenth century royal burial took place in important family churches, often those at the centre of royal estates.[2] Dorset examples are Aethelred at Wimborne, Beorhtric at Wareham, and Aethelbald at Sherborne. The final literary clue is a dedication to a local Anglo-Saxon saint, or the claim to be the resting-place of one, such as Cuthburh at Wimborne (Blair 1995, 203-4). Care has to be taken with such references as relics were accumulated by the reformed monasteries: Athelstan donated relics of Branwallader and Samson to Milton Abbey at its foundation. These, then, are the early literary references pointing to the existence of minster churches.

Economic evidence

The second body of evidence pertains to the wealth and ownership of the churches. Blair examined the Domesday evidence showing that minster churches are indicated by different economic factors such as independent ownership, a separate value, and ownership of land (Blair 1985, 106). In addition to the Domesday Book figures, two taxations, that of Pope Nicholas IV in 1291 and the 1340 *Inquisitiones Nonarum*, give values for many of the Dorset churches (*Taxatio*; *Nonarum*). A minimum value of £20 has been suggested as an indication of minster status (Hinton 1987, 50). By 1291, many church incomes had become fragmented through monastic ownership and in order to assess the total income of the church it is necessary to include the pensions, portions and the separate values of vicarages in the computation: discrepancies between values in the two taxations are often eliminated by this process.[3] Hospitals and churches of low value were exempt from the 1291 taxation (Graham 1929, 298-9). A comparison with the values of churches in the counties surrounding Dorset (see Table 1) indicates that churches in Dorset (and Devon) were generally

County	£0-4	£5-9	£10-14	£15-19	£20-24	£25-29	£30+
Dorset	40 (21%)	87 (45%)	26 (13%)	17 (9%)	15 (8%)	2 (1%)	5 (3%)
Som.	36 (12%)	111 (37%)	77 (26%)	14 (5%)	25 (9%)	10 (3%)	24 (8%)
Hants	14 (6%)	73 (32%)	53 (23%)	14 (6%)	21 (9%)	10 (5%)	44 (19%)
Wilts	20 (15%)	42 (31%)	25 (19%)	5 (4%)	13 (9%)	5 (4%)	24 (18%)
Devon	50 (19%)	119 (46%)	53 (21%)	16 (6%)	7 (3%)	4 (2%)	7 (3%)

Table 1. Numbers of churches of different values recorded in the 1291 *Taxatio* in Dorset and neighbouring counties. Percentages of the county total are shown in brackets.

less wealthy than those of Hampshire, Somerset and Wiltshire. Almost a third of the recorded churches in Hampshire and Wiltshire were worth over £20, whereas only about one eighth of those in Dorset achieved this value. (Devon churches were poorer still with only one twelfth reaching that value). This may indicate that there were fewer minsters in Dorset and Devon; or alternatively, that the minster churches of those two counties did not become as wealthy as those in Hampshire and Wiltshire. It seems safer to assume that there was a lower ratio of wealthy to poor churches in Devon and Dorset than the alternative of fewer minster churches established in the first instance. Therefore, the top third of the churches, *i.e.* those over £10, have been included as possibly having had minster status. The wealth of the churches is shown in Tables 9 and 10 (below pp 27,30).

Minster churches were usually founded either by members of royal families or by bishops (Blair 1985, 104). Consequently, churches in royal or ecclesiastical ownership had a greater chance of having been minsters than those in secular hands - ownership by laymen usually implying manorial church foundation. However, churches in lay ownership cannot be completely dismissed as Bede complained about the secular ownership of monasteries, instances of which are known from the Worcester diocese (Blair 1988a, 2-3).

The minsters were powerful churches overseeing large areas within which they controlled the foundation of lesser churches or chapels. References to chapels occur in many different sources: ecclesiastical records such as bishops' registers, papal letters, and the *Return to the Commission of 1650*; in documents contesting the ownership of advowsons; in antiquarian writings; and in place-name evidence.[4] The status of chapels was not fixed and many grew into fully fledged parish churches, technically known as independent parochial chapels. Some chapels took on all the characteristics of parish churches but did not gain independence: the dependent parochial chapels. Other types of chapels were: chantries, formed to pray for the souls of the departed; oratories which served as private chapels for households; and finally, a group comprising wayside, fishermen's, hilltop and bridge chapels, sometimes served by hermits (Owen 1975, 15). Some chapels occur in the records as 'free' chapels. These were established within the parish or *parochia* of another church but were not dependent on it for service, and they were not involved in cure of souls (with the exception of the King's free chapels which form a special case (Denton 1970, 9)). The free chapels appear to have been mostly either oratories or chantries and whilst they were free from interference from the parish church they were under the control of the bishop. It is important to identify the chapels in the county as these are the least likely group of churches to have been minsters (see Plate 2).[5]

Payments of certain dues and pensions to churches may indicate minster status. The most important of these, church scot, is 'one of the oldest and strongest signs of ancient minster status', and the main source of income of the early minster churches (Blair 1985, 116).[6] The payment of pensions and portions recorded in 1291 mostly reflect the ownership of the rectory or a portion of tithes by another ecclesiastical institution, but in some instances they record the earlier dependence of one church on another. Rose Graham tells us that a pension was a portion of tithes that had been transmuted into a monetary payment (Graham 1929, 273). Hutchins sees some of the pensions as payments in lieu of burial fees.[7] A good variety of economic indications of church superiority survive into the middle ages and, used in conjunction with other evidence, they help to identify the minster churches.

Physical evidence
The physical evidence includes indications such as size of parish, the structure of the church and its relation to other features such as Roman sites. The average size of Dorset parishes is roughly 2250 acres (Minchin 1908, 266-73) and the presence of a larger parish may represent the remnant of a minster *parochiae*. Some parishes have detached areas or tithings possibly indicating the dominance of one church over another, though this is not the only explanation of such links which may also arise through manorial control or commoning rights.[8] Architectural evidence is significant in the case of Saxon remains and cruciform plans where the tower's width is greater than any of the four arms of the church (see Plate 3).[9] Naves of over 50ft are taken to indicate possible signs of early high status (Hinton 1987, 50).[10] As it is has been suggested that there is a relationship between Roman remains and minster churches, especially in Dorset, evidence of Roman remains is included as a possible indication (Blair 1992, 241; Hase 1994, 50).

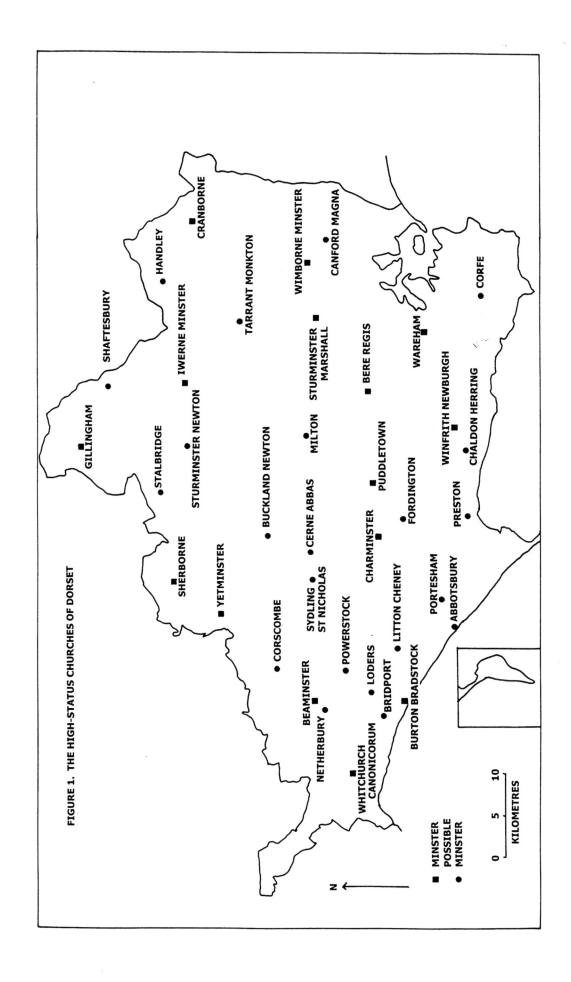

FIGURE 1. THE HIGH-STATUS CHURCHES OF DORSET

MINSTER

POSSIBLE
MINSTER

KILOMETRES

0   5   10

N

CRANBORNE

HANDLEY

WIMBORNE MINSTER

CANFORD MAGNA

TARRANT MONKTON

CORFE

SHAFTESBURY

IWERNE MINSTER

STURMINSTER
MARSHALL

BERE REGIS

WAREHAM

GILLINGHAM

STALBRIDGE

STURMINSTER NEWTON

BUCKLAND NEWTON

MILTON

PUDDLETOWN

WINFRITH NEWBURGH

CHALDON HERRING

SHERBORNE

YETMINSTER

CERNE ABBAS

CHARMINSTER

FORDINGTON

PRESTON

CORSCOMBE

SYDLING
ST NICHOLAS

POWERSTOCK

LITTON CHENEY

PORTESHAM

ABBOTSBURY

BEAMINSTER

LODERS

BRIDPORT

NETHERBURY

WHITCHURCH
CANONICORUM

BURTON BRADSTOCK

| CHURCH | CHARACTERISTICS | | | | | | | | | | | | | | | | | |
| | LITERARY | | | | | | ECONOMIC | | | | | | PHYSICAL | | | | | |
	Religious community before 950	Non-regular community 950-1150	Pre-conquest royal burial	Pre-conquest church reference	Place-name in minster or church	Saint's resting place	Domesday secular minster (after Blair)	Royal / ecclesiastical ownership TRE	Church value 1291 / 1340: £10-20; £20+	Dependant chapels	Pensions from other churches (not chapels)	Receipt of churchscot	Size of parish: 3-5000a; 5000a +	Cruciform church, pre-12C evidence	Saxon architectural remains	Length of nave, 50ft+	Roman remains or site	TOTAL
WIMBORNE	10	7	5	3	3	3	5	3	5	3	2	-	5	3	3	1	1	62
SHERBORNE	10	7	5	3	-	-	-	3	5	13	2	-	5	3	3	1	1	61
WHITCHURCH CANONICORUM	-	-	-	3	3	3	5	3	5	7	-	-	5	-	-	1	1	36
WAREHAM	-	7	5	-	-	-	5	3	-	1	5	-	-	-	3	1	1	31
GILLINGHAM	-	-	-	-	-	-	5	3	5	5	-	1	5	3	3	1	-	31
BERE REGIS	-	-	-	-	-	-	5	3	5	6	1	-	5	3	-	1	-	29
BEAMINSTER	10	-	-	-	3	-	-	3	-	1	-	-	5	3	-	1	-	26
CRANBORNE	-	-	-	-	-	-	3	5	2	4	-	-	5	-	3	1	-	23
STURMINSTER MARSHALL	-	-	-	3	3	-	-	3	5	3	-	-	5	-	-	-	-	22
CHARMINSTER	-	-	-	-	3	-	-	3	5	4	-	-	3	3	-	1	-	22
PUDDLETOWN	-	-	-	-	-	-	5	3	5	2	-	-	5	-	-	1	-	21
YETMINSTER	-	-	-	-	3	-	-	3	5	4	-	-	3	-	3	-	-	21
BURTON BRADSTOCK	-	-	-	-	-	-	5	3	3	5	-	-	3	-	-	1	-	20
IWERNE MINSTER	-	-	-	-	3	-	-	3	5	3	-	-	3	3	-	-	-	20
WINFRITH NEWBURGH	-	-	-	-	-	-	5	3	5	1	-	-	5	-	-	1	-	20
POWERSTOCK	-	2	-	-	-	-	-	3	5	6	-	-	3	-	-	-	-	19
CANFORD MAGNA	-	2	-	-	-	-	-	-	5	3	-	-	5	3	-	1	-	19
MILTON	10	-	-	-	-	-	-	3	3	-	-	-	3	-	-	-	-	19
PRESTON	-	-	-	-	-	-	-	3	3	1	9	-	3	-	-	-	-	19
NETHERBURY	-	-	-	-	-	-	-	3	5	3	1	-	5	-	-	1	-	18
BRIDPORT	-	-	-	-	-	5	-	-	3	4	-	-	-	3	-	1	-	16
BUCKLAND NEWTON	-	-	-	-	-	-	-	3	3	2	-	-	5	3	-	-	-	16
SYDLING ST NICHOLAS	-	-	-	-	-	-	-	3	5	2	-	-	5	-	-	1	-	16
STURMINSTER NEWTON	-	-	-	-	3	-	-	3	5	1	-	-	3	-	-	1	-	16
SHAFTESBURY	10	-	-	-	-	3	-	3	-	-	-	-	-	-	-	-	-	16
FORDINGTON	-	-	-	-	-	-	5	3	5	-	-	-	-	-	-	-	1	14
CHALDON HERRING	-	-	-	-	-	-	5	3	-	1	1	-	3	-	-	-	-	13
SIXPENNY HANDLEY	-	-	-	-	-	-	-	3	3	1	-	1	5	-	-	-	-	13
ABBOTSBURY	-	-	-	-	-	-	-	3	3	1	1	1	3	-	-	1	-	13
PORTESHAM	-	-	-	-	-	-	-	3	3	4	-	-	3	-	-	-	-	13
CORFE	-	-	-	-	-	-	-	3	3	1	-	-	5	-	-	-	-	12
STALBRIDGE	-	-	-	-	-	-	-	3	3	-	-	-	5	-	-	1	-	12
TARRANT MONKTON	-	-	-	-	-	-	-	3	5	1	-	-	3	-	-	-	-	12
CORSCOMBE	-	-	-	-	-	-	-	3	3	-	-	-	5	-	-	-	-	11
LITTON CHENEY	-	-	-	-	-	-	-	?	3	2	-	-	5	-	-	1	-	11
CERNE ABBAS	-	-	-	-	-	-	-	3	-	-	4	-	3	-	-	1	-	11
LODERS	-	-	-	-	-	-	-	3	5	1	-	-	-	-	-	1	-	10

Table 3. The high-status churches of Dorset

Type of Characteristic	Number of points
Literary	
Mention of minster/monastery before 950	10
Mention of group of priests 950-1150	7
Royal burial	5
Church / minster reference or place-name pre-DB	3
Saint's resting place	3
Physical	
Size of parish - 5000 acres +	5
3000-5000acres	3
Cruciform church	3
Saxon architectural remains	3
Nave length over 50ft in length	1
Roman site or remains	1
Economic	
DB reference (after Blair)	5
1291/1340 church valuation - £20+	5
£10-20	3
Royal or ecclesiastical ownership	3
Dependent chapels	1 each
Pension or portion from an independent church	1 each
Receipt of churchscot	1

Table 2 Values assigned to the minster characteristics.

Weighting of evidence (Table 2)

In order to make the best use of these characteristics, they have been weighted according to their importance. The weighting of each indication is relative within its group (literary, economic or physical), and the weighting of evidence of each group is relative to the others. The literary evidence is seen as the most important category. Within it, the authenticity and contemporary nature of the information carries most weight. Consequently a direct early mention warrants a score of 10, whilst a reference to a college of canons during the period 950-1150 scores 7, and a mention of a minster or church in a source predating the Conquest in a place-name merits a score of only three as it more likely to have other implications (such as ownership by a minster). The presence of a royal burial is significant and this scores 5 points. In the group of economic indications value is important. As this is generally lower in Dorset than in Hampshire, Wiltshire and Somerset (see above p 5), all churches valued over £10 have been assigned a score; 3 for a value between £10 and £20, and 5 for over £20. The number of chapels and pensions attached to a church is very relevant and one point is awarded for each chapel and similarly one for each pension or portion that is paid from an independent church to the church in question. A point is also gained for the receipt of church scot. Early evidence of royal or ecclesiastical ownership scores 3 points. In the third category, that of physical evidence, the most significant indication is parish size; a church scores 5 points for a parish

of over 5000 acres, and three points for between 3000 and 5000 acres. Saxon architectural remains and a cruciform church both score 3 points, and the use of a Roman site or materials, one point. Whilst it is a fairly straightforward matter to weight the indications within the groups it is more difficult to compare between them. Some of the features are obviously more indicative than others, however: a minster reference in the *Anglo-Saxon Chronicle* has to be assigned greater weight than a high valuation in 1291 or 1340, which would correspondingly be of more significance than the reuse of Roman material in the church building. This scoring system has to be seen as local to Dorset in its present form because of the differential survival of evidence in disparate localities and locational differences in parish size and wealth of churches, etc. However, it should provide a useful tool by which to produce objectively a list of churches for the county which may have had minster status.

The Possible Dorset Minsters

The characteristics of all the churches in the county have been assessed using the scoring system outlined above. This process resulted in the isolation of a group of thirty-seven high-status churches (see Fig 1 and Table 3) all of which scored over 10 points. A sample of these will be examined in detail below; the remainder are to be found in a gazetteer in Appendix II as the inclusion of them all at this point would lead to too great an interruption in the text.[11]

Wimborne Minster (Fig 2, Plates 1,3,4)

In 718 King Ine founded a monastery for his sister Cuthburh *aet Wimburnan* (ASC, 42-3). An early description of the monastery survives in Rudolf of Fulda's life of Leoba, a Wimborne nun recruited by Boniface. Wimborne was a double monastery, *unum scilicet clericorum et alterum feminarum*. Both communities were surrounded with high and stout walls, the nuns being very strictly enclosed.[12] This description may well exaggerate the divisionary aspect of the *vallum* at Wimborne as it comes from a *vita*, a class of work aimed at providing a good example for its readers and thus not necessarily factually correct (Ridyard 1988, 8-16). Thacker defines the term *clericus* as applying 'generally to all in ecclesiastical grades, or at least all who could not be described as *monachi*' (Thacker 1992, 139). The description of the male occupants of Wimborne as *clerici* implies that the male section of the monastery consisted of a group of clerics with parochial duties rather than enclosed monks. The nunnery was still in existence in 901 when the aetheling Aethelwold abducted one of the nuns when attempting to seize power by holding the royal manors of Wimborne and Christchurch (ASC, 92-3). Royal monasteries played an important role in the control of the kingdom by competing royal factions (Yorke 1990, 174). In 962 King Sigferth, who was possibly being held as a political prisoner at Wimborne, killed himself and was buried there, an indication that the monastery was still functioning at this time with a political role (ASC, 114). The demise of the monastery went unrecorded and the church next emerges as a college of secular canons, founded by Edward the Confessor, who is portrayed on the seal of the deanery (Hutchins 3, 226 and opp. 224). Wimborne thus became a Royal Free Chapel outside the control of the bishop (Denton 1970, 15).

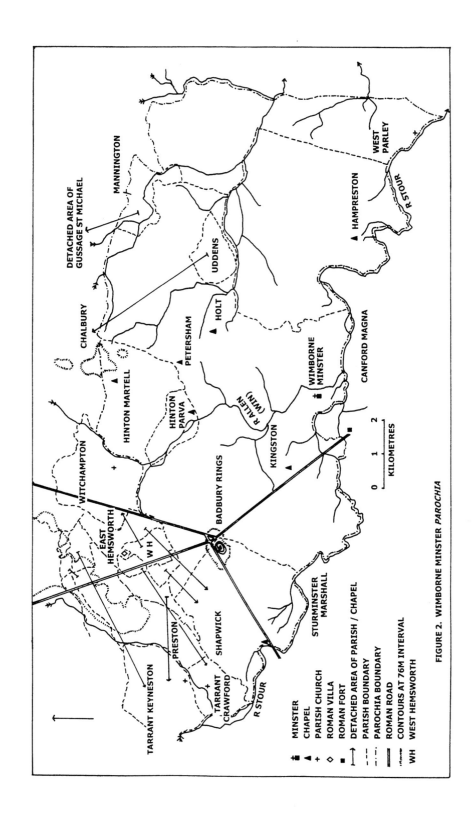

FIGURE 2. WIMBORNE MINSTER *PAROCHIA*

Legend:

MINSTER
CHAPEL
PARISH CHURCH
ROMAN VILLA
ROMAN FORT
DETACHED AREA OF PARISH / CHAPEL
PARISH BOUNDARY
PAROCHIA BOUNDARY
ROMAN ROAD
CONTOURS AT 76M INTERVAL
WH   WEST HEMSWORTH

0   1   2
KILOMETRES

Map labels:

MANNINGTON
DETACHED AREA OF GUSSAGE ST MICHAEL
CHALBURY
UDDENS
HINTON MARTELL
HINTON PARVA
PETERSHAM
HOLT
WEST PARLEY
HAMPRESTON
R STOUR
WIMBORNE MINSTER
CANFORD MAGNA
R ALLEN (WIM)
KINGSTON
WITCHAMPTON
BADBURY RINGS
EAST HEMSWORTH
W H
PRESTON
SHAPWICK
TARRANT KEYNESTON
TARRANT CRAWFORD
R STOUR
STURMINSTER MARSHALL

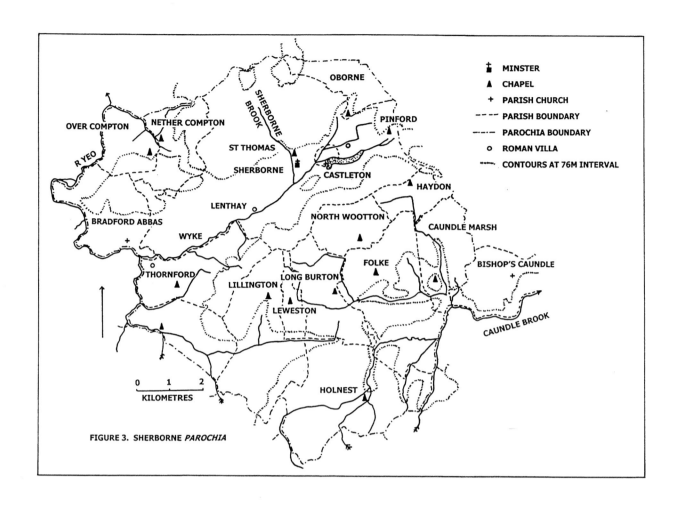

FIGURE 3. SHERBORNE *PAROCHIA*

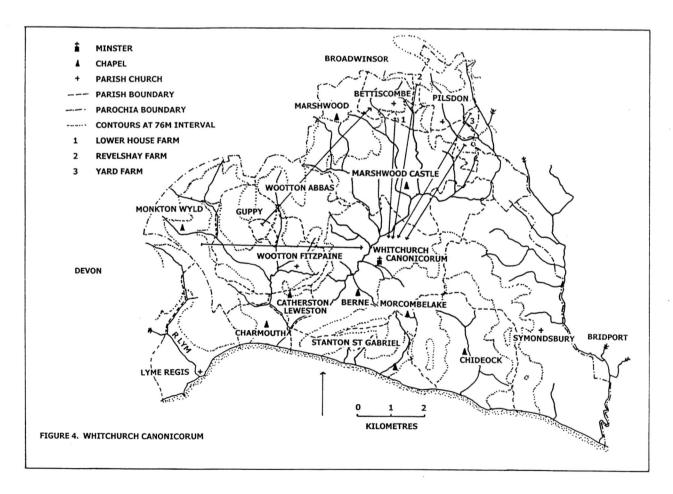

FIGURE 4. WHITCHURCH CANONICORUM

Wimborne's status as a minster church is reflected in the economic and physical aspects of the church and its *parochia* (Taylor 1970, 79; Blair 1985, 108, 131; Keen 1984, 230; Pearce 1978, 184; RCHM Dorset 5, 78; Hinton 1987, 50; Coulstock 1993). The building is cruciform and there are signs of late Saxon structure in the transepts and north-west turret (RCHM Dorset 5, xxxviii; Taylor 1978, 1077). The implications of the Domesday record have been discussed by Blair, who suggests that the landholdings of the minster priests at Hinton Martell may indicate a taking up of residence in outlying areas of the *parochia* (Blair 1985, 131). However, it may bear a different interpretation: the place-name *Hinton - hiwan tun -* 'farm or estate belonging to a religious community', suggests that the area was probably one of the original endowments of the minster possibly along with Hampreston (*DPN* 2, 146-7).

Wimborne Minster had five dependent chapels all of which eventually achieved independent status (Keen 1984, 227). The largest and wealthiest of these chapels was Shapwick, a valuable church with a chapel of its own. Two pensions were paid out of Shapwick church, 13s 4d to the Dean of Wimborne and £5 6s 8d to the prior of Wareham (*Taxatio*, 178). The portion to the Dean of Wimborne denotes its earlier dependency on Wimborne minster whereas that to the prior of Wareham resulted from the donation of the tithes of Shapwick and Kingston to the abbey of Lyre by Robert, Earl of Leicester in 1276 (*CAD* 6, 1915, 395). Blair has shown in Surrey that grants of tithes could 'override existing monastic interests' (Blair 1991, 148). The minster at Wimborne had rights over only the non-demesne tithe within the *parochia*. Hinton suggests that the wealth of Shapwick taken with the length of its nave may indicate minster status. However, as Shapwick was part of the royal demesne in Domesday Book, it is probably fairly safe to assume that it formed part of Wimborne's *parochia*. East Hemsworth was appended to Shapwick in 1356, but had been independent before that date and does not appear to belong in Wimborne's *parochia* (Hall 1993, 124). The place-name of Hampreston, another dependency - the *hamm* of the priests - suggests that it, too, may have formed part of the original endowment of the minster, though it had been alienated by the time of the Domesday record. Within the town of Wimborne, three other chapels are known to have existed: St Mary, owned by Horton Abbey at DB; St Peter, sited in the market place; and St Catherine to the east of the town. The minster at Wimborne, therefore, can be shown to have served a wide surrounding area as well as controlling worship within the town.

Sherborne (Fig 3)
Sherborne became an episcopal seat in 705 (Sherley-Price 1968, 303-4). The West Saxon conquest of the south-west peninsula led to an increase in size of the already large diocese of Wessex. Theodore (668-90) split many of the larger diocese but, possibly because of his friendship with Bishop Haedde, the event did not occur until after his death (Stenton 1971, 134).[13] Both Bede and the *Anglo-Saxon Chronicle* mention the division, but Sherborne itself is not mentioned in either text at that date being first mentioned in the *ASC* in 861 when King Aethelbald was buried there (*ASC*, 40-1, 69). Sherborne's status as a bishopric would undoubtedly mean that it possessed a cathedral church which would have served as a minster for its *parochia*.

The debate on the choice of Sherborne as episcopal seat has engendered suggestions of an already established church at Sherborne. Many of the bishoprics were sited in what formerly had been Roman towns, e.g. Winchester and Dorchester-on Thames, and Campbell suggested the possibility of the continuity of these places as centres of authority though not of population (Campbell 1979a, 119-20). Whilst some Roman remains have been recorded in Sherborne, it was not a Roman town.[14] As Keen points out, the choice of Sherborne may have been influenced by the ability of the king to grant a suitably large area of land to support the bishop (Keen 1984, 208-9). However, as the nearby site of Ilchester could have fulfilled both requirements, being a Roman town and royal demesne (Aston and Leech 1977, 67), Sherborne must have had other attractions. Fowler attributed the use of Sherborne to the presence of an already established ecclesiastical site because of the reputed grant of one hundred hides at *Lanprobi* by Cenwalh in 671, mention of which occurs in a fourteenth-century list of Sherborne Abbey's holdings and benefactors (Fowler 1951, 30-1; O'Donovan 1988, 84-99). The site of *Lanprobi* has been linked with Sherborne and has been, after much debate, convincingly located at the Old Castle site in Sherborne (see below p 53) (Stuart Best 1955; Finberg 1964, 98; Barker 1977, 127; Keen 1984, 209-12; O'Donovan 1988, 84-8).[15] The place-name *Lanprobi* is seen as indicative of the survival of a British Christian enclave in Sherborne: *llan*, an enclosure, especially a churchyard, coupled with *Probus*, a west country saint (*DPN*, 358; Padel 1988, 142-4; Farmer 1978, 408). The newly established bishopric did not centre itself on the old site, however, the cathedral being 0.5km to the west of the castle, on the Sherborne brook, a tributary of the river Yeo. This presents the possibility that the newly-founded Saxon cathedral *displaced* an existing community inheriting its lands. *Lanprobi* is recorded in its genitive form suggesting that the correct interpretation should be that the 100 hides *of Lanprobi* were given by Cenwalh, rather than a 100 hides at *Lanprobus* (which is the form O'Donovan suggests the name should have taken in the list of grants (O'Donovan 1988, 85)). The presence of a British community whose lands could be appropriated may have been the deciding factor in the situation of the bishopric. Having been established, Sherborne remained the head of an episcopal see (though much reduced in size in 909) until 1075 when the seat was transferred to Sarum.[16] The cathedral at Sherborne was staffed by canons until it was reformed by Bishop Wulfsige in 998 when the clerics were replaced by Benedictine monks but the abbacy remained part of the bishopric until 1122 (RCHM Dorset 1, xlvii).

The church of Sherborne has many economic factors indicating its importance including the possession of at least thirteen chapels (*Taxatio*, 182). In 1145, a Bull of Pope Eugenius citing properties of Sherborne Abbey mentions a chapel at Oborne, two appended to St Mary Magdalen next to the castle, and chapels appended to Bradford (*Monasticon* 1, 338). Hutchins lists chapels paying Pentecost money to the vicar of Sherborne as: Oborne, Caundle Marsh, Folke, Stockwood, Lillington, Holnest, Hermitage, Thornford, Beer Hacket, Nether Compton, Over Compton and Haydon (Hutchins 4, 263). In Lincolnshire Pentecost payments were made by parishes to the cathedral (Owen 1971, 107), but these are the only Dorset parishes where they are recorded:

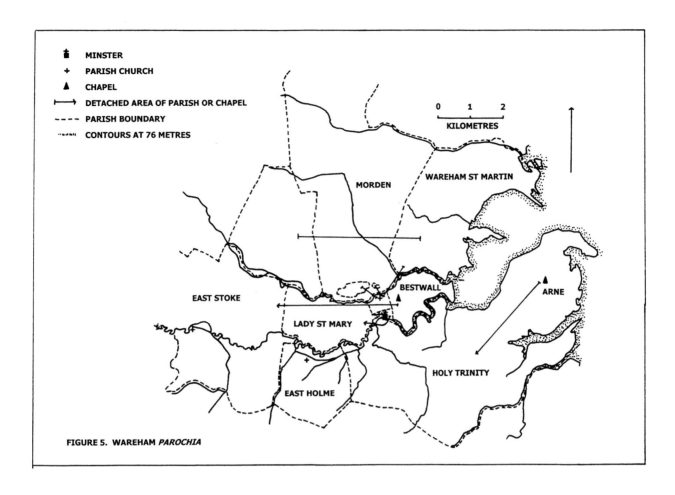

MINSTER
PARISH CHURCH
CHAPEL
DETACHED AREA OF PARISH OR CHAPEL
PARISH BOUNDARY
CONTOURS AT 76 METRES

0 1 2
KILOMETRES

MORDEN

WAREHAM ST MARTIN

EAST STOKE

BESTWALL

ARNE

LADY ST MARY

HOLY TRINITY

EAST HOLME

FIGURE 5. WAREHAM *PAROCHIA*

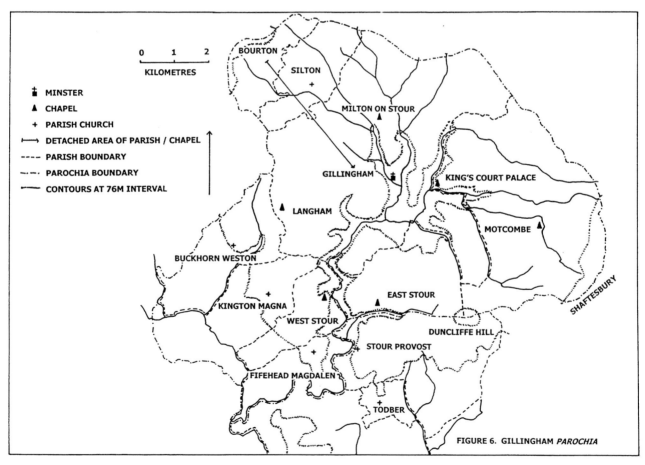

0 1 2
KILOMETRES

MINSTER
CHAPEL
PARISH CHURCH
DETACHED AREA OF PARISH / CHAPEL
PARISH BOUNDARY
PAROCHIA BOUNDARY
CONTOURS AT 76M INTERVAL

BOURTON

SILTON

MILTON ON STOUR

GILLINGHAM

KING'S COURT PALACE

LANGHAM

MOTCOMBE

BUCKHORN WESTON

SHAFTESBURY

KINGTON MAGNA

EAST STOUR

WEST STOUR

DUNCLIFFE HILL

STOUR PROVOST

FIFEHEAD MAGDALEN

TODBER

FIGURE 6. GILLINGHAM *PAROCHIA*

they may be a relict payment, surviving solely in the churches dependent on Sherborne. Of the chapels paying Pentecost money, two belong elsewhere: Stockwood was a chapel of Yetminster, and Hermitage was connected with the estates of the earl of Cornwall. Dean Chandler mentions further chapels at Pinford, Longburton, and St Thomas in the Green (in Sherborne) (*RJC*, 22,24). Other chapels existed in Sherborne itself: St Andrew in the southern part of the town, St Emerenciana on the north side of the town, St John in Castleton, and St Michael and St Probus, two chapels attached to St Mary Magdalen at Castleton (Fowler 1951, 107, 144, 208). Most of the above chapels were dependent on Sherborne for burial: the inhabitants of Over Compton were not granted a licence for sepulture until 1431, a classic, though late example of a parochial chapel gaining in status (*RJC*, 21; Hutchins 4, 170). Sherborne, therefore, can be seen to have had an extensive group of chapels dependent upon it, most of which remained so until after the Reformation.

The minster at Sherborne controlled a large parish which was divided only at the end of last century. The church had a cruciform plan incorporating a large central tower wider than any of its four arms, a feature of pre-Conquest cruciform churches (Gibb 1975, 71-110; RCHM 1, xlix-l). The discovery of a sarcophagus believed to contain the relics of King Aethelbert (d. 866) beneath the floor of the east end in 1840 suggests that the present cathedral stands on the site of the original church of *c*705. A west doorway in the northern aisle is Saxon, possibly dating to the time of Wulfsige who reformed the church. The form of the cathedral is more common on the continent than in this country, perhaps emphasizing the importance of the church at Sherborne (Taylor and Taylor 1965, 540-3; Taylor 1978, 991-2, 1004).

Whitchurch Canonicorum (Fig 4 and Plate 5)
Whilst there are no direct literary references to a minster at Whitchurch Canonicorum, the church, dedicated to St Candida (or St Wite) and the Holy Cross, displays several signs of minster status. Candida, now a unique dedication in this country, was a fourth century Roman martyr (Burne 1969, 272).[17] Both elements of this dedication are seen by Bettey and Arnold-Foster as being early (Bettey 1987, 22; Arnold-Foster 1899, 31-2, 124). The present church contains Roman brick and tile in the twelfth- and thirteenth-century rubble facing of the walls suggesting that a nearby site was robbed for building material at the time of construction of this or an earlier phase, or that the church sits on a villa or Roman building (Woolner and Woolner, 1962, 83). It may, therefore, be an example of a British monastery of fifth- or sixth-century date being subsumed into the minster system (as suggested by Hase, pp 21-4). If this was the case one might expect the saint to have been a male associated with the foundation of the monastery, as for example Carantoc, the founder of the monastery at Carhampton, Somerset. Alternatively, the relics of St Candida, which lie in the north transept of the church, may have been associated with the discovery of Roman remains. There are instances of Roman coffins having been exhumed and sainthood inflicted on the occupant, probably because the Roman processes of burial often preserved bodies, and an indication of sainthood was an incorruptible body (Morris 1989, 42-4). A large abbey such as St Wandrille's, into whose hands Whitchurch came in the tenth century, would have been fully aware of the financial advantages of having such relics and may well have believed they belonged to a saintly founder.[18] The obscurity of the dedication to Candida suggests that it was a back-formation from the Latin word for white, *candidus*, supposing Whitchurch to have been dedicated to St Wite, whereas the *hwit* element probably simply refers to a stone building, though this in itself suggests that it was more important than neighbouring structures (Smith 1956, 273-4).

Alfred bequeathed the royal manor of Whitchurch to his younger son, Athelweard and the superiority of the church is attested by the fiscal records (see below p 27) (*Alfred*, 175, 320). St Wandrille's surrendered the church to Sarum in 1200, and the advowson was acquired by Sir Richard de Mandevil who donated it to the bishop of Bath between 1231 and 1239 (Druitt 1898, 145-9). That bishop's attempt to appropriate the church to the chapter of Wells, led to the partitioning of the rectory. The 1240 appropriation includes a thorough description of the church's property and rights mentioning chapels at Stanton, Chideock and Marshwood served by chaplains appointed by the vicar.[19] Two further chapels, one at Charmouth, and the other *capella Willelmi de Charteray* at Catherston both paid pensions to the vicarage. A perpetual chaplain, appointed by the bishop of Bath, was to be alloted, amongst other things, 20s *p.a.* from the chapel of Wootton Fitzpaine (*Sarum*, 261-6). In addition to these, a chapel is recorded at Berne in Morecombelake in 1362 (Hutchins 2, 254). Controversy arose in the *parochia* as the lords of the manors strained for more independence for their chapels. The abbot of Malmesbury, as arbitrator, decided that William Hieron, lord of Charmouth, should be allowed to present to Charmouth chapel on payment of a mark of silver yearly, 'without contradiction of the mother church: saving the ancient parochial right of the mother church, concerning burials etc' (Hutchins 2, 270). Wootton Fitzpaine attained independence but other chapels such as Catherston, Stanton and Chideock remained dependent on Whitchurch until after the Reformation.

Wareham (Fig 5 and Plate 6, 7)
Evidence suggests that Wareham had a minster church, possibly in the form of a double monastery. Five British inscriptions, tentatively dated from the seventh to the eighth-ninth centuries, point to a British Christian survival at Wareham. The inscriptions came to light with the restoration of Lady St Mary church in 1841-2. The exact provenance of only one of the stones is recorded, being the south nave wall. Pre-restoration notes and pictures have led to a suggested date for the earlier structure, by comparison, in the early eighth century (RCHM Dorset 2, 310-12). Taylor and Taylor put a much later tentative date on the demolished church, 950-1100 (Taylor and Taylor 1965, 634-37). The RCHM date appears to overlap with their suggested dating of some of the inscribed stones, the latest of which is described as being of about 800 or later, but this need not be crucial as the provenance of most of the stones is uncertain. David Hinton's recent review of the evidence supports the RCHM dating of the stones, though Okasha's work on the inscribed stones of the south-west (which unfortunately does not extend to include the Wareham group), emphasizes the difficulties of dating this type of monument (Hinton 1992, 260; Okasha 1993, 50-7). As the problem of dating the stones remains unresolved, an examination of the possible date of construction of the church may be more productive.

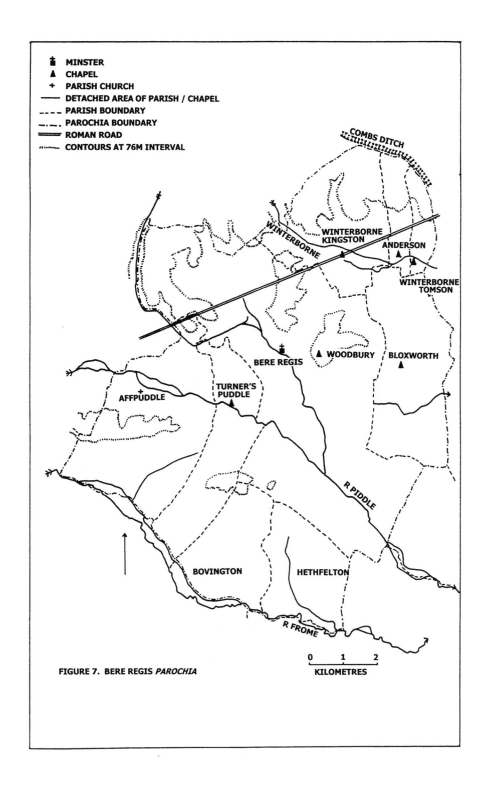

Aldhelm is associated with Wareham by William of Malmesbury who records that he constructed a church near Corfe. William also tells us that he built a church on the river Frome, generally interpreted as the Somerset Frome, but Lapidge and Rosier do not discount Wareham as the site. (Lapidge and Herren 1979, 183). If Aldhelm were the founder of the church that stood virtually unchanged in Wareham until last century, the inclusion of the British Christian memorial stones in the body of its make-up at so immediate a date after the Saxon conquest of Dorset suggests a blatant disregard for those commemorated. As noted above, however, if the latest of the stones is to be dated to about 800 or later this rather precludes a foundation by Aldhelm. Is a later foundation date more likely? The *ASC* records under 784 that King Beorhtric (d.802) was buried in Wareham. His accession to the throne was followed by the first Viking incursion into Wessex recorded under the year 787, fortunately for Beorhtric, the only one during his reign (*ASC*, 53-5). The building of the church by Beorhtric might allow time for the reuse of the latest of the burial stones and could possibly account for his interment there. Following Beorhtric's reign, the Viking attacks resumed in earnest in the south-west, culminating in Guthrum's seizure of Wareham as his raiding base in 875/6. The next possible date of construction, therefore, might be when Alfred's burh was built. By this time the significance of the stones as burial memorials would probably have been lost, a point in its favour: they would have been in service for a very short space of time if the church was constructed in Brictric's reign or earlier. If the unrestored Lady St Mary church were attributed to Alfred an earlier church must have existed in which Brictric was buried. The presence of the large Saxon church of Lady St Mary and associated memorial stones strongly suggest that it was the minster church of Wareham. However, two other churches within the burh both controlled parishes that were larger than that of Lady St Mary. This would be explained if the system was rearranged by Alfred (see below p 35) so the building of Lady St Mary at this date should not be discounted.

What other evidence exists to suggest that Wareham had a minster? Asser's *Life of King Alfred* records a nunnery at Wareham in the year 876 when the burh was breached by Danes, though Smyth has cast doubts on the authenticity of that document, assigning it a date of about 980x1014 (Keynes and Lapidge 1983, 82; Smyth 1995, 312-13).[20] The nunnery was in existence in 982 when the death of one its abbesses is recorded, but it is thought to have perished shortly after due to the continued Danish incursions (*ASC*, 124). In 1086, Lady St Mary was owned by St Wandrille's Abbey in Normandy and shortly afterwards a group of canons was recorded there, suggesting that Wareham developed along similar lines to Wimborne (though not in royal hands) following the demise of the nunnery. The church was given to the abbey of Lyre, with one hide of land attached, by Robert, Earl of Leicester in about 1150, and the canons replaced with monks (*Monasticon* 6, 1092; Levien 1872, 246). With the seizure of lands of the alien priories, Wareham priory was given to the Carthusian priory of Shene whose records recount that the advowsons of St Mary, St Michael, St Martin and St Peter's were attached to the priory suggesting that they were all appended to Lady St Mary (*Monasticon* 6, 29). Holy Trinity church, owned by Sherborne Abbey, paid a pension to the priory in 1291 of 4s

(*Taxatio*, 178). A lost church at Bestwall in Wareham also paid a pension to Lyre (Levien 1872, 246). Lady St Mary now has the only cemetery in Wareham, though St Martin and Holy Trinity are recorded as receiving mortuary payments in 1340, perhaps suggesting that the graveyard was shared rather than burial being solely under the control of Lady St Mary (*Nonarum*, 52-3). Another cemetery existed with a chapel: *cimiterium s'c'i Johannis baptiste* (see below p 56) (Levien 1872, 249). There seems, therefore, to be little doubt that Lady St Mary was Wareham's minster church despite the strange apportionment of lands to the different parishes (below p 35).

Gillingham (Fig 6)
A considerable amount of indirect evidence suggests that St Mary's church at Gillingham was a minster (Blair 1985, 108; Keen 1984, 230)). Anglo-Saxon remains in the form of two ninth-century carved stones, probably from a cross-shaft, are built into the north wall of the vicarage and the church had a pre-Conquest nave before restoration (Hutchins 3, 638; RCHM Dorset 4, 27-8). The church, worth 40s in 1086, was exchanged by William for one hide of Shaftesbury Abbey's land at Kingston, where Corfe Castle was built (*DB*, 19,10). In the early fourteenth century the church is recorded as receiving church scot as part of the endowment of the vicarage (Hutchins 3, 645). Four chapels were appended to Gillingham; East Stour, Motcombe, West Stour and Langham and three other chapels are recorded, one at Milton-on-Stour, a 'free' chapel or oratory, and two in the palace at King's Court (Hutchins 3, 625, 632-3, 636; *DPN* 3, 15; Hutchins 3, 627; *CLR* 3, 1937, 297). Bourton, a detached area of Gillingham parish, had no church until 1813. The intervening parish of Silton must also have originally belonged to Gillingham. Its church, owned by the lord of Silton manor, presumably became independent before 1086 as it would have been unlikely to have gained independence after Gillingham church was given to Shaftesbury. The acquisition of the minster at Gillingham by Shaftesbury just after the Conquest ensured the preservation of its *parochia* as it existed in 1086.

Bere Regis (Fig 7)
St John the Baptist at Bere Regis incorporates 'the remains *in situ* of a cruciform church of c.1050' (RCHM Dorset 2, xlv). The church was held in conjunction with that of Dorchester by Brictward the priest in 1086. In 1091 Bere was formed into a wealthy prebend with Charminster as part of the endowment of Salisbury Cathedral (*Osmund*, 198). Chapels existed at Winterborne Kingston, Bloxworth, Anderson, Winterborne Tomson, Turner's Puddle and Woodbury, and the church received pensions from Affpuddle, Dewlish, and the abbot of Bindon (for the grange of Bovington). Holy Trinity chapel, a classic proprietary foundation by Nicholas Tonere, lord of Turner's Puddle, was endowed with 30 acres and the tithes of the demesne, but was obliged to pay a pension of 6s 8d to the rector of Bere Regis (*RJC*, 3). The manors of Bloxworth and Affpuddle were given to Cerne Abbey in 987, but whilst Bloxworth was a chapel, Affpuddle was an independent church paying only a meagre pension of 20d to Bere (*Monasticon* 2, 621; *RJC*, 3,9). There is no evidence for the foundation dates of these two chapels but, given that both belonged to Cerne and were originally part of Bere's *parochia*, Affpuddle's greater independence might suggest that its church was already in existence when that

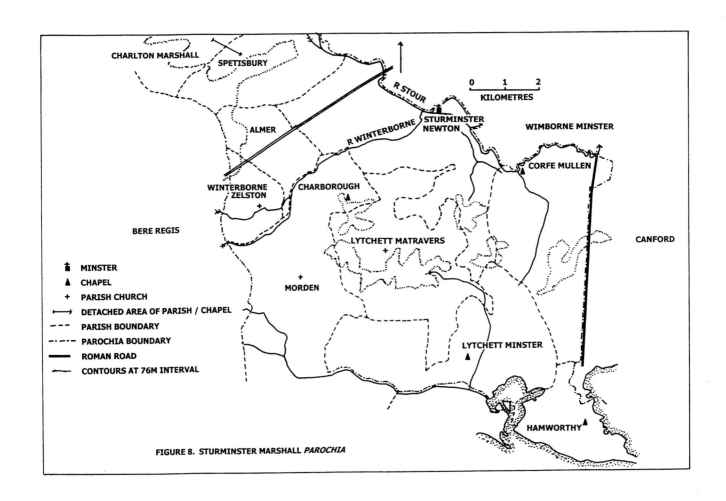

FIGURE 8. STURMINSTER MARSHALL *PAROCHIA*

Legend:
- MINSTER
- CHAPEL
- PARISH CHURCH
- DETACHED AREA OF PARISH / CHAPEL
- PARISH BOUNDARY
- PAROCHIA BOUNDARY
- ROMAN ROAD
- CONTOURS AT 76M INTERVAL

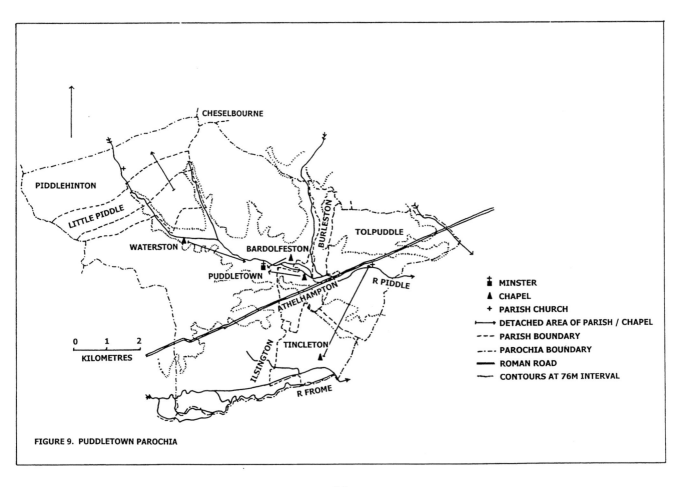

FIGURE 9. PUDDLETOWN PAROCHIA

Legend:
- MINSTER
- CHAPEL
- PARISH CHURCH
- DETACHED AREA OF PARISH / CHAPEL
- PARISH BOUNDARY
- PAROCHIA BOUNDARY
- ROMAN ROAD
- CONTOURS AT 76M INTERVAL

16

vill was given to Cerne. This may also account for the portion of 6s 8d paid by Affpuddle to Cerne Abbey, which may well represent the tithes of the demesne. Winterborne Kingston remained a chapel of ease to Bere until last century. Its position on a Roman road suggests that it may have started life as a wayside chapel.

Sturminster Marshall (Fig 8)

Sturminster Marshall has strong minster church characteristics although the only written indication is a 10th-century place-name reference in Alfred's will, where the estate is left to Athelweard (*DPN* 2, 45). The church had three chapels, two of which, Corfe Mullen and Lytchett Minster remained dependent until the 19th century (*CDF* 1, 85; *Dorset Records* E2, 50). The third, at Hamworthy, is said by Hutchins to have been ruined in the Civil War (Hutchins 3, 360). The *minster* element of Lytchett's place-name is best explained as an indication of ownership by the minster at Sturminster (Taylor 1970, 79; *DPN* 2, 33). Before the Conquest Sturminster belonged to Archbishop Stigand, presumably through royal donation, as implied by Alfred's will (*Alfred*, 175, 320). The tithes of Sturminster, were given by Roger de Beaumont to the Abbey of St Peter, Pratel in c1080.[21] However, by at least the middle of the twelfth century, Sturminster church, with its tithes and appurtenances, was confirmed to the Hospital of St Giles, Pont Audemer, as the gift of Count Robert, Roger's son (*CDF*, 83-7). Earl Robert of Leicester, grandson to Count Robert, wrote to the pope that his grandfather had given 'an estate called Expectesberi' (Spetisbury, just to the north of Sturminster), to Pratel in exchange for a previous gift of tithes from other advowsons, which, because of 'the violence of his officials', the abbot was having problems collecting (Constable 1984, 110). Although Sturminster is not mentioned as part of the exchange, its ownership by Pont Audemer so shortly after its original gift to Pratel, would be neatly explained by this exchange. Sturminster church, therefore, appears to have been an important minster founded at the centre of a royal estate which passed firstly into ecclesiastical and then, following the Norman Conquest, temporarily into lay hands.

Puddletown (Fig 9)

The church of St Mary's, Puddletown has several minster characteristics. The manor was in the king's hands in 1086, but had been held by Earl Harold previously. The third penny of the shire was attached to the manor, and Williams suggests that it was part of the official endowment of the earldom of Wessex (Williams 1968, 28). In 976 a witan was held in Puddletown, further evidence that the land of the earldom was formerly royal demesne (Hill 1981, 90). The church of Puddletown was held by Bolle the priest, together with Chaldon and Fleet, in 1086. All three churches were on Harold's manors and between them they held 1½ hides valued at 57s 6d. Domesday Book also tells us that Ilsington, a unit of land within the parish of Puddletown, had been taken from a clerk by Earl Harold. This might indicate that it had been part of the holding of Puddletown church as Harold is recorded elsewhere in Dorset relieving other religious bodies of their landholdings, a nearby example being Cheselbourne, a Shaftesbury Abbey estate. Harold's accessioning of Cheselbourne and Ilsington can be seen as an attempt to consolidate his holding around Puddletown at the expense of the church.

Puddletown parish was large with chapels at Waterston and Little Piddle (*IPM* 2, 421; Hutchins 2, 620). Little Piddle remained a detached part of Puddletown, separated from the parish by a detached area of Piddlehinton, until 1885 (RCHM Dorset 3, 207). Its chapel possessed land and tithes suggesting it was a manorial foundation (*IPM* 2, 421). The overlap with part of Piddlehinton suggests that that parish was also originally part of Puddletown *parochia*. Athelhampton church appears to have originated within the *parochia* as an oratory which gained some parochial functions though burial remained at Puddletown (Hutchins 2, 588). Burleston, probably an early detachment from the royal manor, was given by Athelstan to Milton Abbey: its church must have been served by the abbey as it had no glebe, parsonage or churchyard (Hutchins 2, 589). The history of Puddletown church is quite in keeping with what one would expect for a minster church although there are no early records of it having been one.

Iwerne Minster (Fig 10)

Iwerne's probable minster status is obviously implied by its name and, though caution is needed as this may only indicate ownership by Shaftesbury Abbey, there are other positive indications such as its wealth and signs of a cruciform plan (*DPN* 3, 123-4; *Taxatio*, 178; RCHM Dorset 4, 36-7). Iwerne has recently been suggested as the site of the mysteriously placed abbey of Abbot Bectun, who was granted 30 hides besides the river Fontmell in 670x676: *de aquilone rivus nomine Funtamel, ex meridie habet terram beatae memoriae Leotheri episcopi* (Murphy 1991, 23-32).[22] The grant does not tell us where either the recipient abbey or the 30 hides were situated, but its inclusion in Shaftesbury Abbey's cartulary led to the supposition that the monastery was a predecessor of Shaftesbury Abbey, a location with which Murphy disagrees, preferring Iwerne Minster.[23] The most obvious solution would still seem to be that proposed by Finberg who suggested that Iwerne Minster was held by Bishop Leuthere and the 30 hides donated to Bectun was Fontmell (Finberg 1964b, 155). Iwerne had probably been donated to Leuthere as the Saxon frontier in Dorset pushed westwards, and the minster may have been founded by Bishop Leuthere (670x676) himself.

Iwerne's minster characteristics are somewhat obscured by the activities of Shaftesbury Abbey which formed the churches in its possession into prebends to support the priests serving the abbey (Hutchins 3, 553). Two charters of the ninth and tenth centuries grant Iwerne, Handley, Compton Abbas and Fontmel to Shaftesbury Abbey, and though the earlier charter is seen as spurious, there is probably little doubt that the lands in question were part of the original endowment of the abbey.[24] Iwerne had five chapels attached to it: East Orchard or Hartgrove, Margaret Marsh, Hinton St Mary, Handley and Gussage St Andrew (*RSG*, 785). Two of these, Hartgrove and Margaret Marsh, are close to home and may be part of the original *parochia* though as both were sited on lands of Shaftesbury Abbey they may have been attached to Iwerne for that reason. Handley, itself a high-status church, was a separate parish until 1327 (Hutchins 3, 553). Hinton St Mary may also have been independent before being granted to Shaftesbury as it had burial rights, or it may have belonged elsewhere as in the tenth century the manor had links with Thornton and Margaret Marsh and it

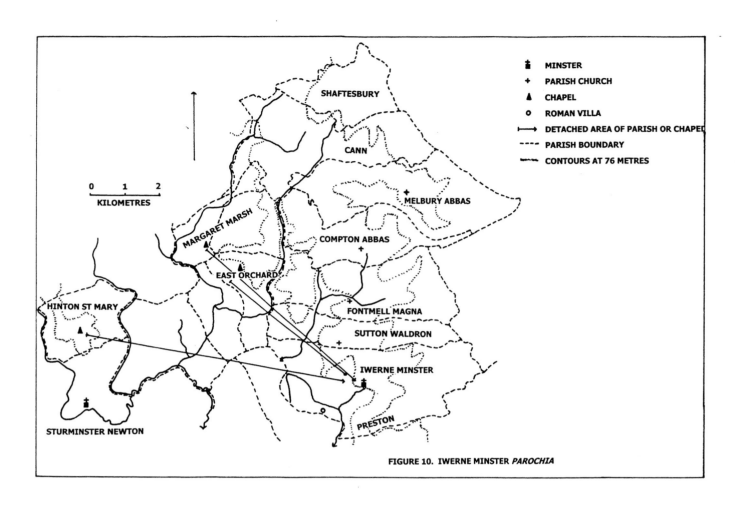

FIGURE 10. IWERNE MINSTER *PAROCHIA*

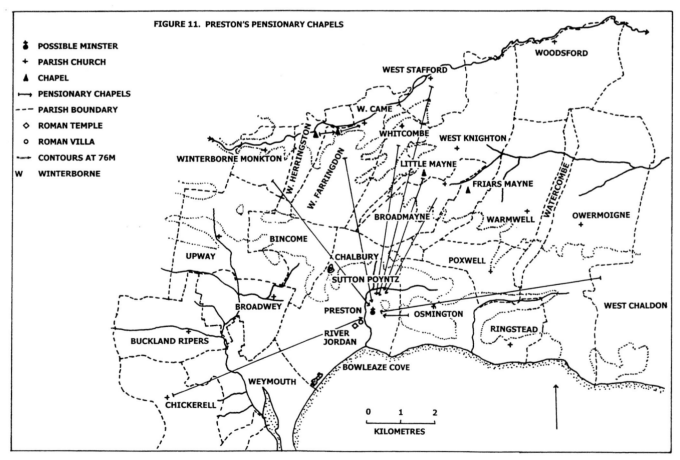

lies very close to Sturminster Newton (Hutchins 3, 549).[25] Neither Handley nor Hinton St Mary, both of which were some distance from Iwerne, can be definitely placed in Iwerne's *parochia*. They appear to have been attached to Iwerne in order to boost the income of the prebend of Iwerne. It is not possible to gauge, therefore, the original extent of Iwerne's *parochia*, as its passage into the hands of Shaftesbury linked it inextricably with the lands donated to the Abbey.

Preston (Fig 11)

The church of St Andrew at Preston lay within the manor of Sutton Poyntz which formed part of an exchange of land by King Alfred in 891.[26] The exchange illustrates Alfred's policy of securing strategic sites (a large number of which had been monastic lands) (Fleming 1985, 247-65). As a land unit, Sutton occupies a good defensive position stretching from the sea at Bowleaze Cove, up the valley of the River Jordan to the South Dorset Ridgeway and containing the hillfort of Chalbury in the west of the parish. Sutton remained royal demesne land until given to the cathedral of Sarum by Henry II, becoming the prebend of Preston.[27] In 1404 Preston church was recorded with ten pensionary chapels most of which were independent churches at that time: Chickerel, Stockwood, Winterborne Monkton, Winterborne Farringdon, Stafford, Whitcombe, Littlemayne, Broadmayne, Chaldon Boys, and Osmington (*RJC*, 11). Stockwood, a possession of Sarum, is situated near Yetminster. Its presence may indicate that these payments were a Sarum innovation to boost the funds of the prebend but none of the other churches belonged to Sarum and it seems unlikely that the bishop could have imposed fines on independent churches at such a late date as 1154x89. Could the pensions represent the last remnants of control of a minster? Unfortunately, Preston is missing some important characteristics of minster churches. Its site is not in keeping with the other early minsters; its *parochia* as described by these churches is not a neat topographical unit; Sutton only appears to have become royal demesne in the tenth century; and its place-name suggests it was a dependent settlement (see below p 25). Another possibility exists: the church of Preston could have been a creation of Alfred following his acquisition of the manor.

Preston is situated in an area of Roman remains. The church lies within 400m of a Roman villa and on the nearby Jordan Hill lay a Roman temple and cemetery. There is no evidence for reuse of Roman material in Preston church, though, which is mainly of fourteenth-century build. Regrettably, doubt has been cast on the authenticity of the reported find spot of a gold Saxon pointer said to have come from Bowleaze Cove as the presence of such a find would boost the case for the church at Preston having been founded by Alfred (Keen 1991, 184).

Abbotsbury and Portesham (Fig 12)

Both Abbotsbury and Portesham are at the lower end of the table of possible minsters. They are examined together as they share several minster characteristics between them. Abbotsbury was first recorded in a grant of 5 hides by King Edmund (939x946) to Sigewulf who gave the land to Glastonbury Abbey.[28] The place-name is thought to derive from this ownership (Fagersten 1978, 245). The foundation of Abbotsbury Abbey by Orc is placed in the second quarter

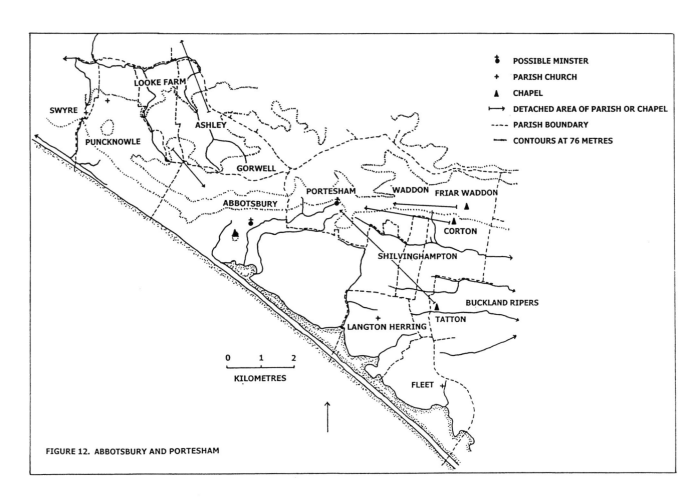

FIGURE 12. ABBOTSBURY AND PORTESHAM

of the eleventh century. Unfortunately, the abbey's cartulary is lost, but it has been partially reconstructed by Keynes from the records of antiquarians who had seen it (1989, 207-43). Reputedly, there was one priest, with his wife, at Abbotsbury when the monastery was founded. A charter of Edward the Confessor gave an account of the foundation, noting that monks were imported from Cerne. This probably accounts for Leland's belief that Orc had expelled canons when founding the monastery: *Orkus ...expulsis canonicus secularibus, introduxit monachus* (Leland, 149). The story in Coker of St Peter bestowing a foundation charter on a holy priest called Bertufus, reputedly of a British church foundation, is plainly a myth and, though these myths often have some grains of truth, in this case the lack of any other evidence to support the presence of a British foundation may point to it simply being an attempt to gain status by the production of an interesting early history (Coker 1732, 30-1).[29]

Is there other evidence to suggest that there might have been a minster at Abbotsbury before the foundation of the abbey? Domesday Book notes that Abbotsbury was owed payments of church scot from Friar Waddon, an indication of minster status. If Friar Waddon depended on Abbotsbury as the church scot payments suggest, the interlying manors must also have been dependent on that minster. However, later records show that Friar Waddon was one of four chapels attached to Portesham church. This presents the possibility that the payment was originally due to Portesham, but was recorded as payable to Abbotsbury because Portesham was owned by that abbey.[30] One of Portesham's chapels, at Tatton, now lies within the parish of Buckland Ripers, showing that Portesham was acting as a mother-church with rights extending beyond its later parish. Unlike Abbotsbury parish which consists almost solely of abbey lands, Portesham had jurisdiction over a considerable area whose ownership lay elsewhere: Corton, two parts of Shilvinghampton, Waddon, and Friars Waddon, all chapels of Portesham, were in lay ownership *TRE,* and Tatton had belonged to Cerne Abbey and was being sub-let in two land units. Portesham, therefore, acted as a mother-church over areas not in the ownership of Abbotsbury Abbey. The most likely explanation appears to be that the abbey took over some of the privileges of a minster at Portesham when it received that church as part of its endowment at its foundation. It is certainly less easy to explain why a minster at Abbotsbury would bestow chapels on Portesham, one of its appropriated churches, whose income went straight into the abbey coffers (*CPL* 4, 342; *CPL* 5, 77).

Summary

The churches examined in detail above and in Appendix II all scored over ten points. Not all of them would have been early minster churches. Within Table 3 a division exists whereby those with scores of 20 and over have written sources to support their minster status. For those scoring between 10 and 20 the evidence is more circumstantial, suggesting that they should be viewed as possible minsters for the present. Other churches have been suggested as minsters by previous writers and these will be examined briefly.

Other possible minsters

Past research has suggested as minsters several churches that do not score highly enough to appear on Table 3. Symondsbury was proposed by Barker, but evidence suggests that it lay within Whitchurch's *parochia* originally (below p 31, & Fig 4) (Barker 1988a, 36). Pearce suggested Halstock, Hinton St Mary, and Tarrant Crawford were minsters (Pearce 1978, 99). Halstock (see Fig 50) was an early estate of the episcopal see which formed a prebend with Lyme Regis and in 1291 Halstock was described as a chapel of Lyme (*Taxatio*, 181). Pearce proposed that Halstock was a minster for several reasons: firstly, because mention is made of a *monasteriunculo*, in a ninth-century charter; secondly, the presence of a Roman villa in the parish suggested a Roman estate given to support a minster church; and thirdly because of the place-name Halstock - 'holy place'.[31] The diminutive form of *monasteria* probably refers to a hermitage rather than a minster, and may be a reference to the chapel, dedicated to St Juthware, on the ridge which forms Halstock's parish and the county boundary. The *monasteriunculo* of the charter was dedicated to St Michael, whereas the parish church is dedicated to St Mary and sits in the valley, making the chapel a more appropriate setting for this dedication. A rededication to Juthware could easily have come about following the translation of that saint's relics to Sherborne in the 10th century (Talbot 1959, 85).[32] Excavation of the villa, some 800m from the church, showed no evidence for use of the site in the post-Roman period contrary to Hase's suggestion that it was a British monastery (Lucas 1993, 140; Hase 1994, 50). Hinton St Mary (see Fig 76) was a chapelry of Iwerne Minster and the priests mistakenly assigned to it by Pearce belong to Hinton Martell. Its neat topographic unit, recorded by charter boundaries in the tenth century, is too small for a minster parish. The church's proximity to a Roman villa has to be seen as one of the major reasons Pearce suggested it as a minster, a relationship which will be examined below. The final minster candidate suggested by Pearce is the church of Tarrant Crawford (Fig 2) sited near the confluence of the Tarrant with the River Stour, a seemingly encouraging site for a minster serving the Tarrant valley. However, the church has no minster characteristics: its parish is one of the smallest in Dorset, only 600 acres. The church itself is small with no signs of wealth or chapels. Domesday Book tells us that a priest living at Tarrant held one and a third hides in Hinton Martell. Pearce allots this priest to a minster at Tarrant Crawford, an identification which is mistaken as the Hinton Martell land belonged to the community at Wimborne (Pearce 1978, 99). There is not enough evidence, therefore, to assign minster status to any of these three churches.

The final church in Dorset previously suggested as a minster is Studland, put forward by Pitfield on the grounds that it was the most likely church to have had minster status within the hundred of Ailwood (Pitfield 1985, 25). Whilst no minster place-names in Dorset have the suffix -*land*, the name Studland may indicate an ancient land unit as in Hartland, Devon (Orme 1991, 9-10). Studland parish (see Fig 71) is of considerable size with a detached area to the west of Langton Matravers (DRO, T/SW). Its southerly neighbour, Swanage, however, was a chapel of Worth Matravers.

Studland had a chapel on Brownsea Island in Leland's day but the church was of no great value being worth only £5 in 1291. The evidence for a minster at Studland, therefore, is inconclusive.

Discussion of Certain Minster Characteristics
In the following section some of the minster characteristics are examined further, and another two characteristics, place-names and dedications, are suggested as useful diagnostic features which have arisen from the analysis of this group of high-scoring churches.

The reuse of Roman sites and its implications
There has long been a suggested correlation between Roman sites and minster churches (above p 1). Various reasons have been mooted to account for the postulated link: firstly, continuity from Roman Christianity, sometimes evinced in continuity of cult sites from Roman Britain as at St Albans; secondly, continuity of use from pagan religious sites, possibly brought about by Gregory's instructions to Augustine to assimilate pagan sites; thirdly, an attempt to strengthen the church's claim to antiquity by association; fourthly, the siting of churches at centres of secular power which had been Roman sites; fifthly, the availability of building material, or the presence of a ready-made Roman enclosure for use as a *vallum monasterii*; and sixthly, the endowment of minster churches with surviving Roman estates (Pearce 1978, 99-100; Aston 1985, 50; Morris 1989, 40, 42; Blair 1992, 240-6; Finberg 1955). Recently the link with villas has taken a new turn; Hase now sees it as a possible phenomenon of the fifth/sixth century mission from Wales, along the lines of St Illtud's reuse of the Roman villa at Llanilltyd Fawr (Hase 1994, 49-50).

In central and eastern England there are examples of churches placed in walled Roman forts or small towns at an early date such as Reculver and Dorchester-on-Thames. In the west the coincidence appears to be more one of villas and minster: Blair, synthesizing the work of Pearce, refers to the 'English appropriations of villas', which include a remarkable number in the south-west', and 'the large number of minsters on villas in Dorset' (Blair 1992, 240-1; Pearce 1978, 99, 100, 111; Pearce 1982a, 117). Hase, synthesizing the work of Pearce and Taylor, also holds the view that 'churches are built on top of, or immediately alongside, villas' in Somerset and Dorset (Hase 1994, 50; Taylor 1970, 73). This data needs to be re-examined because, as has been shown above (p 20), three of Pearce's examples are not minster churches.

Having ascertained which churches in the county have minster status it is possible to approach the question of a relationship from a new angle. Table 4 correlates the evidence for Roman villas and their proximity to the nearest church and its status. All parishes with villa or temple sites are included in the table, along with churches associated with Roman remains (see also, Figs 13-15). Two definite minster churches are directly associated with Roman remains, Sherborne and Wimborne, three other definite minsters have a villa within their parish and one has reused Roman building material. Two of the possible minsters, Corfe and Preston, both have villas within their parishes, though, as shown above p 19, Preston is unlikely to have been a primary minster. Fordington church is built on one of Dorchester's Roman cemeteries and incorporates some Roman material in its foundations. Moving onto the parochial churches, there are eleven instances; four direct associations with Roman

Church type	Roman remains in fabric	Roman remains under church	Parishes with villas or temples	
Minster	Whitchurch Canonicorum	Sherborne Wimborne Minster	Charminster Iwerne Minster Sherborne	V: 2.4km V: 1.4km V: 1.8km
Possible minsters	Fordington	Fordington	Corfe Preston	V: 2km + 1km V - 0.4km + T - 1.1km
Church	Godmanston	Chalbury Piddletrenthide Tarrant Crawford	Church Knowle Fifehead Neville Frampton Rampisham Tarrant Hinton Winterborne St Martin Witchampton	V: 1km V: 0.5km V: 1km V: 1.5km V:1.3km T - 2.4km V - 2.5km + T- 0.2km
Chapel	Gussage St Andrew		Gussage St Andrew Charlton Marshall - V site unknown Halstock Dewlish Hinton St Mary Thornford Wynford Eagle	V: 0.3km V: 0.8km V: 1.2km V: 0.1km V: 0.9km V: 0.4km

Table 4. Relation of minsters, churches and chapels to Roman remains. T - temple site   V - villa site.

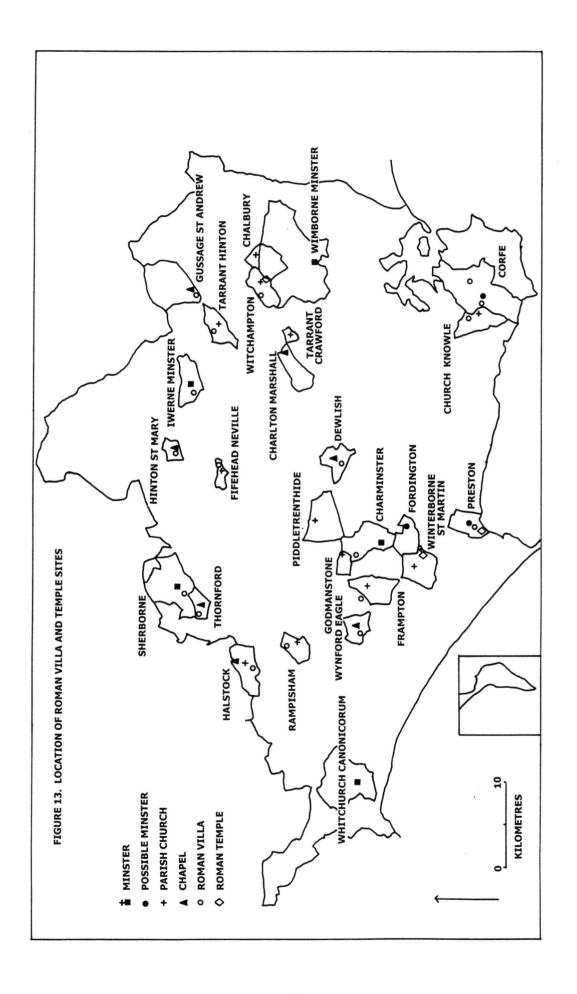

FIGURE 13. LOCATION OF ROMAN VILLA AND TEMPLE SITES

MINSTER

POSSIBLE MINSTER

PARISH CHURCH

CHAPEL

ROMAN VILLA

ROMAN TEMPLE

WHITCHURCH CANONICORUM

RAMPISHAM

HALSTOCK

SHERBORNE

THORNFORD

WYNFORD EAGLE

GODMANSTONE

FRAMPTON

PIDDLETRENTHIDE

CHARMINSTER

FORDINGTON

WINTERBORNE
ST MARTIN

PRESTON

DEWLISH

CHARLTON MARSHALL

HINTON ST MARY

FIFEHEAD NEVILLE

IWERNE MINSTER

TARRANT
CRAWFORD

WITCHAMPTON

GUSSAGE ST ANDREW

TARRANT HINTON

CHALBURY

WIMBORNE MINSTER

CORFE

CHURCH KNOWLE

10

0

KILOMETRES

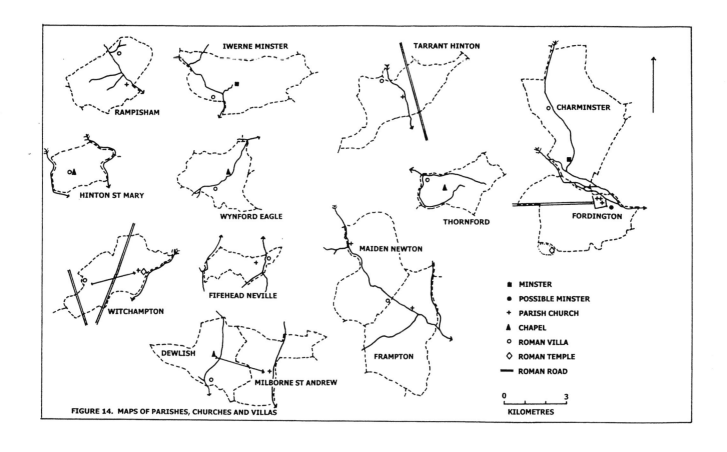

FIGURE 14. MAPS OF PARISHES, CHURCHES AND VILLAS

Legend (Figure 14):

- ■ MINSTER
- ● POSSIBLE MINSTER
- + PARISH CHURCH
- ▲ CHAPEL
- ○ ROMAN VILLA
- ◇ ROMAN TEMPLE
- ▬ ROMAN ROAD

Parish labels (Figure 14): IWERNE MINSTER, TARRANT HINTON, CHARMINSTER, RAMPISHAM, HINTON ST MARY, WYNFORD EAGLE, THORNFORD, FORDINGTON, WITCHAMPTON, FIFEHEAD NEVILLE, MAIDEN NEWTON, DEWLISH, MILBORNE ST ANDREW, FRAMPTON

0 3
KILOMETRES

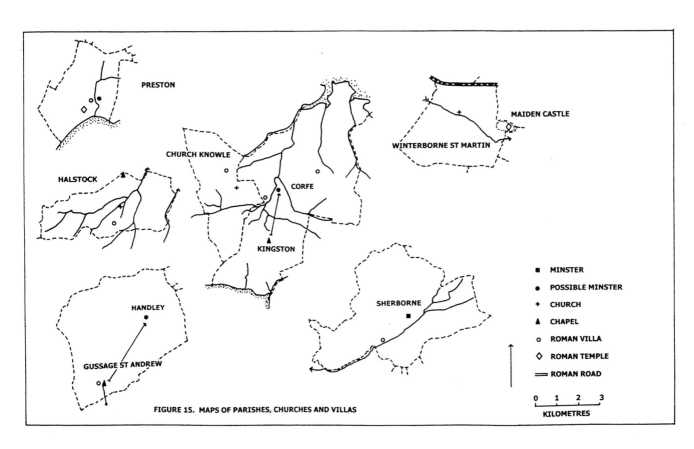

FIGURE 15. MAPS OF PARISHES, CHURCHES AND VILLAS

Legend (Figure 15):

- ■ MINSTER
- ● POSSIBLE MINSTER
- + CHURCH
- ▲ CHAPEL
- ○ ROMAN VILLA
- ◇ ROMAN TEMPLE
- ▬ ROMAN ROAD

Parish labels (Figure 15): PRESTON, MAIDEN CASTLE, WINTERBORNE ST MARTIN, CHURCH KNOWLE, HALSTOCK, CORFE, KINGSTON, SHERBORNE, HANDLEY, GUSSAGE ST ANDREW

0 1 2 3
KILOMETRES

remains, and seven cases of villas or temples within the parish. Parochial chapels are also well represented: one with Roman remains in the fabric and seven cases of villas within parishes. The association of Roman remains, therefore, is not significantly linked with minster churches.

Where Roman remains definitely exist under churches, there is not enough evidence in any of the cases to say with certainty that they belong to a villa. At Sherborne, part of a Roman pavement was reputedly found 'on the site of the abbey' (Stuart 1892, xxii). The portion of pavement found under the minster at Wimborne (see Plate 4) is of very poor quality and it has been suggested as the possible floor of the original Saxon minster, rather than a Roman building (RCHM Dorset 5, 80). With the remaining three churches on Roman remains, none has any pretensions towards minster status: at Chalbury a pit associated with a Roman tile was found in a keyhole excavation in the nave, with similar results from Piddletrenthide (Hall 1990, 43; Keen 1983, 152). Only at Tarrant Crawford do the remains suggest a Roman building. Four churches in the county have Roman remains incorporated into their fabric: Whitchurch Canonicorum, where the provenance of the material is unknown; Fordington; Godmanston, which has part of a Roman altar in the chancel arch (provenance unknown); and Gussage St Andrew, from a villa site near the chapel. Medieval pottery from the villa site at Gussage, along with the twelfth-century build of the chapel, led Martin Green to suggest that robbing of the Roman remains took place during that period (Green 1990, 117). In defence of the reuse of building material which Pearce sees as a trivial and naive reason for the coincidence of Roman remains and churches, the thirteenth-century manor house at Witchampton incorporates Roman materials in its fabric, robbed from an adjacent temple site (Pearce 1982, 118; Sumner 1924, 235). Is it right to attribute more significance to the material in Whitchurch, a known minster, than to that in Gussage St Andrew, a chapelry of Handley, or indeed to that in the manor house at Witchampton? As the Roman material is incorporated into construction work of the twelfth and thirteenth centuries these cases cannot be said to represent anything more than the reuse of readily accessible building materials. The siting of Fordington over one of Dorchester's Roman cemeteries is, however, more significant and may be an example of the survival of a cult site from the fifth century though none is known and there is, as yet, no evidence of continuity.

Turning to the continuity of Roman estates into Saxon times as suggested by Finberg at Withington, Fowler has suggested a similar pattern in the Vale of Wrington (Som.), where the villas are distributed evenly between the Saxon estates (Hingley 1989, 102-5). These examples are, however, both areas which are dense in villas. Pearce suggests that this phenomenon might occur in parts of Dorset but does not present enough evidence for a convincing argument (Pearce 1982, 119-23). In the vast majority of Dorset parishes with villas, villa and church are over 0.5km apart and many villas are situated in peripheral positions in the parish (see Figs 13-15) suggesting that the parishes do not represent Roman land units.

In Dorset, therefore, as elsewhere, a variety of reasons may exist to account for the coincidence of Roman remains and churches. At Sherborne, the Saxons may have been making a point of associating their new church with Roman remains (the British site was at the Old Castle); Gussage St Andrew and Whitchurch appear to illustrate reuse of building material; Fordington, perhaps the continuation of a cult site; and Hinton St Mary may represent the continuation of an estate centre. Morris and Roxan have suggested that the relationship between church and villa is likely to reflect the relationship between manor and villa as estate centres, and that churches, most of which are proprietary in nature, are incidental to the equation (Morris and Roxan, 1980, 191-2). The reuse of Roman villas as monasteries is based on the example of St Illtud at Llanilltyd Fawr. As Blair notes, however, the gift of Roman sites to the church is not confined to the British sector; 'the practice was too generalized to constitute in itself a means of distinguishing between British and Anglo-Saxon origins' (Blair 1992, 241). Additionally, three of Hase's Dorset sites, Halstock, Whitchurch Canonicorum and Tarrant Crawford, are dismissed above and there is no evidence for a villa at the site of his fourth example, Beaminster, where the only Roman finds recorded on the SMR are pottery sherds from a site 150m east of the church.[33] Most of Pearce's examples have been shown above to be equally suspect. The reported high association of villa and minster in Dorset, therefore, cannot at present be shown to have a sound factual basis.

Place-Names of the Minster settlements
The high incidence of place-names in Dorset incorporating the element *minster* suggests that an examination of place-names may be fruitful. The minster names are divided into two groups for analysis: those that have been positively identified as minsters, and the possible minsters. The place-names are grouped according to the type of name: topographical, with a sub-set of river-names; personal, those referring to a person or group of people; and other names which includes status and habitative names, ownership by classes of persons or groups, and references to administrative arrangements.

The composition of the place-names of the definite minsters (Table 5) is very biased towards river names; nine out of fifteen settlements take their name from the river on which they lie. This is a familiar pattern in many areas. Hoskins suggested that the initial Saxon settlement of Devon consisted of the establishment of caputs centred on large riverine estates where both the settlement and the estate took their names from the river. He noted that amongst other characteristics these settlements often possessed minster churches (Hoskins 1952, 300-10 and map facing 307). Gelling proposed that topographical names should be considered as 'potentially the earliest English ones in any region' and notes that in addition to referring to the main settlement they often apply to the surrounding estates: e.g. Lambourn in Berkshire (Gelling 1978, 123-4, 126). In Kent, Everitt has detected a similar pattern (though some two centuries earlier that the Saxon conquest of Dorset) when the Jutes took over riverine sites as royal centres of large estates. Many of these became minster sites with the conversion to

River-names	Topographical	Personal	Other
Sherborne - OE - bright stream **Wimborne** - OE - meadow stream **Cranborne** - OE- stream frequented by cranes **Charminster** - C/OE - river name from heap of stones **Sturminster M.** - C/OE- strong or powerful one **Iwerne** - C - the yew river **Burton** *-Bridetone* - C/OE - estate on the gushing stream **Puddletown** - OE- river-name from marsh or fen **Winfrith** - C- white or bright stream	**Bere** - OE/L - wood	**Beaminster** - OE - Bebbe's church **Yetminster** - OE - Eata's church **Gillingham** - OE - homestead of Gylla's people	**Whitchurch Canon.** - OE/L - white stone church **Wareham** - OE - estate by the weir

Table 5. Categories of minster place-names (interpretations from Mills 1986). OE – Old English: C – Celtic: L - Latin

Christianity (Everitt 1977, 4-10; Everitt 1986, 72-92). Seminal Saxon settlements in southern England took their names from rivers and this pattern can be clearly seen in the first flush of Dorset minster settlements.

The river-names are divided fairly evenly between Celtic and Old English names. There are six occurrences of the *minster* element but it is only recorded prior to Domesday book in three instances, Sturminster Marshall, Wimborne and Beaminster, with Charminster, Yetminster and Iwerne Minster being first mentioned in Domesday Book (*DPN* 1, 338; *DPN* 2, 45, 183; *DPN* 3, 123; Mills 1986, 33, 165). *Tun* has been shown to indicate royal settlements in certain cases, especially where the name applies to the estate as well as the settlement itself (Campbell 1979b, 49-50). The fact that Burton and Puddletown acquired *ton* rather than *minster* may imply that they were more important as royal estate centres than as minster sites. This interpretation is supported by the fact that the three places mentioned as minsters in Domesday Book are all in ecclesiastical hands at that time; Charminster and Yetminster belonged to the bishop and Iwerne Minster to Shaftesbury abbey. Two of the Somerset *minster* names, Pitminster and Ilminster, were also in ecclesiastical hands in 1086.

Turning to the remaining names of the definite minsters: Bere has topographical origins; Gillingham, Beaminster and Yetminster include personal names; and Whitchurch is a status name, describing the church. Of the three personal names, two are combined with the element *minster*, both of which belonged to the bishop of Sherborne. The minster at Beaminster is known to have existed before 705 (see below p 90), and it is possible that Yetminster church was also founded before the estate was donated to the bishopric as the personal element suggests commemoration of its founder. The place-name of Whitchurch, if referring to an early stone church rather than simply a white-washed building, might be indicative of the importance of the church (Ekwall 1960, 513; Mills 1986, 154, 158).

Moving on to the place-names of the possible minsters (Table 6), these are much more evenly distributed between river-names, topographical and other types. The majority are topographical, but the river-names that were so prominent in the definite minsters are much less in evidence here, only 6 out of the 21 names. Within this second group of high-scoring churches, there are many more status names, the least likely place-names for early minster settlements. Milton and Netherbury are situational implying that they are secondary settlements. Preston, originally known as Sutton, also falls within this group of secondary settlements. *Buckland* refers to an administrative arrangement and, as Gelling notes, cannot be early (Gelling 1978, 125). Abbotsbury was named before the foundation of the Benedictine monastery in the eleventh century, referring to an earlier ownership by Glastonbury abbey (Mills 1986, 25). Abbotsbury is one of only two instances in the county where the *abbot* affix is Old English. In seven other cases it is a Latin addition of about the 13th century. A similar OE use occurs in Abbotstone in Hampshire an estate held by Romsey Abbey (Coates 1989, 19). It seems unlikely that the OE *abbod* referred to a minster in existence before the eleventh century foundation, its name being more likely to imply ownership by a monastery elsewhere.

As noted above, Hoskins, Gelling and Everitt have drawn attention to primary riverine settlements. The Devon names suggested by Hoskins show a striking difference from the Dorset names because of the frequent addition of the *tun* element in Devon. Dorset has only two examples of this as minster names, Puddletown and Burton, whereas Devon has many; Torrington, Cullompton, Crediton, Plympton, Colyton and Tawton. Hoskins notes that 'In nearly all these instances, we can show from other evidence that *tuns* compounded with a river-name are the oldest settlements in their respective districts' (Hoskins 1952, 303). An examination of Somerset shows a similar, if not so pronounced, picture. Of the 29 possible minsters identified by Costen in Somerset, 13 bear river-names, six of which are also coupled with *tun*, these being mostly in the south of the county. A further five have topographical names with the suffix *tun* (Costen 1992a, 106). In comparison, the small incidence of river-names with *tun* in Dorset is quite striking. Everitt suggests that the riverine settlements in Kent were formed before *tun* came into common usage, accounting for the lack of its application in Kent (Everitt 1977, 7). River-names with the suffix *tun*, therefore, seem to take over from the simpler form of river-name alone.[34] This chronology is supported by Cox's work on the earliest English place-names which concludes that those in *tun* were formed for the most part after c.730 (Cox 1976, 63). The evidence from the river-names suggests, therefore, that the major riverine estates in Dorset, nearly all of which had minsters, were established before 730 and earlier than those of Devon, which one would expect, but also before those of southern Somerset. There is one other place-name in Dorset comprising of river-name coupled with *tun* - Frampton. Whilst its church does not have enough characteristics to be included in the table of high-scoring churches it does have one of the important features being originally a royal manor as it belonged to Harold's family and it is possible that it might be an example of a failed minster.

To summarize, the place-name evidence presents a broad outline of settlement chronology in Dorset. The primary settlements, which appear to have had minsters soon after their establishment, have river-names and were probably all in existence by 730 at the latest. The settlements with topographical names and with the element *tun* appear to be a second layer of important estates, which in turn are followed by those in *tun* linked with personal names representing small personal estates formed from the tenth century onwards. The minsters linked with the personal names of their founders or owners were probably early establishments, possibly before or at the same time as the river-name settlements. The coupling of the *minster* affix with the river-name may indicate a greater importance of the church in these particular settlements than in those where the river-name is linked with *tun*.

The survival of minsters and their wealth

In Hampshire the mother-churches had values of 8-15 times that of the average church (Hase 1975, 37). It has already been noted that the value of minsters is generally less in Dorset than in Hampshire and Wiltshire (above pp 4,5). In order to look at the difference in values between minsters and their dependent churches, two *parochiae*, Wimborne and Gillingham are examined (see Tables 7 & 8).

These have been chosen as many of the lesser churches in the other *parochiae* are not given values in 1291 or 1340. Whilst Wimborne was worth between 3 to 14 times that of its former chapels, Gillingham was only worth 5 to 6 times as much. These figures do not represent the whole picture, however, as they do not include values for some of the chapels still dependent on the minsters which would have been worth considerably less. In addition, Wimborne Minster is not an average example, having the highest wealth of all the minsters in 1291 (see Table 9). The ratio shows less divergence of values in Dorset, supporting the view that the minsters did not accumulate as much wealth in Dorset as in Hampshire and Wiltshire.

As well as recording the taxable income of the churches, the 1340 taxation is, in some cases, one of the earliest records of the amount of glebe which is recorded for 105 of the 229 churches. The average holding was 44a, but ranges from 2a at Wareham St Martin to 2 carucates at Whitchurch Canonicorum. Table 9 shows the glebe of the definite minsters and Table 10 that of the possible minsters. Only a few of the minster glebes are recorded in 1340.[35]

River-Names	Topographical	Other
Cerne – C – cairn	**Sydling** - OE - broad ridge	**Milton Abbas** - OE -middle settlement
Powerstock - C/OE - ?river + place	**Corfe** - OE - gap	**Netherbury** - OE - lower fortified place
Sturminster N. - C/OE – strong or powerful one + church	**Fordington** - OE - farm at the ford	**Preston / Sutton** - OE -Priests' farm or south settlement
Tarrant M. – C – tresspasser	**Chaldon** - OE - hill where calves are pastured	**Buckland** - OE- book land
Loders - ?C – pool stream	**Stalbridge** - OE -bridge on posts	**Abbotsbury** – OE - fortified house or manor of the Abbot
Litton – OE – estate by the noisy stream	**Corscombe** - OE-valley of the road in the pass	**Portesham** - OE - the enclosure of the port
	Canford - OE - Cana's ford	**Handley** - OE - high wood or clearing
		Shaftesbury -OE- fortified place of Sceaft

Table 6. Categories of the possible minsters place-names (interpretations from Mills 1986). OE - Old English: C – Celtic

Church	1291 value	1340 value
Wimborne Minster	£74 3s 4d	£32
Hampreston	£8	£8 2s
Hinton Martell	£5	£5
Hinton Parva	£5	£5
Shapwick	£20	£20

Table 7. Comparison of the value of the minster at Wimborne with churches within its *parochia*.

Church	1291 value	1340 value
Gillingham	£30	£30
Silton	£6	£6
Kington Magna	£6	£6
Buckhorn Weston	£5	£5
Fifehead Magdalen	£4 6s 8d	-

Table 8. Comparison of the value of the minster of Gillingham with churches within its *parochia*.

Minster	DB value	DB landholding	1291 value	1340 value	1340 glebe
Sherborne	-	-	£46. 13s 4d	£41. 6s 11d	-
Wimborne	-	1½h ½v	£73.3s.4d	£32	?
Whitchurch C	(1)	(1)	£36	£24. 6s. 8d.	240a
Sturminster M	-	-	£20	£40	147a
Gillingham	40s	-	£30	£30	-
Bere Regis	(2)	(2)	(4)	(4)	-
Wareham LSM	70s	1h	£1. 10s.	-	-
Beaminster	-	-	(5)	(5)	(5)
Puddletown	(3)	(3)	£17	£47	-
Cranborne	-	-	£10	£21	12a
Charminster	-	-	(4)	(4)	-
Yetminster	-	-	£20	£20	60a
Burton B	(1)	(1)	£10	£10	-
Iwerne M	-	-	£20	£20	100a
Winfrith N	10s	1v	£20	£20	128a

Table 9. The wealth of the Dorset minsters and their landholdings.

    (1) Held together with Bridport: £7, 4h.

    (2)Held with 'Dorchester': £4, 1h 20a.

    (3) Held with Fleet and Chaldon: 57s 6d, 1½h.

    (4) Charminster was held with Bere: 1291 -£5; 1340 - £105 (at least £55 of which was Bere)

    (5) Beaminster was held with Netherbury: 1291 - £73 6s 8d; 1340 - £73 6s 8d; 130a glebe.

Possible minster	DB value	DB landholding	1291 value	1340 value	Glebe 1340
Milton			£6 13s 4d	£6 13s 4d	-
Preston			£16 13s 4d	£16 13s 4d	98a
Netherbury			(1)	(1)	(1)
Powerstock			£22 13s 4d	£22 13s 4d	-
Canford			£20	£20	55a
Bridport	(2)	(2)	£6 13s 4d	-	-
Buckland N			£14 6s 8d	£14 6s 8d	-
Sydling St N			£20	£20	30a
Sturminster N			£13 6s 8d	£23 6s 8d	-
Corfe			£10	£10	40a
Fordington			£21 6s 8d	£21 6s 8d	-
Chaldon H	(3)	(3)	£5 6s 8d	£5 6s 8d	-
Handley			£13 6s 8d	£13 6s 8d	60a
Abbotsbury			£18 13s 4d	£18 13s 4d	32a
Portesham			£17	£17	24a
Shaftesbury			-	-	-
Stalbridge			£13 6s 8d	-	61a
Tarrant M			£20	£20	-
Corscombe			£11	£11	50a
Litton Cheney			£10	£10	50a
Loders			£25	£25	-
Cerne Abbas			£6 13s 4d	£6 13s 4d	10a

Table 10. The wealth of the possible minsters and their landholdings.
(1) Held with Beaminster. 1291 - £73 6s 8d, 1340 - £73 6s 8d; glebe 1340 130a.
(2) Held with Whitchurch, DB value £7, 4h.
(3) Held with Puddletown and Fleet, DB value 57s 6d, 1½ h.

Of those that are, the average of the holdings was 114a, well above the total average. The landholding of Winfrith was recorded in both Domesday Book and in 1340, showing an increase from 1 virgate (30a) to 128a, presumably through endowments. This is the only minster where it is possible to directly compare the landholdings of 1086 and 1340. A holding of 2 carucates is recorded in 1340 for Whitchurch which in 1086 held 4 hides together with Bridport.

The glebe of Bridport church is recorded at the time of the tithe survey as 8a 16p. (Whilst the tithe record is very late, in certain cases, such as Sturminster Marshall, the figures are very similar to those of 1340: 130 acres in the tithe apportionment, and 147 acres in 1340). It seems safe to assume that Whitchurch held at least 2 carucates in 1086, if not more. The tithe map records that of the Wareham churches only Lady St Mary had any glebe, a total of 3a 2r 34p (not including the churchyard). However, an area of 58a 2r 30p of tithe free land in Holy Trinity parish was held by one Elizabeth Smith who held the site of the Priory. The names of her holdings include Priory Mead and Priory Garden, indicating that this formerly belonged to Wareham Priory. It may have been part of the minster's original endowment, though the position of most of this land within the parish of Holy Trinity may imply it was a later gift. Iwerne had a total of just over 76a on the tithe map, some 30 acres less than in 1340. Many of the churches examined as possible minsters have values that are less than those in the group of definite minsters and they generally have smaller

glebes (see Table 10). The average glebe for this group is 47 acres, just 3 acres more than that of the whole group of churches, and less than half of that of the average of the definite minsters (114a). Glebe, therefore, seems to be significantly larger in the case of the minster churches where early records exist.

Conclusion

The utilization of an objective system to identify minster churches by means of their various characteristics has helped to locate both definite and possible minster churches in the county. The definite minsters seem to have additional characteristics that set them apart from some of the possible minsters. Their place-names, for the most part, are quite distinctive, and analysis of them presents an hypothesis for the order of conquest of the south-west, suggesting that Dorset and north Somerset were settled before the southern part of Somerset. The additional evidence of the place-names shows that many of the positively identified minsters were founded on the large primary riverine estates that formed the core of the royal demesne of the newly conquered land in Dorset. It seems sensible to christen these *primary* minsters. Is there any evidence for the genesis of the remaining high-scoring churches? One explanation for this group of possible minsters may be that some of them belong to a group of secondary minsters possibly founded by Alfred: two of the churches associated with Alfredian burhs belong in this group. Many of the remaining high-scoring churches are founded on large monastic estates indicating they may be of ecclesiastical rather than royal foundation. It is possible, therefore, that at least three layers of minster foundation are apparent here. Firstly, the primary minsters, those founded at the centre of royal estates shortly after the Saxon conquest of Dorset. Secondly, a group of churches serving large estates donated to various early monastic houses; and thirdly, churches that were founded at about the time of the building of the burhs. It has been possible tentatively to identify successive layers of foundation through the different characteristics present. This being so, the distinction between primary and secondary refutes Cambridge and Rollason's claim that the characteristics associated with minster churches were possibly all Alfredian or later. This can be illustrated by the case of Preston, a possible foundation of Alfred, where the place-name evidence suggests that the church was not a primary minster. Preston's *parochia* shows no signs of the pattern of fragmentation where land-units gained chapels which gradually became independent, a pattern apparent in most of the primary minsters. There is no evidence for any of the ten churches paying pensions to Preston ever having been dependent upon it and they do not form a coherent topographical unit. This appears to be a case of a church being founded by Alfred and being given a *parochia* containing pre-existing churches. The distinctive pattern of the burhs also suggests a difference in development from the primary minsters and this will be examined further in the next chapter where the high-scoring churches will be looked at from the point of view of their *parochiae* and their relation to royal demesne and the hundredal system, to see if this helps illuminate the picture.

Another important point to note on this theme of the foundation and function of the minsters is that, to all intents and purposes, Sherborne, the cathedral *parochia,* appears to have functioned in exactly the same manner as the primary minsters on royal estates, apart from the fact that it retained a tighter control over its *parochia* suggesting that the pastoral role of the bishop's church did not differ from the other minsters. Evidence for pastoral care within the *parochiae* of the monastic houses is sparse but may be supported by Rudolf of Fulda's use of the term *clericus* to describe the male occupants of the double monastery at Wimborne, suggesting that the priests served the royal estate (above p 8).

Much has been made, recently, of the possibility of the continuity of the British church in the region. Hase uses the suggested correlation of minsters and villas, along with survival of Celtic saints, to suggest that the Saxon church only filled in the gaps in a system put in place in the fifth/sixth centuries by the Irish missionaries. In Somerset there is a distinct group of churches with Celtic dedications: St Kea, at Llantocai (now Street); St Decuman at Watchet; St Kew, Kewstoke and St Carantoc, at Carhampton, to name some. In Dorset the only Celtic dedication of this type was that of *Lanprobi*. Evidence suggests that this church was suppressed and its lands confiscated to form the basis of the bishopric of Sherborne. Investigation of the dedications of the primary minsters show that the vast majority were dedicated to Mary and there are no Celtic dedications in the group. The Dorset evidence hardly supports the statement that 'The middle Saxon church in the west of the region must have been based almost entirely on a sub-roman foundation' (Hase 1994, 51). Even the site of *Lanprobi* cannot be called upon to support this argument. Whilst there are Roman remains under Sherborne cathedral the putative British site was 1.2km to the east at the site of the Old Castle. In Chapter 4 the plan forms of the minster settlements of Dorset will be examined and this may indicate whether there are any likely sites of continuity from a supposed British system.

---

[1] Gerrard and Costen have ranked the Somerset churches using some of the minster characteristics (Gerrard 1987, 15, 16; Costen 1992a, 106-7).

[2] As, for example, Aethelred at Wimborne (Yorke 1990, 145).

[3] As for instance at Portesham which is recorded as £12 plus the vicarage worth £5 in 1291, but as £17 in 1340: *Taxatio,* 182, and *Nonarum,* 46.

[4] The *Return to the Commission of 1650* is a set of documents, quoted by Hutchins, which record the replies of churches to a Commission set up during the Commonwealth to deal with ecclesiastical affairs. See also, Fry 1915, 'The Augmentation Books: 1650-1660 in Lambeth Palace', 48-105.

[5] Beaminster is a possible exception, see below p 90.

[6] See also Blair (1988a, 12,19) where he notes that this view of its importance may have to be modified as in Hampshire Hase had instances of church-scot being attached to later monasteries which had never been minsters.

[7] As, for example, at Edmondsham, Hutchins 3, 427.

[8] On the tithe map Mannington was attached to Gussage All Saints, a link which may date to 1086 when both properties were in the hands of the Count of Mortain: DRO, T/GUS.

[9] There are no Dorset churches of the clasped-tower form that Franklin identifies as suggesting minster-status in Northampton (Franklin 1986, 69-88).

[10] Hinton suggests that a long nave may indicate a minster church though he notes that this factor may be linked to benefactions.

[11] The churches are dealt with in order of rank within this chapter, but alphabetically in the Appendix.

[12] The *vita* was written in 836: RCHM, *Dorset* 5, 78-80, quote at 80.

[13] Theodore's only known surviving poem is dedicated to Haedde (Bischoff and Lapidge 1994, 186).

[14] SMR, Sherborne.

[15] The case was first argued by W Stuart Best 1955, 189-190.

[16] This displacement is one of several that occur about this time, all of which are moved to *defended* sites such as the hill-fort at Old Sarum which would not have been a larger centre of population at that date.

[17] There was a chapel dedicated to St Candida at the western end of the Windwhistle Ridge in the *parochia* of Crewkerne, Somerset (Dunning and Bush 1978, 33).

[18] The skull of St Wandrille is still on display in a reliquary in the abbey of that name in Normandy.

[19] The vicarage was to remain in the hands of Sarum.

[20] Smyth considers the description of Wareham as one of the factors supporting the writing of the work by Bryhtferth.

[21] The church was worth £20 in 1291 and £40 in 1340, the discrepancy resulting from the exemption of hospitals from the 1291 taxation, so only the vicarage is taxed at that date: *Taxation*, 178; *Nonarum*, 56; Graham 1929, 299; *CDF*, 108.

[22] S.1164, thought to be authentic.

[23] Murphy attempts to locate Bectun's monastery and the 30 hides of the grant. However, she examines the question with the belief that the community of Bectun had to be local, considering that they would have been personally involved in the 'husbandry of land' thus ruling out a monastery at Shaftesbury: Murphy, 'Bectun's base', p.25. It is unlikely that the members of the community would have worked much land: this task would fall on those who had lived on the estates before they were acquired by the minster (Foot 1989, 212).

[24] S.357, S.630.

[25] S.656, seen as authentic.

[26] S.347, considered authentic.

[27] *Osmund* 2, 203, where *ecclesiam de Sutton* is confirmed as a previous endowment of the cathedral.

[28] S.1727: the charter is lost but recorded in a list of contents of a lost Glastonbury cartulary. William of Malmesbury also claimed to have seen the document (Scott 1981, 117, 143, 202).

[29] Dunning has suggested that Glastonbury's invention of the Joseph of Arimethea legend was an attempt to gain status in the Benedictine world: lecture in Glastonbury 20th October 1995.

[30] Pershore Abbey appears to have assumed mother-church rights over land acquired in 972, including the right to exact church-scot: Graham Jones, pers. comm.

[31] S.290: the charter is considered authentic.

[32] The parish church is dedicated to St Mary.

[33] I believe that this is a misreading of one of Pearce's symbols (Pearce 1982a, 122, fig.8.3).

[34] Examples of this are Ashbourne which became Ashburton, and Carhampton which was originally Carrum (Ekwall 1960 (4th edn), 14, 87).

[35] Hutchins helps explain this discrepancy: apparently the 1291 tax was used a guide in levying that of 1340, and if the income of great tithes in 1340 did not exceed 1291 value then other articles such as glebe, mortuary payments and lesser tithes were included. As the minsters had large incomes, they would have been able to meet the tax from their greater tithes: Hutchins 1, 102.

CHAPTER THREE:
THE MINSTER *PAROCHIAE*

In the previous chapter examination of the high status churches enabled the identification of definite and possible minsters in Dorset. This chapter will examine these churches further, from the point of view of the areas they controlled, their *parochiae*. Some examples of *parochiae* will be reconstructed, and their boundaries analyzed to see if they follow natural features. The areas under the control of the definite and possible minsters will be compared to see if this gives any clues to the origin of the possible minsters. Do the lesser churches appear thus because of poor survival of evidence or were they different from the outset, perhaps being founded at a later date, and possibly equating with the lesser minsters of Aethelred's law code of 1014 (Whitelock, Brett and Brooke 1981, 390)? In other parts of the country it has been suggested that the tenth-century hundredal systems were based on that of the *parochiae* of the minsters (Hase 1988, 45-8; Blair 1991, 104). The two systems will be examined for signs of correlation, and to see if they relate to the royal demesne. In certain areas of the country, such as eastern England, it has been suggested that there is a relationship between rural deaneries and the *parochiae* of the minsters, but an examination of the rural deaneries in Dorset proved to be of little worth as there are only four in comparison with possibly as many as 37 *parochiae*.[1]

The *parochiae*

The reconstruction of the areas controlled by the minsters is based mainly on the identification of the areas served by their dependent chapels. This process is limited by our knowledge of the origins of most proprietary churches. Only where minster control remained sufficiently strong to retain these churches as chapels, or where they were founded or gained their freedom late enough to appear in the records, do we know to which minster *parochiae* they owed allegiance. In some cases the reconstruction of the *parochiae* can be taken further as detached areas of parish existed, often to be found on the tithe maps. Furthermore, in some instances, the landscape suggests that certain areas belong to one *parochia* rather than another. There are other situations, however, where there is evidence for the existence of a minster church with no or very few chapels recorded to define its *parochia*. The *parochiae* of Whitchurch Canonicorum and Sherborne are examined as they can be reconstructed further. The burhs of Wareham, Bridport, and Shaftesbury then are considered as a group as they show minster characteristics but have only small, poorly-defined *parochiae*. Other comments on the extent of individual *parochiae* are included in the descriptions in Appendix II.

Whitchurch Canonicorum

It has already been established that Whitchurch controlled the area comprising the present parishes of Chideock, Stanton St Gabriel, Charmouth, Catherston Leweston, Wootton Fitzpaine and Marshwood (above p 13). Can any other parishes in the vicinity be assigned to its *parochia*? The tithe maps of Whitchurch, Wootton Fitzpaine and Bettiscombe show six detached areas of tithing (see Fig 4). Two portions of the parish of Bettiscombe remained dependent on Whitchurch, Revelshay Farm and a small area to the south-west of Lower House Farm. In addition,

Bettiscombe has a small detached area to the south of Guppy in the centre of Wootton Fitzpaine (DRO, T/WCC, T/BET, T/WFP). Bettiscombe was given to St Stephen's, Caen, by William, from the royal estate described as Chideock in Domesday Book, and can be safely included in Whitchurch's *parochia*. Though later attached to Burstock, Pilsdon may also originally have been within Whitchurch's jurisdiction as in the 1240 appropriation of Whitchurch, tithes are recorded as due from Pilsdon (Hutchins 2, 211-12; *Sarum*, 264). The Burstock connection was probably brought about through monastic ownership: in 1323 the Abbot of Forde presented one *Ammericus de Gorton* to the chapel of Pilsdon which was attached to Burstock according to the 1340 Inquisition (Hutchins 2, 236; *Nonarum*, 44). As Forde owned both churches, Pilsdon may have been appended to Burstock so they could be served by one priest. Broadwindsor, a large parish to the north of Whitchurch, surrounds Burstock on three sides, suggesting that Burstock was cut out of Broadwindsor. The split had taken place before 1086. The topography suggests that Broadwindsor and Burstock did not lie in this *parochia*. From just west of Monkton Wyld, to the east of Bettiscombe the northern boundary of the *parochia* is determined by the watershed, which also forms the county boundary for part of its length. Pilsdon lies to the south of this divide, including within it the hillfort of Pilsdon Pen, the highest point in Dorset, whereas Broadwindsor and Burstock lie to the north of the watershed (Finberg 1964b, 166).[2]

To the east of Chideock lies the large parish of Symondsbury. At Domesday it belonged to Cerne Abbey though it was not one of its original endowments.[3] Symondsbury was one of the best livings in the county with a glebe of one carucate in 1340 (*Nonarum*, 44). The church is cruciform but was completely rebuilt in the 14th century so it is not possible to tell if this reflects an earlier form (RCHM Dorset 1, 237). However, the narrowness of the central tower suggests that it did not possess the significant pre-Conquest form. Symondsbury had no chapels and its position appears to be peripheral to the surrounding royal estates. In addition, its place-name, 'hill or barrow of a man called Sigemund', suggests that it was a site of strategic importance farmed out to a trustworthy thegn rather than a primary estate (Mills 1986, 141). Symondsbury appears to have been in lay hands when it was given to Cerne in the tenth century, possibly being one of Aethelmaer's estates. Symondsbury is an example of a church on a large monastic estate, acquiring minster characteristics because of the size of its parish.

Lyme Regis lies wedged between the Devon border and the *parochia* of Whitchurch. Its early donation to Sherborne abbey in 774 to provide salt for the community may have removed it from Whitchurch's jurisdiction.[4] However, as the county boundary at this point diverges from its route along the watershed which surrounds the *parochia* of Whitchurch to take in the lower reaches of the river Lim, the unit originally may have looked westwards. In the adjacent parish of Uplyme in Devon, Glastonbury possessed six hides granted by Athelstan to an ealdorman who took it with him when he entered the monastery. Shapwick Grange, which lies within this area, was originally a detached tithing of Axminster, showing that it lay within Axminster's *parochia* (Fox 1970, 39). It seems probable that these two land units named after the river Lyme and now separated by the county

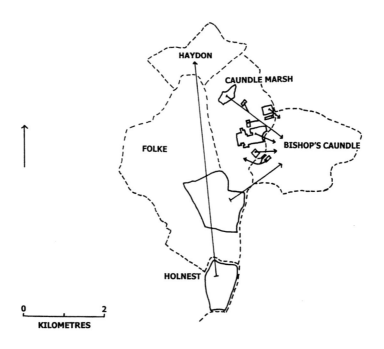

FIGURE 16. DETACHED LAND IN CAUNDLE MARSH

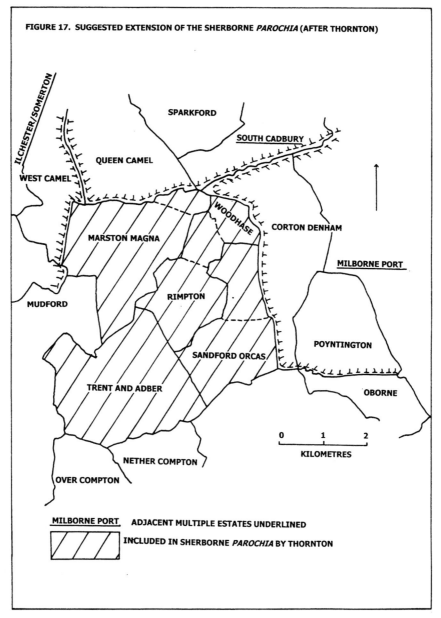

FIGURE 17. SUGGESTED EXTENSION OF THE SHERBORNE *PAROCHIA* (AFTER THORNTON)

boundary were once part of the same land unit. The topography and Axminster's interest in Uplyme favour their connection with that minster rather than with Whitchurch. The *parochia* of Whitchurch, therefore, appears originally to have covered the area comprising the basin of the river Char, running from the river Lim in the west to the river Simene in the east.

Sherborne

The retention of so many of Sherborne's dependent chapels through the middle ages makes it possible to reconstruct its *parochia* with apparent ease (see Fig 3). However, two parishes, Bradford Abbas and Bishop's Caundle, need further examination. Because of its name it has been assumed that Bishop's Caundle was always in the ownership of the bishop but in 1224, the church was given to Sarum by the priory of Breamore (*Sarum*, 163-4). The first record of the name Bishop's Caundle is in 1268 in its Latin form *Kandle Episcopi*. Four of the five Caundle names have manorial additions: Wake, Stourton, Bishop, and Purse. Personal names indicating manorial ownership appear to be the common way of differentiating between manors with river-names, the affix often changing with ownership, a differentiation which probably worked perfectly well at the time, but has led to problems centuries later; witness the mostly unidentifiable Winterborne entries in Domesday Book. If, therefore, Bishop's Caundle only came into the hands of the bishop in the thirteenth century, it is perfectly plausible that its name should have changed at that date along with its ownership, and the fact that the church was in the hands of Breamore Priory before 1224 suggests that this was the case. Had this church always been part of the out-hundred of Sherborne, of which the southern half of the *parochia* was composed, there is no reason why it would not have remained a chapel along with all the others. In addition, Bishop's Caundle was not in the peculiar jurisdiction of the Dean of Salisbury as was the rest of the *parochiae* (Hutchins 4, 235). The interdependence of land between this parish and its neighbour, Caundle Marsh (see Fig 16), is undoubtedly due to land reclamation which probably took place after the manor was joined to the bishop's estates. It seems unlikely, therefore, that Bishop's Caundle was originally part of Sherborne's *parochia*.

Bradford Abbas, whilst being in the hands of the bishop, is notably absent from Sherborne's list of chapelries and, as with Bishop's Caundle, it was not included in the peculiar jurisdiction of the Dean of Salisbury (Hutchins 4, 235). The estate is recorded in the fourteenth century lists of endowments as being given to Sherborne by Athelwulf (839x58) though a charter places it as the gift of Athelstan in 933 (O'Donovan 1988, xlii).[5] A papal bull of 1145 records the church of Bradford *cum capellis*, implying that the church had at least two chapels dependent on it (*Monasticon* 1, 338). A possible explanation for its independence and mother-church status is the existence of the church before the estate was given to Sherborne in the ninth century. It may have been built to serve the remains of the royal estate from which Sherborne was originally granted as geographically it appears to lie within Sherborne's *parochia*.

The question of the extent of Sherborne's *parochia* has been touched upon by Keen and Thornton (Keen 1980, 216-21; Thornton 1988, 32-46). Keen suggested that the area of the

mother-church's *parochia* was the same as that of the original endowment of the bishopric, comprising Sherborne and Castleton, with the royal grants of Oborne, Compton, Bradford Abbas and Thornford added at a slightly later date, but he did not mention the area of the out-hundred of Sherborne, to the south of the town (Keen 1980, 221). The Domesday record makes no mention of the chapelries of Sherborne that formed the out-hundred, but they are almost certainly included in the 43 hides attributed to the Bishop's holding of Sherborne and must have formed part of the original gift of land to the bishopric.

Thornton looked at the *parochia* of Sherborne in his examination of the estate of Rimpton (Somerset) as its church showed no signs of dependence on any of the adjacent Somerset minsters (Thornton 1988, 32-46). He argued that Marston Magna, Trent, Adber, Rimpton and Sandford Orcas belonged in Sherborne's *parochia* but acknowledged that there is insufficient evidence to secure his case as none of these parishes can be shown to have had any ecclesiastical dependence on Sherborne. The 26 hides of Thornton's parishes are seen by him as forming part of the 100 hides of *Lanprobi*, in addition to the 25½ carucates of demesne. However, as the hidage of the land of the monks and bishop adds up to 74, the inclusion of the 25½ carucates of demesne would bring the total to 99½ hides. There seems therefore, to be no good reason for supposing that the carucates were not part of the original 100 hides especially if, as suggested above (p 11), the 100 hides that Cenwalh gave to *Lanprobi* are seen as the foundation grant of the Saxon church of Sherborne. The exemption from tax on the 25½ carucates of demesne might then be seen as originating with the endowment of the bishopric.

Thornton suggests that Marston Magna, Trent, Adber and Rimpton do not belong in the adjacent Somerset multiple-estates (see Fig 17) (Thornton 1988, 32-3). From the geographical point of view, these parishes lie beyond the east-west watershed that forms the northern boundary of the Sherborne *parochia*, a boundary that appears to be as strong as those suggested by Thornton. It is a primary boundary up to which all the smaller parish unit boundaries run. In which case Thornton's parishes appear to be left out in the cold. Two possible solutions to the problem spring to mind. Firstly, these parishes may indeed have been part of the original *parochia* of Sherborne, but not as possessions of the minster. They may well have been included in a royal estate only part of which was given to the bishopric, some of the rest being given to thegns, thus becoming independent at an early date. Alternatively they may only ever have been marginal land in between *parochiae*/royal estates that was colonized at a later date and thus never came under the dominance of the surrounding minsters. Costen showed that a small area in the north of the present parish of Rimpton was a separate one hide estate before 938, and Thornton shows that another hide at Woodhouse only became part of the manor of Rimpton between 953x955 and 964x980 (Thornton 1988, 30). Instead, therefore, of representing fission of multiple estates, this may in fact represent a fusion of small independent units in an area of later expansion onto poorer land that was not covered by the minster system. In view of the fact that Sherborne was the bishopric and that it was so successful at retaining the main body of its *parochia*, an area which adds up to 99½ hides thus almost exactly

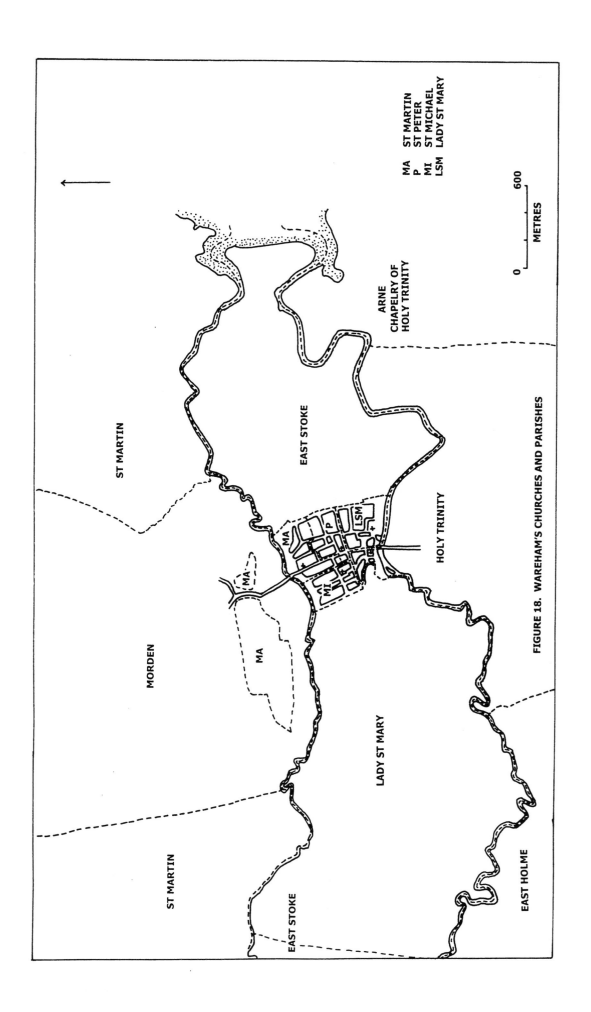

FIGURE 18. WAREHAM'S CHURCHES AND PARISHES

ST MARTIN

EAST STOKE

MORDEN

MA

MA

MA

MI

P

LSM

LADY ST MARY

HOLY TRINITY

ARNE
CHAPELRY OF
HOLY TRINITY

ST MARTIN

EAST STOKE

EAST HOLME

MA   ST MARTIN
P   ST PETER
MI   ST MICHAEL
LSM   LADY ST MARY

600

METRES

0

corresponding with the 100 hides of *Lanprobi*, it seems unlikely that the Somerset parishes were originally part of Sherborne's *parochia*.

Wareham, Bridport and Shaftesbury

The *parochia* of a minster at Lady St Mary, Wareham, is problematical and has been discussed by Keen and Hinton (Keen 1984, 224-7; Hinton 1987, 52-3). The parish of Lady St Mary contains only 823 acres – a very small area for a minster church. Wareham's other two parishes are both much larger; Holy Trinity, 2614 acres, and St Martins, 4053 acres. The fragmentary nature of these parishes (see Fig 18) suggests that reorganization took place at some time after the foundation of the minster. A possible date for such a scheme would be at the establishment of the burh by Alfred. An examination of the parishes within the walls of Wareham shows that the inter-mural area of Lady St Mary parish around the church itself does not extend beyond the walls of the town as might be expected: Lady St Mary's extra-mural parish lies beyond the west wall of the burh. The parish seems to have been reformed either at the time of, or at some time after, the building of the walls. East Stoke parish, which lies to the west of Wareham, had an outlier consisting of the Bestwall peninsula to the east of the burh, an arrangement apparently pre-dating the Conquest as Domesday Book records that Bestwall and East Stoke were both held by Edmer *TRE*. The reorganization of parishes at the time of burh construction is argued by Haslam for London and *Wigingamere* and he proposes that the founding of new churches was 'an integral part of Alfred's burghal policy' (Haslam 1988a, 29; 1988b, 38). Haslam suggests that the wards in East London which were coterminous with the parishes bore the responsibility of maintaining and defending the walls of the burh (Haslam 1988b, 36). The extension of Morden parish southwards to the river Piddle, and the detached area of East Stoke parish to the east of Wareham may be explained as the association of more parishes with the burh as part of the defence strategy. Because of these alterations to the original pattern, it is difficult to gauge the extent of Wareham's *parochia*. A relationship between the hundred and *parochia,* if such exists, would suggest that Wareham sat on the northern edge of a *parochia* extending southwards into Purbeck. The area to the north of Wareham, covered by the parishes of Morden and St Martin's, is a poor area of heathland which has probably only ever been sparsely populated up until modern times. There is some suggestion that it formed part of Bere Regis. Much of Holy Trinity parish is similar and in 1086, very few manors are recorded in the area: Worgret was divided into 3 holdings of about 1 hide each, the biggest being worth 28s; at Stanborough, all that is recorded is ½ hide and a mill worth 40s; and at Bestwall Edmer held 3 hides worth 30s. Wareham's main importance was as a port and access point to the centre of the county. Its *parochia* cannot be reconstructed with any certainty probably because of restructuring at the time of the formation of the burh.

Turning to the other two Dorset burhs, there is no evidence of an early minster at Bridport and this is reflected in the absence of a *parochia* (see below p 90). Bridport, by all appearances, did not exist as a minster church before its establishment as a burh, and its parish seems to have been formed from the adjacent royal estate of Burton Bradstock. The existence of a pre-Alfredian minster at Shaftesbury is also questionable (Figs 10 & 24). If such a church existed, its *parochia* must have extended to the south of the town as the well-defined *parochia* of Gillingham runs up to the northern edge of the town of Shaftesbury. As Alfred's newly founded abbey at Shaftesbury was in possession of virtually all of the lands (excepting Sutton Waldon) stretching southwards to Iwerne Minster, a primary minster, it might be expected that this area was all originally dependent on Iwerne which would account for its northerly chapels of Margaret Marsh and East Orchard. It seems unlikely, therefore, that either Shaftesbury or Bridport had minster churches before their establishment as burhs. Both occupy defensive positions at the edges of *parochiae,* pointing to a reorganization of the minster system with the establishment of burhs by Alfred. Wareham also shows signs of its parochial system having been rearranged at the time of the establishment of the burh. Fordington, another possible minster with a very small *parochia* lying just outside the Roman walled town of Dorchester, may also belong in this category. It may have been promoted to the status of minster when Dorchester became a burh.

Analysis of the *parochiae* boundaries

A glance at a map of the physical geography of Dorset suggests that some of the *parochiae* boundaries appear to follow very distinctive landscape features. In some instances the boundaries of these units can be described as primary boundaries as they run for long distances along natural features such as rivers and watersheds, and other 'lesser' boundaries run up to them. In order to examine the *parochiae* boundaries the parish boundaries (as recorded by the tithe maps) have been measured and divided into the following four main categories of features: definite landscape features, such as rivers, dry valleys, ridges, watersheds, etc.; a lack of any specific features, such as those crossing spurs or heath; man-made features of early date, such as Roman roads or iron-age dykes; and later man-made features, such as field boundaries or roads. Pie charts have been constructed to show the percentage composition of each section of parish boundary for the *parochiae* examined, including the internal parish boundaries. The main drawback in comparing the *parochiae* boundaries to the internal later parish boundaries is that for many of the *parochiae* the boundaries are uncertain, so this exercise has only been undertaken with the three best-defined *parochiae*.

Sherborne (Fig 19)

The examination of the bounds of Sherborne shows that most of the *parochia* bounds follow strong topographical features. The western edge in particular is very distinctive in this respect, being composed almost entirely of river. The two most obvious anomalies in the make-up of the boundary are the northern edge of Oborne and parts of the boundary of Caundle Marsh. The western extremity of Oborne's northern boundary is very dog-legged in nature for over a distance of about 500m suggesting that it follows a line of interlocking fields. The size of the plots indicated by the zig-zagging boundary seems to indicate part of an open field structure with the boundary running around furlongs suggesting late formation. There may be another explanation however. As this boundary is at the highest point of Oborne parish, 150-165m above sea level, it seems unlikely that it was part of the open fields of Oborne, and the boundary at this point may

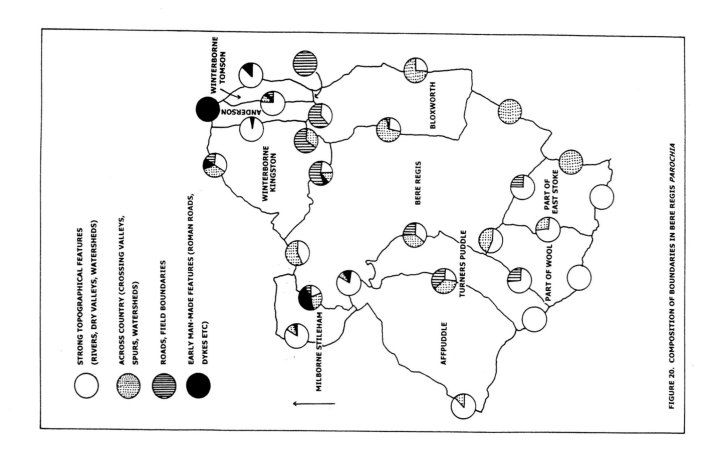

STRONG TOPOGRAPHICAL FEATURES
(RIVERS, DRY VALLEYS, WATERSHEDS)

ACROSS COUNTRY (CROSSING VALLEYS, SPURS, WATERSHEDS)

ROADS, FIELD BOUNDARIES

EARLY MAN-MADE FEATURES (ROMAN ROADS, DYKES ETC)

FIGURE 20. COMPOSITION OF BOUNDARIES IN BERE REGIS *PAROCHIA*

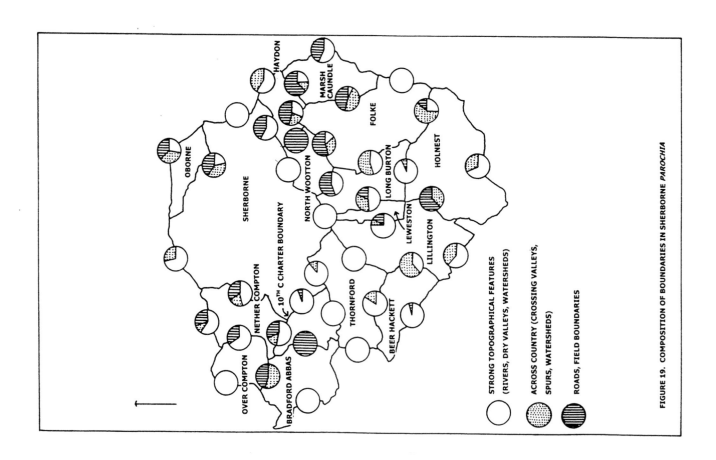

STRONG TOPOGRAPHICAL FEATURES
(RIVERS, DRY VALLEYS, WATERSHEDS)

ACROSS COUNTRY (CROSSING VALLEYS, SPURS, WATERSHEDS)

ROADS, FIELD BOUNDARIES

FIGURE 19. COMPOSITION OF BOUNDARIES IN SHERBORNE *PAROCHIA*

follow the remnants of a Celtic field system, as noted elsewhere by Hooke (Hooke 1988, 128-33). On Poyntington hill, slightly to the north-west of Oborne, the remnants of Celtic field boundaries can be seen on the unploughed downland at about the same altitude as this part of Oborne parish. The jagged interlocking part of Caundle Marsh's boundary also requires explanation. The tithe maps of Caundle Marsh and Bishop's Caundle show a great deal of detached land belonging to Bishop's Caundle in Caundle Marsh (Fig 16) (DRO, T/BCD, T/CDM). Most of the detached land lies to the west of a north-south stream running from Poll Bridge northwards to Ashcombe Farm, with one larger area called Bishop's Down in the corner of the parish of Folke. Given that the boundary between the parishes appears to be late as it follows the field boundaries, and given the late date of the bishop's acquisition of Bishop's Caundle, the boundary may have been altered following that acquisition. The land that forms the detached areas of parish in Marsh Caundle looks very much like land that was reclaimed in the middle ages, and if this occurred after the bishop acquired the land it may explain the interdependent areas of parish. The stream in Marsh Caundle may have provided the original *parochia* boundary. The eastern *parochia* boundary of Sherborne, therefore, appears to have been altered with the acquisition of Bishop's Caundle in the thirteenth century.

Within the *parochia* the boundaries show some interesting features. To the south of Sherborne, the parish boundaries follow the watershed which runs east-west across the *parochia*, forming the junction between the in- and out-hundreds of Sherborne. The boundary appears to have been laid out at one time. Most of the land to the north of the watershed was the demesne land of the manor of Sherborne held between the bishop and monks, along with other separate manors mostly belonging to the monks of Sherborne, whilst that to the south was sub-infeudinated land. The composition of some of the internal boundaries of the *parochia* show signs of late formation. The present boundary between Bradford Abbas and Sherborne is a particularly good example. We know that it is later than the boundary recorded in the 10th century charter of Bradford Abbas which was further east and included Wyke Farm now no longer in Bradford parish.[6] The charter boundary for this stretch follows a dry valley as far as Keeper's Cottage and then a small stream to join the river Yeo on the Thornford boundary. In contrast, the newer boundary follows two long stretches of road and a section of field boundaries joining them.

The composition of the internal boundaries may help with the interpretation of the formation of the parishes. An initial glance at the small parish of Leweston - the farm of Leofwig - suggests that it was carved out of Lillington parish. However, its boundary with Longburton appears to be of later formation: it is winding and takes man-made features much more into account than the boundary with Lillington which follows the watershed for virtually all of its length before dropping down the end of the spur to a stream.

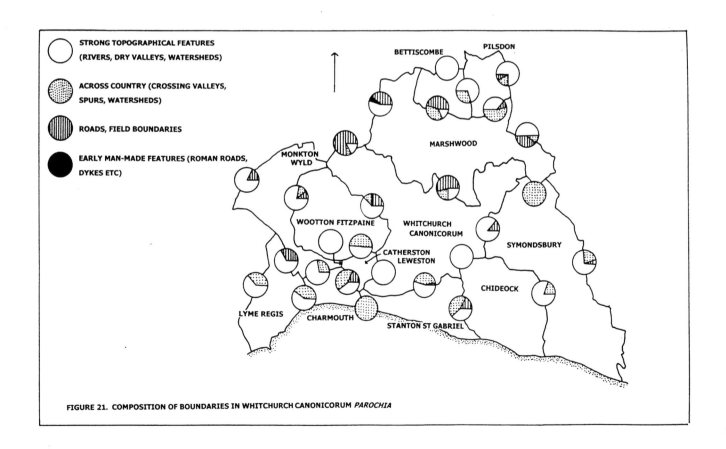

FIGURE 21. COMPOSITION OF BOUNDARIES IN WHITCHURCH CANONICORUM *PAROCHIA*

Lillington is divided roughly in two by an east-west stream, the two parts being marked as inner and outer districts on the tithe map. The southern boundary of Longburton also follows the stream for part of its length. The parish to the south of Longburton is Holnest, a chapel of Longburton. This arrangement, and the nature of the landscape south of the stream, suggests that this area was probably originally waste belonging to the manors in the north. The fields are irregular and there is a larger amount of woodland than to the north of the stream. In summary, the large *parochiae* unit of Sherborne can be seen to be well-defined externally by river and watershed boundaries, whilst internally it is divided in the south into small manorial units.

Bere Regis (Fig 20)

The *parochia* of Bere Regis has less distinctive boundaries than that of Sherborne partly because of the lack of suitable features in places for it to follow. The southern boundary follows the river Frome before turning northwards across the heath. The hundred of Bere continued eastwards past this point to the shores of Poole harbour, but there is no evidence to place the area within the *parochia* of Bere Regis. In the north, the *parochia* boundary follows Combs Ditch, a pre-Saxon feature, running along the watershed. The southern part of the western boundary, which is fairly well-defined, follows rivers, valleys and a ridge. In the north, the *parochia* takes in part of the Winterborne valley and the parishes run from the crest of the chalk down to the river: here the internal boundaries follow natural features. Anderson and Tomson show signs of having been carved out of Winterborne Kingston being typical of the units in many of the chalk valleys, which seem naturally to lend themselves to fission, often producing very small units such as these. Milborne Stileham was part of Bere Regis parish, but its name and position suggest that it was originally part of the unit to the north-west of Bere, probably centred on the Milborne Brook. The boundary between Bere and Milborne Stileham follows a pre-Saxon ditch for a great part of its length which also represents the tithing boundary, so preserving the original *parochia* boundary. As in the case of Sherborne, the internal boundaries follow a higher proportion of later man-made feature.

Whitchurch Canonicorum (Fig 21)

The external boundaries of Whitchurch have a higher proportion of roads in their make-up than the previous two *parochiae*. However, as the roads themselves follow the watersheds and one in particular is mentioned in a charter as a *herepath*, this does not necessarily indicate that the boundaries are not ancient.[7] The western boundary, which also forms the county boundary, divides the *parochiae* of Whitchurch and Axminster. As mentioned above (pp 31,33) Lyme Regis topographically appears to lie in the land unit to the west of Whitchurch. The northern boundary of Whitchurch *parochia* is composed mostly of ridge and watershed, making a small northwards extension to include the Iron Age hill-fort of Pilsdon Pen, the highest point in Dorset. The eastern boundary has a high amount of stream and river in its composition, joining the river Simene at Atrim, which flows into the river Brit (formerly the Woth). Within the *parochia* the parishes of Stanton St Gabriel, Chideock and Symondsbury are topographically well-defined units. Most of the rest of the parish units appear to have been carved out of Whitchurch at a late date; Abbots Wootton was given to Orc in 1044 and Bettiscombe by William the Conqueror to St Stephen's, Caen, though a small part around Revelshay Farm remained as part of the tithable land of Whitchurch. The late formation of such boundaries as that between Marshwood and Whitchurch, and Bettiscombe and Marshwood is illustrated by their greater use of minor roads and field boundaries.

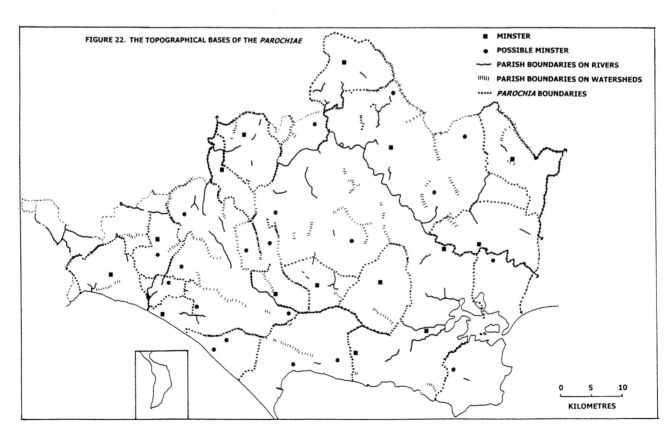

FIGURE 22. THE TOPOGRAPHICAL BASES OF THE *PAROCHIAE*

■ MINSTER
● POSSIBLE MINSTER
⌒ PARISH BOUNDARIES ON RIVERS
⅏ PARISH BOUNDARIES ON WATERSHEDS
⋯ *PAROCHIA* BOUNDARIES

0 5 10
KILOMETRES

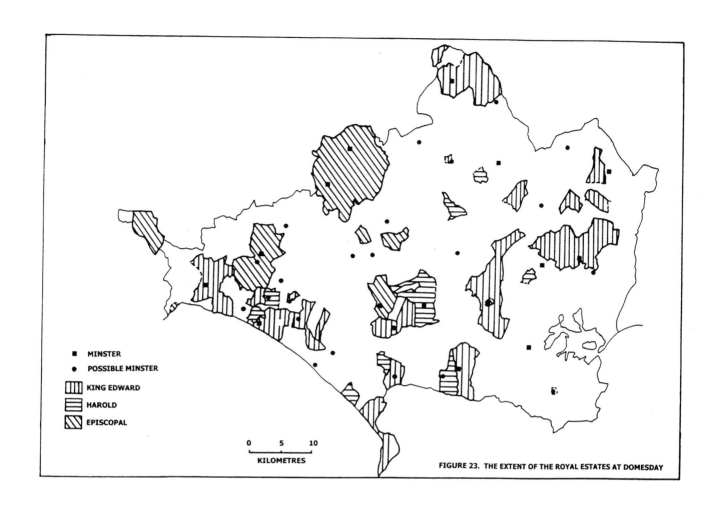

MINSTER

POSSIBLE MINSTER

KING EDWARD

HAROLD

EPISCOPAL

0   5   10
KILOMETRES

FIGURE 23. THE EXTENT OF THE ROYAL ESTATES AT DOMESDAY

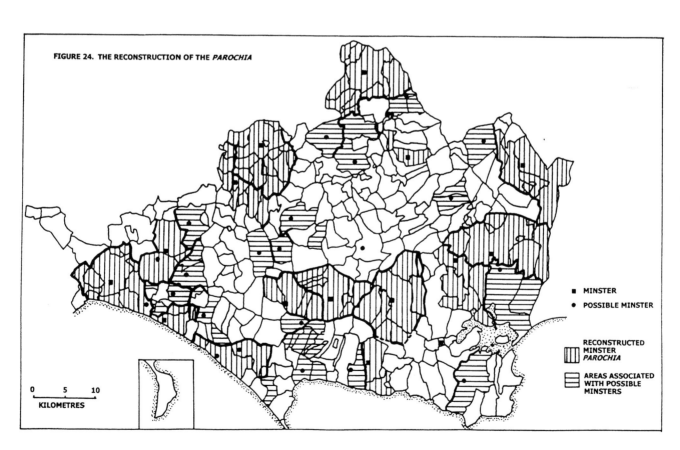

FIGURE 24. THE RECONSTRUCTION OF THE *PAROCHIA*

MINSTER

POSSIBLE MINSTER

RECONSTRUCTED
MINSTER
PAROCHIA

AREAS ASSOCIATED
WITH POSSIBLE
MINSTERS

0   5   10
KILOMETRES

The topographical bases of the parochiae (Fig 22)

The boundaries of the *parochiae* use more major topographical features than the internal boundaries of the later parishes into which the *parochiae* split and it is very noticeable that some of the *parochiae* consist of natural land units such as river basins; Gillingham and Whitchurch Canonicorum are good examples. In her study of Leicestershire, Richardson found that many of the dominant parish boundaries 'were related to memorable landscape features', but was unable to link them to *parochiae* boundaries because of the sparsity of Leicestershire minster evidence (Richardson 1996, 52). In Dorset the minsters served royal or episcopal estates and their *parochiae* reflect the boundaries of those estates. The royal estates (Fig 23), therefore, appear to have been based on geographically defined land-units, which elsewhere in the country have been shown to function as multiple estates.[8] Hall notes for Raunds that the external boundary of the estate 'consists of smooth segments following watersheds or brooks, but within, the boundaries of each township have many right-angle irregularities' (Hall 1988, 107). The internal irregularities suggesting late formation can be seen within other Dorset *parochia*, for example, in the southern part of the parish of Yetminster, and the north-south section of boundary between Abbotsbury and Portesham. It would appear that the Saxon conquerors had a preference for certain types of land unit; generally compact, well-defined river basins, bordered by watersheds. The long, narrow chalk valleys do not seem to have been to their taste at all, as none of these form royal demesne, nor is there any sign of primary minsters in them.

The minsters, royal demesne and monastic lands

The reconstruction of the *parochiae* shows that the minsters of the county are mostly situated at the centre of royal or episcopal estates (see Figs 23 & 24). Significantly, the more definite the minster status the more likely the church is to be associated with royal or episcopal estates. This may be an accident of survival in that those churches may have retained superior status through being at the centre of such important estates. Alternatively, as suggested in Chapter 2, they may represent an initial layer of primary minster foundations, the *ealden* minsters of Edgar (Whitelock, Brett and Brooke 1981, 97-98). If this were the case it might be possible to detect characteristics in the remaining high-scoring churches which would throw light on their origins. The ownership of the high-scoring churches will, therefore, be examined more thoroughly. The churches as a whole can be sub-divided into five groups according to the type of estate on which they were situated in 1086, or earlier if known; royal, episcopal, monastic houses founded before 950, monastic houses founded post 950, and lay (see Table 11). The table very clearly shows the predominance of definite minsters on royal and episcopal lands: 13 of the 16 positively identified minsters were founded on either royal or episcopal estates.

The remaining groups have churches with minster characteristics but few or no chapels, and *parochiae* consisting of usually only the later parish, albeit usually a large area, in the hands of an ecclesiastical body at the time of DB. Corscombe and Stalbridge are two good examples of this type of church. Both in the hands of Sherborne Abbey, they have very large parishes, belonging almost entirely to the abbey. The churches of Glastonbury at Buckland Newton, Milton at Sydling St Nicholas, and Shaftesbury at Handley and Corfe Castle may be further examples. These 'pseudo-minsters' appear to be churches founded by monastic owners on large estates in their ownership. Alternatively, they may represent defunct primary minsters or minsters that had become ineffectual beyond their immediate area. However, they lack some of the characteristics of minsters, in particular, they are not founded on primary riverine sites in well-defined topographical territories and they do not have riverine place-names. Those belonging to early foundations such as Glastonbury would almost certainly have been established following the gift of the land to the abbey. Evidence suggests that the first layer of minsters in the county represented only a partial covering which was extended by these pseudo-minsters planted on monastic estates.

Royal	Episcopal	Monastic Pre-950	Monastic Post-950	Lay
Wimborne *	Sherborne *	Shaftesbury	Sydling St N	Canford *
Whitchurch *	Beaminster *	Iwerne Minster *	Milton	Powerstock
Sturminster M *	Charminster *	Corfe	Abbotsbury	Chaldon
Gillingham *	Yetminster *	Handley	Portesham	Loders
Bere Regis *	Netherbury	Sturminster N	Cranborne *	Preston
Puddletown *	?Iwerne Minster*	Buckland Newton	Tarrant Monkton	
Burton B *		Stalbridge	Cerne	
Winfrith *		Corscombe		
Wareham *				
Fordington				
Litton Cheney				
Bridport				

Table 11. Categorization of high-status churches by earliest recorded ownership. * Definite minster.

Glastonbury appears to have had a policy of minster foundation on its estates: the estate of Shapwick in Somerset illustrates this point. In some senses its church functioned as a minster but, its place-name is secondary in nature; its situation is unlike the royal minsters which sit at focal points within well-defined topographical territories; and the church and parish were both small. In addition, whilst the great abbey had relatively few estates in its early days, acquiring many of them in the ninth and tenth centuries, Shapwick was on one of the abbey's early acquisitions (Costen 1992b, 29).

The picture painted by this division of high-scoring churches into primary and pseudo-minsters indicates a partial covering of the county in the first instance with minsters founded at the centre of royal and episcopal estates (see Fig 23). The gaps in this system may result purely from the loss of intervening minsters. However, the difference in the topographical nature of the pseudo-minsters implies that they were not part of the first flush of royal / episcopal minsters, suggesting gaps between the royal foundations, especially in the less intensely exploited part of the county, for example areas around the Caundle brook, and the area to the west of Dorchester around Maiden Newton and Toller Porcorum. Monastic estate churches seem to have filled in some of the gaps, providing a secondary layer of high-status churches.

Endowment of the minsters
Very little evidence survives concerning the original endowment of the Dorset minsters. Sherborne had its reputed grant of 100 hides but, even if genuine, this cannot be taken as representative as it formed the endowment of the bishopric. Keen has suggested that all the lands that formed Wimborne's *parochia* were part of that monastery's original endowment. A possible problem is highlighted with this interpretation as it would infer that the royal *tun* of Wimborne stood on a monastic estate (Coulstock 1993, 4). This seems to be putting the cart before the horse. Wimborne's inclusion in the ancient demesne lands of Domesday Book and the place-names within the *parochia* suggest a different interpretation. Two estates within the *parochia* have names associated with ecclesiastical ownership; Hinton - *hiwan tun* - (Martell and Parva); and Hampreston - the *ham* of the priests. If the whole of the *parochia* were in the hands of the monastery, these place names would have been superfluous. Instead, they must indicate the land on the royal estate that was apportioned to the monastery. The parish of Piddlehinton within the *parochia* of Puddletown may be another example. Everitt notes that in Kent several minsters have Preston names in their immediate environs suggesting the original estates of the minsters (Everitt 1986, 266), a Dorset example of which is the Preston in the southern part of Iwerne Minster parish. The suggested pattern of minsters founded at the centre of royal estates (and all the main royal estates of Dorset have minsters) must preclude all those estates forming the endowments of the minsters or there would be no royal estates. Not all early monasteries were endowed with large estates: Bede tells us that when Hild was recalled to Northumberland by Bishop Aidan, she was granted one hide on the edge of the river Wear, where she lived with her companions under the monastic rule (*Bede*, 246). These early minsters would have been endowed with a portion of the lands within the royal estates to supplement their income from the church-scot which Ine's laws enforced as a compulsory payment (Whitelock 1955, 399).

Minster *parochiae* and the hundredal system
A link was suggested between the hundredal system and mother-churches in 1915 by Page in his work on the Domesday churches (Page 1915, 66, 67, 71). More recent work has emphasized this relationship: in Hampshire the two systems share common boundaries, a relationship which is also present in Surrey (Hase 1988, 46-47; Blair 1991, 104). For Devon, there is conflicting opinion: Reichel, writing some twenty years after Page, dismissed the postulated link between hundred and minster with the statement, 'it is difficult to see what possible connection there can be between the organization of the hundred and the organization of the church' (Reichel 1939, 336). Writing more recently, however, Orme identifies fourteen minsters in Devon, most of which are central to hundreds (Orme 1991, 9). Reichel's objections to a link between the two systems, which were mostly concerned with the discrepancy in date between the formation of the two, can be easily overcome if a link between the area of the *parochiae* and the estates of royal vills is taken as acceptable. The correlation between the royal and ecclesiastical geography links the minster system with the hundredal system. Page noted that Dorset 'is not satisfactory for an investigation of this nature' and that 'the hundred system apparently had not fully developed' by the Conquest (Page 1915, 71). However, whilst Domesday Book itself reveals little information on the minster system or the hundreds of Dorset, both can be reconstructed to some extent from other sources.

The early composition of the hundreds in the south-western counties is elusive: Domesday Book does not group manors under hundreds, mentioning only two Dorset hundreds: Buckland and Purbeck. The source for the Dorset hundreds is the Geld Rolls which, whilst not listing the manors in each hundred, describe the hidage, the total exempt demesne of the tenants-in-chief, and their demesne. This has enabled Thorn to reconstruct most of the Dorset hundreds for the eleventh century. His reconstruction (Fig 25) and Table 12 will be used to compare the hundredal and minster systems (Thorn 1988; 1991). There is a total of 39 Geld Roll hundreds in Dorset but only 15 churches with definite minster status (shown in bold). Looking firstly at the distribution of minsters within the hundreds, it will be immediately apparent, that while some hundreds have one minster, there are also many with no minster and others that have more than their fair share such as Beaminster. Turning to the relationship between the reconstructable *parochiae* and the hundreds, Table 12 shows a mixed correlation. Sherborne is probably the best fit, with only one discrepancy. Whitchurch Canonicorum, Gillingham, Cranborne and Puddletown *parochiae* are all fairly similar to their hundreds. The minsters of Sturminster Marshall and Canford Magna, taken together, cover the area of Cogdean hundred almost exactly. Bere Regis *parochia* has lost its north-eastern corner but has gained Wareham. Dorchester hundred had within it two high-status churches, Fordington and Charminster, but only Charminster was definitely a minster.

HUNDRED	MINSTER	PARISHES ADDITIONAL TO HUNDRED
1 Gillingham	**Gillingham**	Stour Provost, Todber, Margaret Marsh
2a-b Sherborne	**Sherborne**	Bishop's Caundle, Lydlinch (pt)
3 Brunsell	Stalbridge	Purse Caundle, Lydlinch (pt), Stourton Caundle
4 Newton	Sturminster Newton	Hinton St Mary, Belchalwell, Okeford Fitzpaine
5a-b Farrington	---	---
6 Sixpenny	**Iwerne Minster** (Shaftesbury)	Shaftesbury, Cann, Melbury Abbas, Compton Abbas -
7 Handley	Sixpenny Handley	-
8 *Alvredesberge*	Cranborne	Woodyates, Pentridge
9 Yetminster	**Yetminster**	Melbury Osmund, Melbury Sampford, Melbury Bubb, Batcombe (Leigh is in the *parochia* but not the hundred)
10 Buckland	Buckland Newton	Wootton Glanville, Mappowder, Pulham (pt), Minterne Magna (pt), (Plush is part of Buckland *parochia*)
11a-b *Hundesburge*	---	-
12 Pimperne	---	-
13 *Langeburge*	Tarrant Monkton	Ashmore, Tarrant Gunville, Farnham, Chettle, Tarrant Hinton, Langton Long, Tarrant Rawston, Tarrant Keyneston
14a-b Knowlton	---	-
15a-b Beaminster	**Beaminster** (Netherbury) (Corscombe)	Crawley, Wambrook, Chardstock, Broadwindsor (pt), Stoke Abbot, Halstock, Corscombe, Mosterton, South Perrott, Cheddington
16a-c *Modbury*	Sydling St Nicholas	-
17a-b *Stana*	Cerne Abbas	Evershot, Frome St Quintin, Cattistock, Leigh, Compton Abbas, Hawkchurch (pt), Minterne Magna (pt), Godmanstone, Alton Pancras, Piddletrenthide
18 Hilton	Milton Abbas	Stoke Wake, Woolland, Ibberton, Melcombe Horsey, Hilton, Cheselbourne
19 Combsditch	---	-
20 Badbury	**Wimborne Minster**	Tarrant Crawford, Tarrant Rushton, Witchampton, Gussage All Saints
21 *Canendone*	---	-
22a-b Whitchurch	**Whitchurch Canonicorum**	Burstock, Broadwindsor (pt), Lyme Regis, (Bettiscombe was in the *parochia*)
22 Redhove	---	-
24a-d Eggardon	Powerstock	Hawkchurch (pt), Toller Porcorum, Askerswell (pt), Long Bredy, Winterborne Abbas
25a-b Tollerford	---	-
26a-b Frampton	---	-
27a-c Dorchester	**Charminster** (Fordington)	Hermitage, Stickland (Devon), Fordington, Bradford Peverell, Winterborne St Martin (pt)
28 Puddletown	**Puddletown**	Dewlish, Milborne St Andrew, Tolpuddle
29 Bere Regis	**Bere Regis** (Wareham)	Wareham St Martin, Morden (pt), (Anderson, Winterborne Tomson and Bloxworth were part of the *parochia*)
30 Charborough	---	-
31 Cogdean	**Sturminster Marshall** Canford Magna	- -
32 Loders	Loders	-
33 *Goderthorne*	**Burton Bradstock**	Swyre
34 *Uggescombe*	Portesham/Abbotsbury	Winterborne Steepleton, Littlebredy, Kinston Russell, Langton Herring, Fleet
35 Cullifordtree	Preston	Wyke Regis, Portland, Broadway, Radipole, Upway, Bincombe, West Knighton
36 Chilbury	---	-
37 Winfrith	**Winfrith Newburgh**	Combe Keynes, East Lulworth, Wool (pt)
38 Hasler	---	-
39 Ailwood	Corfe Castle	Studland, Swanage, Worth Matravers (pt), Langton Matravers

Table 12. A comparison of *parochiae* and hundreds. Primary minsters shown in bold.

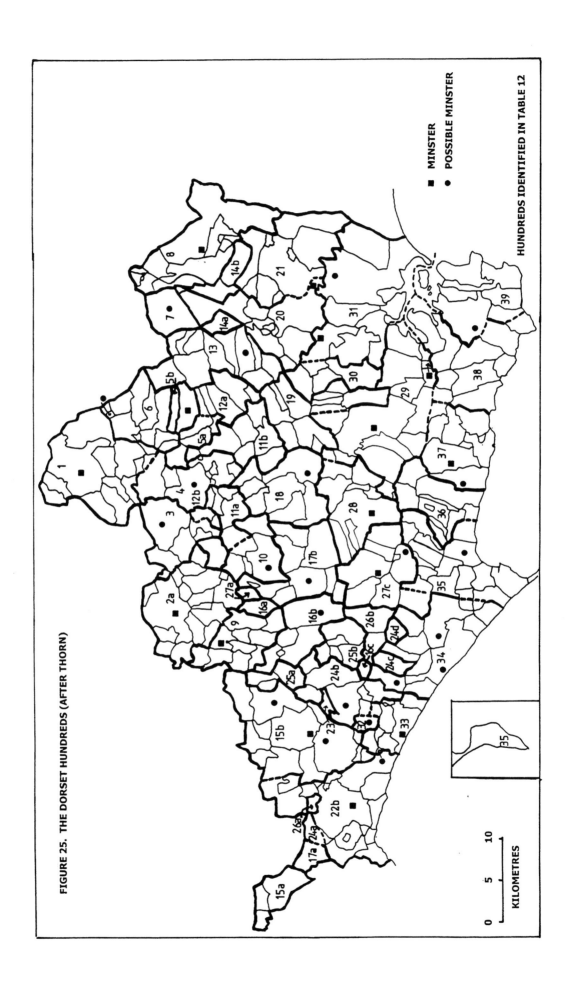

FIGURE 25. THE DORSET HUNDREDS (AFTER THORN)

■ MINSTER

● POSSIBLE MINSTER

HUNDREDS IDENTIFIED IN TABLE 12

KILOMETRES

0   5   10

In virtually all cases, the *parochiae* cover less area than their corresponding hundreds. It may be that the evidence for the attachment of the other areas within the hundred to the minsters has simply disappeared and that the *parochiae* originally covered larger areas. This does not appear to have been true for all cases, however: it does not explain the loss of Bloxworth to Bere hundred or the inclusion of the land north of Wareham, which was served by the minster at Wareham, in Bere hundred.

Is it possible to account for the poor correlation? Hinton showed that in the east of the county there appeared to have been some reorganization of the royal demesne, affecting the hundredal system, which Stafford attributes to the period just before the Conquest (Hinton 1987, 51; Stafford 1980, 491-502, at 499). A clue to the reorganization may lie in the ownership of the hundreds. Thorn noted that it was not possible to tell in Dorset if the hundreds had descended to private ownership by the time of DB (Thorn 1991, 38). Eyton, however, writing at the end of last century was quite ready to divide up the ownership of the hundreds along the lines of their later fate distributing them between the king and ecclesiastical bodies. He sub-divided the king's hundreds into three distinct groups: those that were based on units of ancient demesne; those that had belonged to Queen Matilda; and those wherein the main manors belonged to Harold, Earl of Wessex.[9] *Langeberge* and *Albretesberge*, which he credited to Queen Matilda, were formed around lands that had belonged to Brictric, an important English thegn. An analysis of the hundreds may determine if any were in hands other than the king in 1086.

An examination of the land-holdings of Earl Harold suggests that some hundreds were in private ownership. Eyton attributes the hundreds of Puddletown, Hilton, Charborough, Ailwood, Farringdon, Frampton and Loders to Harold. Barring those recently acquired manors that he held illegally, all but three of Harold's Domesday manors (Chaldon in Winfrith, Shillingstone in *Hunesberga*, and Fleet in *Uggescombe*) lie within these hundreds. Puddletown was Harold's main Dorset manor to which the third penny of the shire was attached. Ailwood and Hilton hundreds do not appear to have been in Harold's ownership, however. In the entry for Puddletown, we are told that 1½ hides in Purbeck, which Thorn locates at Leeson, are attached to Puddletown (*DB*, note 1,8). As Harold's manor in Ailwood hundred was attached to his Puddletown manor, it seems unlikely that he was in control of Ailwood Hundred, where Shaftesbury Abbey was the main landholder. There seems little reason to suppose that Harold controlled Hilton Hundred, either, as his manor of Ibberton was small and marginal, although the only member of the hundred not in ecclesiastical hands.

Three of the hundreds attributed to Harold by Eyton, Charborough, Frampton and Loders have the appearance of recent creations, unlike Puddletown, Hilton and Ailwood, which look like ancient geographical land units: Puddletown and Hilton both consist of large parts of drainage basins; and Ailwood comprises most of the Purbeck peninsula. Hinton has argued that Charborough hundred resulted from a reorganization and that most of the southern manors within it were probably originally attached to Sturminster Marshall in Cogdean hundred (Hinton 1987, 53). Loders and Frampton both consist of single manors, Loders in Harold's ownership

and Frampton in that of his mother, Gytha. As Loders reverted to royal ownership with the Conquest, its existence as a separate hundred can only be accounted for if it was formed before 1066 for the convenience of Harold. The land immediately to its south in Godderthorn Hundred was part of the ancient royal demesne and there would have been no point in creating a separate hundred consisting solely of Loders manor after the Conquest. Frampton may be a similar case, but as these lands of the Godwin family were given to St Stephen's, Caen, there is a possibility that the Hundred was created after the Conquest, though it is probably more likely that St Stephen's inherited an already existing hundred. These hundreds, apparently newly created in the pre-Conquest period, reflect a trend of hundreds organized on a tenurial basis rather than a geographical one (Thorn 1991, 37). Whilst their origins are obscure, it may be speculated that the manorial hundreds owned by Harold came about after the creation of the earldom of Wessex by Cnut in c.1018 (Lawson 1993, 177). The earldom would probably have been endowed with land from royal demesne, prompting a re-organization of the hundredal arrangements. Hinton suggests that Charborough hundred came into existence following the alienation of the main part of the royal manor of Sturminster Marshall to Archbishop Stigand, an event which probably occurred when he came to prominency in the reign of Edward the Confessor. However, the creation of the hundred may have pre-dated the alienation of the remaining royal land of Sturminster Marshall, and be attributable to the time of the gift of Charborough to Earl Godwin. Thus we can see a gradual change in the hundreds as the ancient, topographically-based land units are broken down, and a more piecemeal collection of units based on ownership take their place.

The fragmentation of hundreds can also be seen in the western part of the county, where a highly interconnected area of hundreds existed around Litton Cheney. Some of the outliers in this region can be accounted for on manorial grounds. West Compton was an outlier of Modbury hundred, which was later in the ownership of Milton Abbey. Similarly, Bettiscombe was an outlier of Frampton hundred, both properties of St Stephen's, Caen. This must have been a post-Conquest arrangement as Bettiscombe was part of the royal demesne of Whitchurch before the Conquest. Both examples illustrate the disintegration of a geographically based system in favour of a tenurial one. The interlocking hundreds of Eggardon and *Uggescombe* may also result from this process. Eggardon has two outliers amidst the hundred of *Uggescombe*, Winterborne Abbas and Long Bredy, both properties of Cerne Abbey. As both hundreds were held by the king, it seems difficult to fathom why they should be attached to one other than where they are situated. A great deal of Uggescombe hundred was in the possession of Abbotsbury Abbey and this may have influenced the placement of the Cerne manors. In north Dorset, Iwerne Courtney formed an outlier of Farringdon hundred probably because it was surrounded on all sides by the properties of Shaftesbury Abbey in Sixpenny hundred. Cerne may have preferred their manors to be included in a hundred that was not so overwhelmingly composed of another abbey's estates. Once again, as the ancient demesne units broke up, new manorial links were dictating a new hundredal pattern. The pattern shown in Dorset, therefore, is one where the hundredal system and that of the *parochiae* do not show a high degree of correlation. This was probably not always the case, however, as the discrepancies appear to have been brought about by alterations to the hundredal system as it started to become more tenurially based in the immediate pre-Conquest period. Rather than showing a lack of development of the hundredal system as Page suggested, the Dorset hundreds appear to have development beyond the initial geographical stage (though this may be seen as a deterioration of the system rather than development). The result is that the *parochiae* and hundreds have little in common for much of the county, and that the hundreds do not provide a key to the form of lost minster *parochiae* (if such exist).

The Grouping of Hundreds
Thorn has collated evidence showing that hundreds were grouped around royal manors at an early date in the south-west (Thorn 1991, 39). The same appears to be true of the manors of the bishop. The bishop of Sherborne owned all of the land within the hundred of Sherborne and would have been in control of the hundred. In the thirteenth century he was also in control of Beaminster and Yetminster hundreds. The *ASC* informs us that hundreds were grouped into three in 1008 in order to provide ships for the royal fleet (*ASC*, 138). The writ of Bishop Aethelric of Sherborne, written between the years 1001/2 and 1009/12, concerning lands from which he was paying ship-scot suggests that the bishop owned all three hundreds before the Conquest. Aethelric wrote to Ealdorman Aethelmaer in an attempt to reclaim 33 hides of land which was part of the 300 hides from which he had previously received shipscot. The lands are listed geographically (see Table 13 and Figs 26 & 27), and all but one fall within the hundreds of Sherborne, Yetminster and Beaminster.[10] *Bubbancumbe*, identified as Bookham in Buckland Newton, is the only place not later in one of the bishop's hundreds but it is immediately adjacent to Alton Pancras so may well have originally formed part of that manor (*DPN* 3, 241). The OS map shows two manors

adjacent to Dibberford just to the north of Beaminster Down: Buckham and Wellwood. All three units are of a similar size, and have definitive hedge boundaries. Just to their north lies another unit, what is now called Pickett farm in South Perrott, defined by parish boundaries on three sides. This is probably the unit called *Peder* in the writ (Ordnance Survey, 1st edn 6" map, Dorset Sheet XX SW). Buckham was held by three thegns *TRE* and attached to it was 1 hide of land in *Welle* which Thorn identifies as Wellwood (*DB*, note 3,18). We are told that this land is amongst some that the bishop had had in exchange for 'Shipley' which remains unidentified. It would seem that with the Conquest the bishop finally managed to regain control of two of his missing manors. As all the places mentioned in the writ lay within the bishop's three hundreds from which he was collecting tax at the beginning of the 11th century, the evidence strongly suggests that they must have been in his ownership from at least that date, presenting an example of hundreds grouped into three. This group of hundreds correlates fairly well with the minsters and their *parochiae*, probably because the ownership remained concentrated in the hands of the bishop thus retaining the earlier form of the *parochiae*.

A second grouping of hundreds appears around the manor of Wimborne. However, the hundredal system is strongly at odds with the minster system in this area. The hundreds of Badbury and *Canedone* divide Wimborne's *parochia* into two, representing demesne and non-demesne lands. The two hundreds stretch further north than the *parochia* and interlock with a third small hundred, Knowlton, comprising mostly royal land. This must result from the rearrangement of the night's farm groups suggested by Stafford (1980). *Canedone* hundred contained land that had been part of Wimborne's *parochia* but was no longer royal demesne, along with two monastic properties, Chalbury and Horton, in the north. Knowlton hundred was very small, containing

Hundred	Place	Identity	DB entry
Sherborne	*Bubbancumbe*	Bookham	-
	Awultune	Alton Pancras	2.2
	Upcerl(e)	Upcerne	2.3
Yetminster	*Cliftun(e)*	Clifton Maybank	27.6
	Hiwis(ce)	Huish Dairy Farm	-
	Tril	Trill	27.6
Beaminster	*Wyllon*	Wellwood	3.18
	Buchaematune	Buckham	3.18
	Dibberwurðe	Dibberford	-

Table 13. Bishop Aethelric's lost properties.

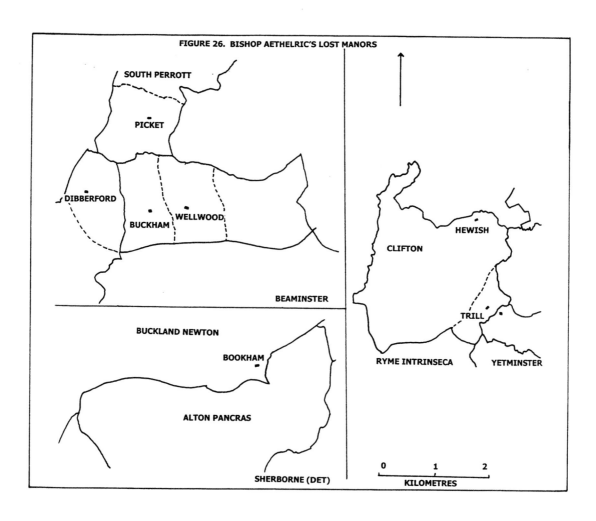

FIGURE 26. BISHOP AETHELRIC'S LOST MANORS

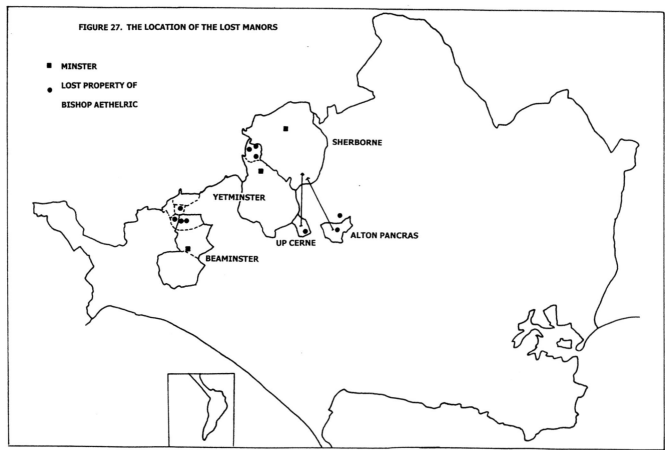

FIGURE 27. THE LOCATION OF THE LOST MANORS

■ MINSTER

● LOST PROPERTY OF
BISHOP AETHELRIC

only Knowlton, Gussage All Saints and Long Crichel. It is difficult to see why this should have been a separate hundred unless it was the remnants of a previously larger hundred which may have additionally included Horton, Chalbury, Gussage St Michael, More Crichel and Witchampton. It may be, therefore, that two original hundreds existed, one coterminous with Wimborne's *parochia* and the other encompassing the parishes between it and the *parochia* of Cranborne which formed the hundred of *Albretesberge*. However, there are no high-status churches in this intermediate area. These examples show some evidence for the grouping of hundreds in Dorset. The case of Wimborne where the old *parochia* is rearranged into hundreds, one containing royal demesne and the other properties that had left royal ownership, suggests a fairly late date for this arrangement, which possibly occurred with the regrouping of the night's farms in the immediate pre-Conquest period. In contrast, the three hundreds of the bishop retained a distinct resemblance to the *parochiae,* though as noted above p 33, the hundred of Sherborne was divided into and in- and out-hundreds, representing the demesne and non-demesne land.

Conclusion

The reconstruction of the *parochiae* of Dorset presents a very piecemeal picture, reflecting the survival of the strong minster churches. Despite the paucity of the evidence it is still possible to gain some insight into the layout of the minster system and its spatial relationship with other administrative units, the royal demesne and the hundredal system. Where the *parochiae* can be reconstructed the minsters can be shown to have been focal points in what were either large estates of royal demesne or holdings of the episcopacy.

The poor state of survival of many of the *parochiae* makes it difficult to come to any conclusions about the extent of the minster system as it first existed in the county. There are several large gaps without any churches of significantly high status to have been minsters suggesting either an initial absence or non-survival, such as the area to the west of Dorchester where Frampton may have filled in one of the gaps. More than one stage of minster construction seems to be evident from the existence of a class of lesser minsters with small parochiae, usually with no or very few chapels, serving large monastic estates. The fact that these lesser or pseudo-minsters are in settlements with topographical place-names but are not in the river-name category isolated as being so important in Dorset in Chapter 2, suggests that they are indeed later foundations on smaller, less important estates, probably filling in the gaps between the large royal primary estates served by the *ealden* minsters. The reconstructed *parochiae* show that they covered areas that formed strong topographical units. A third layer of high status churches can be recognized in association with the burhs. The Dorset burhs all appear to have had new high-status churches created for them thus altering the existing minster *parochiae* by the creation of new parishes, a process which is most clearly seen at Wareham. Alfred may also have been responsible for other churches such as that at Preston in Sutton Poyntz which has all the appearances of a *created* minster church: the churches contributing to its upkeep appear to have been assigned to it rather than evolved from it. These differences in origin have been discovered through the examination of the *parochiae* under the control of the high-scoring churches. In the following chapter, a study of the siting and topography of the settlements of the primary minsters and other high-status churches will be undertaken to see if the three distinct types of minsters are apparent in the immediate environs of the churches.

The units of the *parochiae* seem to correlate fairly well with the ancient royal demesne lands but the flux in the hundredal units before the Conquest has prevented the survival of any great correlation between the minster and hundredal systems in Dorset. The restructuring of the hundreds along manorial lines was probably intensified if not initiated by the creation of the earldom of Wessex and by the depletion of the royal demesne caused by large grants to the church such as that of Sturminster Marshall to Archbishop Stigand. The onset of the break-up of the geographically-based hundredal system into smaller units in private ownership implies less political restraint in Dorset than in neighbouring Hampshire, and further east in Surrey, where Hase and Blair have shown a high degree of similarity between the minster *parochiae* and the hundreds. This may suggest that Dorset had become more marginal in importance to the crown, perhaps brought about by the creation of the earldom.

The *parochiae* and, therefore, presumably also the ancient demesne on which they were based, were estates with strong geographical boundaries as has been shown by the analysis of those *parochiae* that it is possible to reconstruct with some certainty. It would be useful to examine the charter boundaries of the county along similar lines to see if there was a tendency to use more topographical bounds at earlier dates, though by the time the charters were being written the fragmentation of the large royal estates was already well underway, suggesting that they would have less geographically defined boundaries than the larger units. Phythian-Adams has proposed a model of societies operating against a broad geographical base of cultural areas in the post-Reformation period (Phythian-Adams 1993). The division of the county into royal demesne/*parochiae* units based on local topographical components presents a picture of society operating against this background at a local level as well as a regional one, albeit at an earlier date.

---

[1] Hudson put the formation of the rural deaneries in immediate post-Conquest period following William's separation of the civil and ecclesiastical courts. He showed that for Norfolk the deanery boundaries respect those of the hundreds and suggested that the deaneries were based on the hundredal unit (Hudson 1908, 52-62); Winchester 1990, 73-75; a strong relationship has also been suggested by Dr Dunning for Somerset, pers. comm.

[2] S.1706.

[3] S.1217, thought authentic by Finberg.

[4] S.263, basis considered authentic.

[5] S.422.

[6] S. 422; Finberg 1964, no.578: Finberg sees the charter as authentic.

[7] S.1004. The *herepath* is mentioned in King Edward's grant of land at Wootton Abbas to Orc which Finberg sees as authentic; Finberg 1964, no. 625.

[8] For example South Malling in Sussex and the Raunds estate in Northamptonshire (Jones 1979, pp.20-29; Hall 1988, 106-7).

[9] Eyton divides the king's hundreds into those held *Jure Coronae*, as *Comes* and 'by courtesy of England' in which he places the two hundreds of Albretesberge and Langaberge because they were largely composed of lands held by Brictric which were inherited by Queen Matilda at the Conquest (Eyton 1878, 143).

[10] Harmer 1989 (2nd edn), 266-70, 482-486; Yorke has suggested, on the strength of previous identifications of the places in the writ and the example of New Minster, Hampshire, that the allowance of holding far-flung properties in private hundreds by the bishops may have been granted in part exchange for the provision of ships by the bishops (Yorke 1995, 129). However, barring Alton Pancras, the bishop's Dorset holdings are not dispersed .

CHAPTER FOUR
THE LAYOUT OF MINSTER SETTLEMENTS

Introduction: Problems and Methods

This chapter will discuss the topography of the settlements associated with the minsters and possible minsters identified in Chapter Two and Appendix II. The siting of the churches will be examined to see if they fit the pattern suggested by Blair for early minsters. Favoured sites, according to Blair, were: the confluence of rivers; bends in rivers, often on gravel promontories; low hills; islands and headlands. Proximity to a navigable water source appears to have been important, possibly partly for baptismal purposes, and Blair has recently suggested that waterfronts may have been exploited by the minsters for profit (Blair 1992, 227-31; 1994, 61-3, 67; 1995, 110). The layout of the settlements will be examined using retrogressive town plan analysis developed by Conzen in an attempt to identify the circuits of the minsters (Conzen 1960).

What type of topographical characteristics might we expect to be associated with minster churches? Blair in his review of minster topography points to several diagnostic features. Firstly, minsters were normally situated independently from the *villae regales* with which they were often associated, and settlement was more likely to develop around the minster than the royal vill. Secondly, the minster sites were enclosed with a *vallum monasterii* of some form, whether ditch and bank or thorn hedge. Whilst often insubstantial physically, the *vallum* provided a boundary to the precinct of the minster denoting a 'spiritual and legal' delineation (Thomas 1971, 29). The typical enclosure was round or oval except where Roman sites were reused, a common practice where they were available. In the south-west Blair suggests that the minster system assimilated the British church though no examples of minsters situated in a *llan* spring to mind in Somerset, Dorset or Devon. Thirdly, domestic buildings, used for eating and sleeping etc., associated with minsters were rectilinear where Anglo-Saxon traditions prevail and circular in areas where they did not. Finally, a common feature of minster sites was the presence of a row of churches, on an east-west alignment as at Canterbury and Northampton (Blair 1992, 246-58).

Approaching the problem from another angle, the topographical characteristics of lesser churches or chapels can be expected to differ considerably from those of the minsters. One of the main characteristics of secondary churches or chapels is their proprietary nature. Founded for the convenience of the local lord, proprietary churches were often sited within, or very close to, the *curia* of the manor: this characteristic should not apply to the siting of minster churches. Two examples, taken from amongst the chapels of the Dorset minsters, Wootton Fitzpaine (Plate 8), a chapel of Whitchurch Canonicorum, and Caundle Marsh, a chapel of Sherborne (see Fig 28), both illustrate the dependence of these secondary churches on their manors. Chapels and lesser churches are often marginal to the settlement in which they are situated, whereas minster churches, probably

founded before the nucleation of settlement into vills and towns, are more likely to have been a focus for that development. Most chapels did not have burial rites whereas the minsters, due to their large *parochiae*, can be expected to have large graveyards.

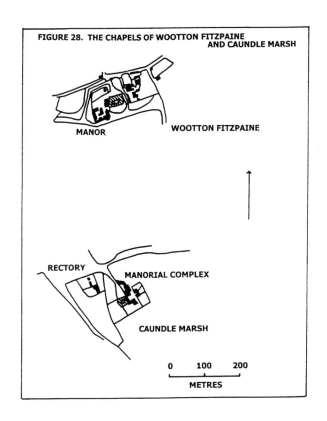

FIGURE 28. THE CHAPELS OF WOOTTON FITZPAINE AND CAUNDLE MARSH

MANOR

WOOTTON FITZPAINE

RECTORY

MANORIAL COMPLEX

CAUNDLE MARSH

0   100   200
METRES

Many of the Dorset minster sites have developed into central places. In the analysis of towns, Conzen's work on Alnwick has been pivotal, initiating examples of plan analysis such as that of Pershore by Bond and Hunt, Witham by Rodwell, and work by Slater on the topography of various towns including Lichfield, much of which centres on the use of metrological analysis (Bond 1977, 2-38; Slater 1986, 11-35; Slater 1990, 60-82; Rodwell 1993). Conzen showed that layout, particularly of the streets, is the most conservative element, buildings and land-use both being more adaptable and consequently more susceptible to change (Conzen 1960, 6-7). One of his most important achievements is the recognition that growth takes place in periodic phases, rather than gradually and uniformly. Plan-units are often apparent, distinguishable by their regularity; areas of burgage plots or other regular tenements are examples. The boundary of a phase of growth sometimes taking, for example, the physical form of town walls, castle defences or monastic enclosures, is often preserved in the layout. Such boundaries are known as 'fixation lines' and are respected by roads and boundary alignments even after their physical aspects have vanished. Fixation lines sometimes form a morphological frame which exerts an influence over subsequent development. A well-known example of this is the effect of Roman walls on the growth of a town. At Dorchester the Roman wall provided a morphological frame controlling the growth of the town and leaving a fossilized presence in the roads and boundaries even after the wall disappeared. The convergence of roads at certain points may indicate the former presence of a physical barrier, a result of the funnelling of traffic through certain points of entry. Markets often develop at such places, for example, outside castle walls or monastic enclosures. The plans of the minster and possible minster settlements will be examined for evidence of these features which might indicate the presence of a *vallum monasterii*.

Taylor has noted that some of the minster settlements are now quite small, and should probably be classed as villages rather than towns (Taylor 1970, 174). Much work has been done over the last twenty years on village origins ranging from that of Sheppard in Yorkshire, through Taylor on polyfocal villages and settlement shift, and Roberts on the classification of plan types, to ongoing work on individual settlements such as that by Aston on Shapwick (Sheppard 1976, 3-20; Taylor 1977, 189-93 and 1983; Roberts 1985, 7-25, 1987, and 1989, 59-75; Aston et al, 1989-1995). In the analysis of the plan, the same analytical techniques apply to the village settlement as to the town, though obviously on a lesser scale, and whereas towns are more prone to continuous growth, villages often have periods of contraction that show up in the field as earthworks.

Plans of the minster and possible minster settlements have been produced by retrogressive analysis, transcribing tithe and pre-19th century estate maps (where they exist) successively onto an early edition of the 25" Ordnance Survey map. Churchyards are shown by diagonal shading throughout. The resulting maps represent the earliest accurate picture of the layout of the settlement that is available. The accuracy can obviously never be a hundred *per cent*, but the plans thus produced are a better tool for analysis than the direct use of estate maps where the precision of the cartography is sometimes questionable. The same scale of reproduction has been used for all the plans making direct comparisons possible. Roberts has described the process of transcription and the problems associated with it (Roberts 1987, 16-17). In the case of many of the smaller Dorset settlements, transcription has been fairly straightforward as there was little change during the 40-60 years between the making of the tithe maps and the 1st or 2nd edition 25" OS maps in 1887-90 and 1901-2. In some cases, large-scale alterations were caused by toll roads and railways, as at Puddletown; however, generally, the road systems appear mostly unaltered. A greater problem, which is brought to light by the transcription, is the poor quality of the cartography of a few of the tithe maps.[1] As Roberts notes, this is an important reason for using transcribed maps in examining the topography rather than a rescaling of the earlier map which would not pick up such errors (Roberts 1987, 16-17). Maps earlier than the tithe maps have been examined and made use of where they exist, though some are drawn in a stylized manner which provides little additional useful information. In addition to the study of the cartographic evidence, field visits have been undertaken and earthworks indicating areas of desertion or shrunken areas of settlement noted. Some of the minsters sit in large settlements of some complexity which could in themselves form the bases of individual studies. Unfortunately the constraints of time and the number of settlements involved have limited the amount of fieldwork undertaken and many of the sites would profit from a more thorough investigation. The examination of the settlements is divided into two parts: the first deals with the minster settlements following the order imposed by the scoring system; the remaining high-status churches are examined in less detail in groups with similar characteristics.

The topography of the minster settlements

Wimborne Minster (Figs 29 & 30)

Wimborne lies just on the north bank of the river Stour at its junction with the Allen (previously the Win). The Stour is bridged to the south and west of the town which sits at a focal point of routeways on a site just above the floodplain. Wimborne had three medieval suburbs. To the south-west of the town lies the short-lived suburb of the Leaze probably created by the Dean of Wimborne (Field 1972, 49-62). To the north, lie the twin streets of East and West Borough, created by the lord of Kingston Lacy, the manor of which ran up to the edge of the medieval town which was under the Dean's control (Hutchins 3, 230). Across the river Allen lay East Brook first mentioned in 1286 (*DPN* 2, 188). The removal of these elements of the plan leaves an area within which the roads and boundaries are all aligned east-west / north-south, in the southern part of which sits the Minster. In the sixties Taylor identified a fixation line bordering this area which he suggested represents the 'high and stout walls' surrounding the monastery described by Rudolf of Fulda in the eighth century (Taylor 1967, 168-70; RCHM Dorset 5, 78). In 900 Aethelwold hid in Wimborne barricading all the gates, suggesting that a defensible barrier, possibly the *vallum monasterii*, was still in existence at that date (*ASC*, 92). Within this large rectangular area there are two main north-south divisions which appear to have originally divided the area in three lengthwise. The western line is represented by Redcotts Lane, then property boundaries as far the Corn Market. The division then cuts across an excavated area marked by a positive lynchet at the edge of an accumulation of soil: 'The alignment of the field edge may relate to an earlier circuit or land-division' (Woodward 1983, 61). It is then picked up by property boundaries as far as the walled garden of Dean's Court. The eastern division proceeds from the end of East Borough, just after the bend, a stretch of road previously known as Pillory Street, across a group of burgage plots which have grown into the area of the market, and along the end of the High Street and Dean's Court Lane. Several east-west divisions also exist: the line of King Street; West Street - Mill Lane; the Corn Market - Cook Row (this boundary has now been shown to have continued as a ditch under the property opposite Cook Row (Coe and Hawkes 1992, 143)); and the boundaries at the edge of Dean's Court. The excavation in the tourist bureau opposite Cook Row also showed no twelfth/thirteenth century frontage, suggesting that the area has been infilled from an original frontage further to the east. The Priest's House also has an earlier frontage incorporated inside the

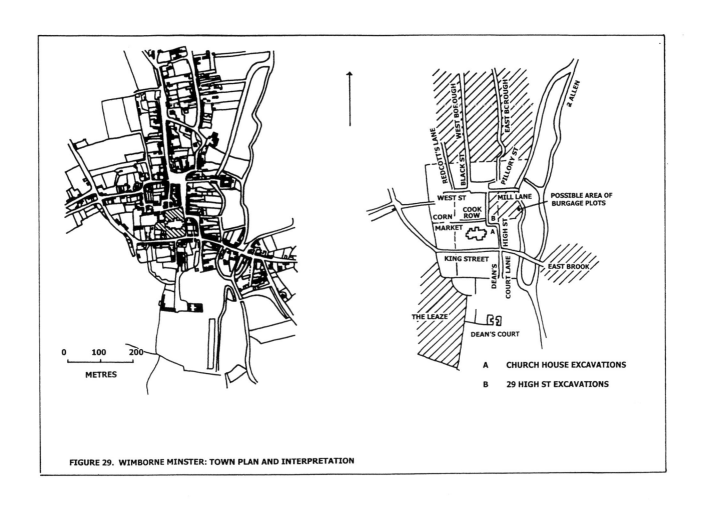

FIGURE 29. WIMBORNE MINSTER: TOWN PLAN AND INTERPRETATION

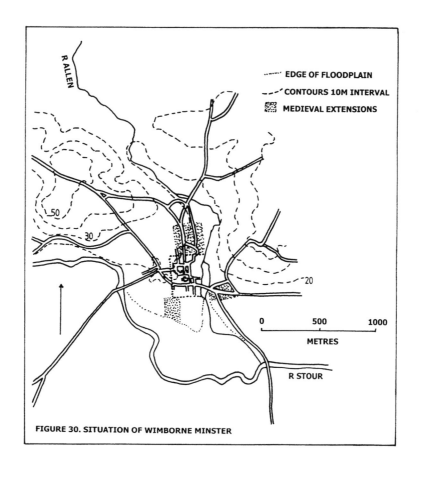

FIGURE 30. SITUATION OF WIMBORNE MINSTER

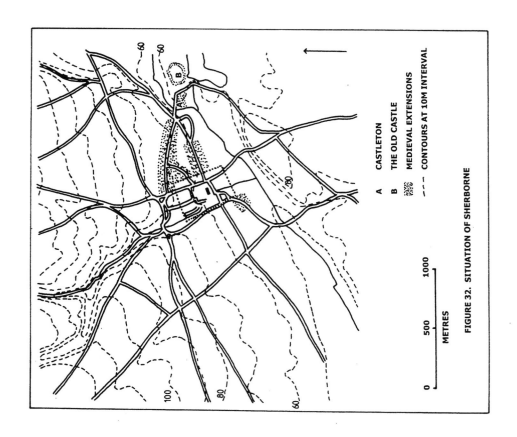

FIGURE 32. SITUATION OF SHERBORNE

A   CASTLETON

B   THE OLD CASTLE

    MEDIEVAL EXTENSIONS

- - - - CONTOURS AT 10M INTERVAL

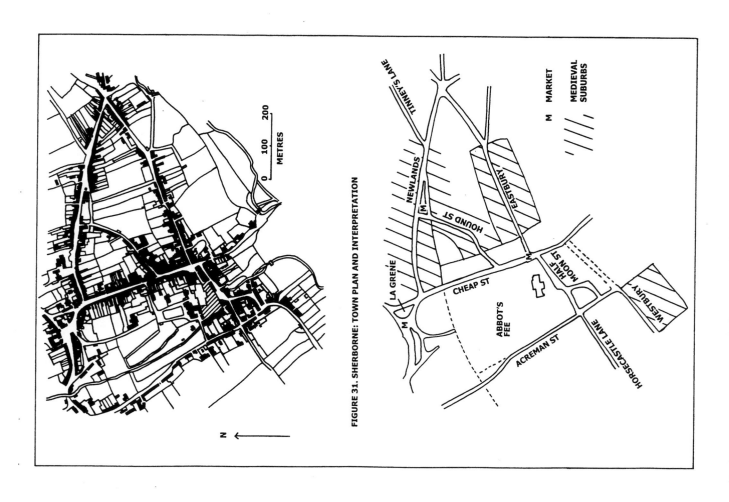

FIGURE 31. SHERBORNE: TOWN PLAN AND INTERPRETATION

M   MARKET

    MEDIEVAL SUBURBS

building. The grounds of the minster must have continued further eastwards in the past as burials were uncovered in a small excavation in the passage between Church House and the Minster (see Fig 29). This, together with the lack of evidence for a high street frontage along the present line, reinforces the possibility that the north-south route originally ran along the line of Dean's Court Lane - northern East Borough (before it turns west into the Square). At Domesday, Bishop Maurice had eight burgesses in the town of Wimborne. Their burgages might be represented by the area to the east of the High Street between Mill Lane and the east-west portion of the High Street, the plots running from the High Street to the river Allen. A watching brief adjacent to Mill Lane revealed a boundary ditch running back from the High Street approximately 5m from Mill Lane, and may have represented the edge of one of the plots (Hall and Sims 1984, 123). Other roads have intruded into the original grid pattern. Some of the areas have been sub-divided and others encroached upon, but the street and boundary pattern show Wimborne to consist of a large, internally divided rectilinear area probably of one ownership originally, against which suburbs have accreted. The grid-like pattern of the centre of Wimborne has led to various suggestions for the line of the circuit of the ancient monastery (Woodward 1983, 58-9). Further excavations have tested some of these proposed circuits but no boundary has been revealed so far (Graham 1984, 77-86; Cox 1992, 145-50). The proposed enclosure on the side of Rowlands Hill bears no relationship to the minster at all and would have been a most unlikely site. [2]

Sherborne

Sherborne (Figs 31 & 32) is situated on the northern bank of the river Yeo at a point where the Combe stream joins the river. Two main east-west routes encompass most of the medieval town, and these are linked by two main north-south streets, Acreman St and Cheap St. In the immediate area of the Abbey church there is a high degree of rectilinearity based roughly on a north-south / east-west alignment. Sherborne's medieval tithings consisting of Abbot's Fee, Westbury, Eastbury, and Houndstreet, present a clue to the growth of the town. In addition to these areas, there are known to have been two boroughs, Newlands and Castleton (Fowler 1951, 147). The tithing called Abbot's Fee may represent the extent of the town in 1122, when the abbacy was separated from the episcopacy of Salisbury. To William of Malmesbury, writing at about that time, Sherborne was a small village with few people and not a fit place to have been a bishop's seat.[3] Westbury is first mentioned in 1280, Hound Street in 1288 and Eastbury in 1332 (DPN 3, 361-63; Penn 1980, 96). These 'suburbs' are shown on Figs 31 and 32. Half Moon St is known to be a new creation of Bishop Roger, at some time between 1122 and 1139, allowing access to the main road (Cheap St), across part of what was the cemetery of the Abbey church. As Fowler notes, this implies that unless the precinct extended somewhat further to the south, the exercise would have been pointless (Fowler 1951, 109-110). The former route to Cheap St may well have continued directly eastwards along the line of Westbury where the road now bends northwards, joining up with the fragment of lane to the south of Eastbury. The northern boundary of the Abbot's Fee tithing appears to have been the

strong east-west boundary line running westwards from the market in Newlands. This line has been suggested by Keen as part of a middle-Saxon field system laid out in the 8th century (Keen 1984, 238). The area around the chapel of St Thomas in the Green, dedicated in 1177, suggests a focus developed at the north end of the monastic enclosure (Fowler 1951, 132). The borough of Newlands was laid out by Bishop Richard le Poore in 1227x1228. According to the charter three areas of burgage plots of differing size were created, two along the road from the chapel of St Thomas on the Green towards the castle, measuring 24 x 4 and 20 x 4 perches, and the third between the Green and the abbot's barn, the site of which is lost, measuring 2 x 2 perches (Ballard and Tait 1923, 54-55). Unfortunately, the measurements do not correlate with any of the regular blocks of development along that road if the perch is taken to measure 5½ yds. As this measurement was not standardized until c.1305, varying before that date between 9 and 26 feet, an alternative measurement may have been in use here. Fowler argues that this piece of speculation by the bishop was laid out on a green-field site on the edge of town, as the name Newland implies (Fowler 1951, 153-54). The *bury* names of the tithings to the east and west of Abbot's Fee may be referring to the monastic enclosure as has been suggested for *bury* names elsewhere.[4] The removal of these later elements leaves a core area consisting of the Abbot's Fee which may represent the area of the original minster precinct and the developed area of the town by 1122.

The debate on the site of *Lanprobi* and its relation to the site of the newly created cathedral of 705 (above p 11) led to the conclusion that the pre-Saxon site was situated at the Old Castle, rather than to the north of the present abbey inside a curvilinear enclosure proposed by Barker. Barker saw the curving line of Hound St and that of the north part of Acreman St as part of the *llan* of a British monastery. The bend in Hound St, however, may have been caused by its diversion northwards following the creation of the market in Newlands. The high degree of rectilinearity in the street plan of Sherborne suggests that it was originally planned thus, on a new site at a discrete distance from the site of the British monastery.

Whitchurch Canonicorum (Figs 33 & 34)

Whitchurch Canonicorum is a large polyfocal village in the middle of an area of dispersed settlement. The parish of Marshwood, which formed the northern part of Whitchurch until the 19th century, had no nucleated settlement at the time of the tithe commutation consisting totally of separate farm units. Whitchurch is situated beside a small tributary stream of the river Char. It is the focus of numerous roads which enter the village at various points. The church sits in a large rectangular churchyard adjacent to the stream, and the settlement concentrates in two main areas to either side of this area. To the east it occupies the rising ground along the road climbing to Ryall and to the ridge along which the main east-west road (A35) now runs. To the west of the church the settlement follows the road as far as Whitchurch Cross, where roads from Morecombelake, Charmouth, and Wootton Fitzpaine meet. The orientation of the roads and boundaries indicates a rectilinear block of land around the church to the

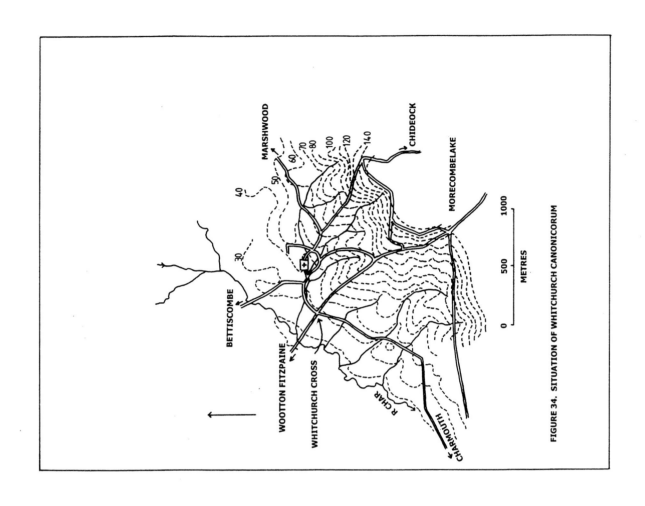

FIGURE 34. SITUATION OF WHITCHURCH CANONICORUM

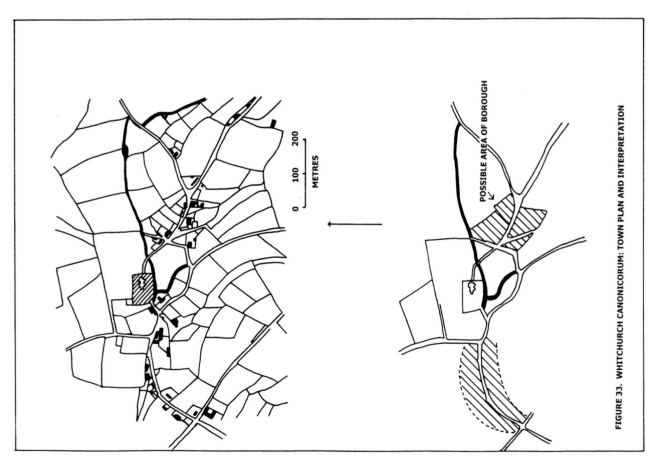

FIGURE 33. WHITCHURCH CANONICORUM: TOWN PLAN AND INTERPRETATION

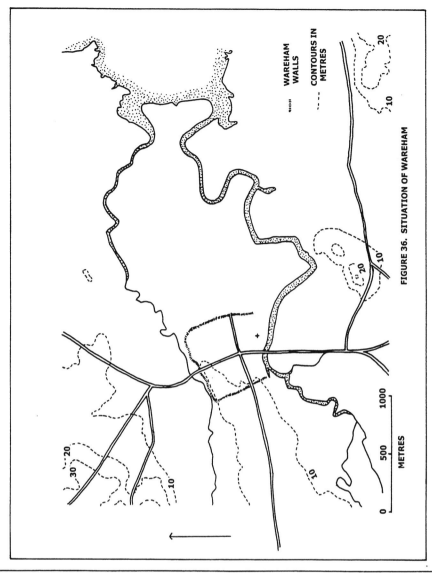

FIGURE 36. SITUATION OF WAREHAM

WAREHAM
WALLS

CONTOURS IN
METRES

0   500   1000
|___|___|___|___|___|
METRES

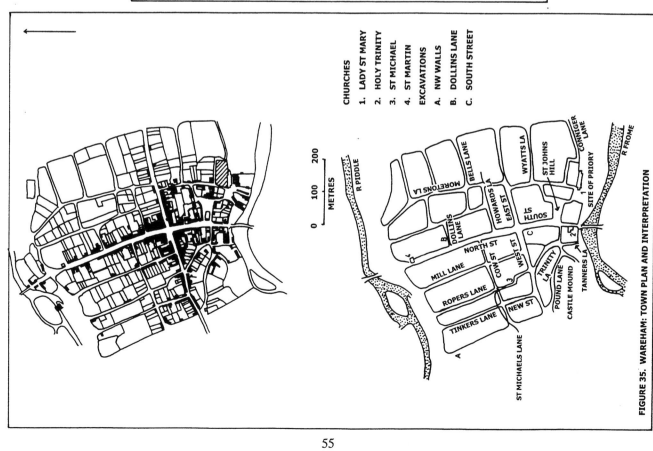

CHURCHES

1. LADY ST MARY
2. HOLY TRINITY
3. ST MICHAEL
4. ST MARTIN

EXCAVATIONS

A. NW WALLS
B. DOLLINS LANE
C. SOUTH STREET

0   100   200
|___|___|___|
METRES

R PIDDLE

ST MICHAELS LANE

MILL LANE

ROPERS LANE

TINKERS LANE

NORTH ST

COW ST

WEST ST

NEW ST

DOLLINS LANE

MORETONS LA

BELLS LANE

HOWARDS LA

EAST ST

SOUTH ST

WYATTS LA

ST JOHNS HILL

CONNIGER LANE

SITE OF PRIORY

R FROME

TRINITY LA

POUND LANE

CASTLE MOUND

TANNERS LA

FIGURE 35. WAREHAM: TOWN PLAN AND INTERPRETATION

55

north of the stream within which there is very little settlement. To the south of the stream the roads and boundaries are more irregular. In 1265 an inquisition was recorded as being held in the borough of Whitchurch (Beresford and Finberg 1973, 105). The small area to the east of the church has a slightly planned appearance, but if there was a borough here the lack of surviving burgage plots indicates that it was an unsuccessful attempt at expanding the settlement.

Wareham (Figs 35 & 36)

Wareham is situated between the rivers Frome and Piddle about 1.5km from the point where they discharge into Poole harbour. The town straddles an important north-south routeway at the lowest bridging point of the rivers. Wareham, recorded in the burghal hidage, is surrounded by impressive earthen banks on three sides, the fourth side abutting the river Frome. Wareham commands a strategic position and was captured by Guthrum. The Vikings' attempt to overwinter in the town in 867 implies that it had some defences by that date (ASC, 74). Excavations across the north-west corner of the walls by the RCHM in 1959 were somewhat inconclusive, placing the first phase of development between the late Roman period and possibly after c700 (RCHM 1959, 137).

Topographically, the town is divided into four quarters by the two main streets. Each of these has developed different characteristics. The south-west corner is dominated by the castle mound. Thought to date from just after the Conquest, the line of its defences is preserved in Pound Lane and Trinity Lane (RCHM Dorset 2, 325). The castle has obviously obliterated the earlier pattern in this quarter, though Tanner's Lane is aligned with Mill Lane suggesting that the three north-south lanes in the north-west quarter probably continued into the southern quarter, down to the river Frome. In the north-west corner the division into blocks of land is the most regular and in this area the lanes are fairly sunken in places. The main diversion from this pattern is the kink in St Michael's Lane, which may have developed as the result of the alteration of the street pattern by the imposition of the castle. In the north-east corner the division into blocks of land is much less regular. This is the largest quarter and the least developed. The south-east quarter is dominated by the church of Lady St Mary. The development immediately to the west of the church is marked by a group of radial lanes leading from church, and by the area of St John's Hill, the former site of a chapel of that name. Many burials have been found in this vicinity during building works and it must have been the site of the cemetery attached to the chapel of St John (see above p 15). The British inscribed stones from Lady St Mary church suggest that the area immediately around the church may have been a British llan. To the south of Lady St Mary is the site of the priory possibly also the site of the Saxon nunnery (ASC, 124). The street names within the different quarters also have differing characteristics. The only occupational names are found in the western half of the burh, mostly to the north of West Street. Tinker's Lane, Roper's Lane and Mill Lane all suggest a certain degree of industry in this quarter, as does Tanner's Lane to the west of Holy Trinity

church. To the east of North Street the lanes appear to be named after the landholders: Dollins Lane; Bells Lane; Mortons Lane; Howards Lane and the most southerly, Wyats Lane. Lanes named after churches are common to all four quarters.

In the Domesday record, the borough of Wareham is divided into three main holdings: that of the King, being the largest, with 143 dwellings in Edward's day, reduced to 70; the area of St Wandrille's with 62 dwellings, 17 of which were derelict; and the parts in the hands of the barons where there were 20 houses, 60 having been destroyed. The area of St Wandrille is undoubtedly that surrounding Lady St Mary. The area of the king is probably represented by that of the castle and the north-west quarter with its artisans. The area of the barons would then be in the east stretching northwards from Wyatt's Lane where the majority of personal names have survived.[5] Archaeological recording shows two concentrations of Roman finds, one in the north-west corner and the other around Lady St Mary where Field considered that an early Roman fort may have been situated (Field 1992, 135-7, 246-9). Hinton's excavations in Dollin's Lane, which might have been expected to locate pre-Conquest settlement, showed that the area did not develop until at least the 13th century (Hinton 1977, 42-83). Excavations at the rear of 5 South Street have produced a similar picture (CBA Wessex News, April 1996). The fragmentation of units is greatest in the north-western quarter suggesting that the western half of the burh may have been the most important commercially. If Lady St Mary had British Christian origins, this area may have been the site of a royal vill placed next to the British site. The walls of the burh at Wareham are not as regular as those of Cricklade with which it is often compared, and the RCHM excavation suggests that the north-west corner may have had defences from before the time of Alfred, perhaps implying that there was more than one stage of development of Wareham as a fortified site.

Keen has noted that the three churches of Lady St Mary, St Martin and Holy Trinity were probably all in existence before the creation of the Alfredian burh defences, as all three have extra-mural areas as well as internal areas of parish (Keen 1984, 224-7). As noted above (p 35) it seems likely that the parochia was rearranged with the founding of the burh and that Holy Trinity and St Martin may have been created at that time. Strangely, only Holy Trinity has contiguous internal and external parish. That of Lady St Mary covers the smallest area and its intramural parish area stops at the edge of the town along the line of the defences. The extra-mural area of St Martin is split into two by the parish of Morden. The whole system appears to have been juggled to enable the more distant parishes of Morden and East Stoke to abut the burh. This rearrangement may have been part of the defensive strategy of the burh at Wareham, increasing the manpower resources in order to meet the required number for the defence of the 2,200 yards of rampart.

Wareham may have had a line of churches as has been suggested for Canterbury and Northampton. Holy Trinity, originally dedicated to St Andrew, is on the same axis as

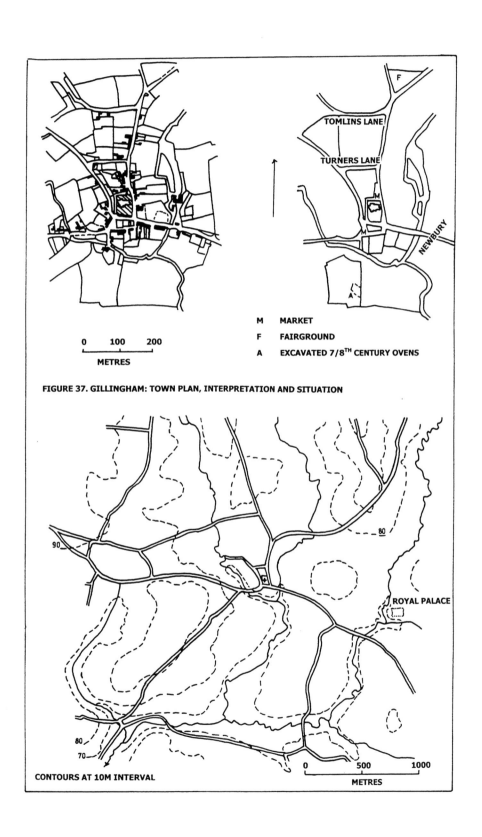

M   MARKET

F   FAIRGROUND

A   EXCAVATED 7/8TH CENTURY OVENS

FIGURE 37. GILLINGHAM: TOWN PLAN, INTERPRETATION AND SITUATION

CONTOURS AT 10M INTERVAL

Lady St Mary, and the area in between these two churches crosses just to the south of St John's Hill. The site of the chapel of St John was in this vicinity and may well have lain to the south of St John's Hill.

Gillingham (Fig 37)

The town of Gillingham lies on a neck of land at the confluence of two branches of the river Stour. The church and its churchyard are surrounded by roads on two sides and paths on the others. Market areas exist to the north and south of the church. There is some degree of rectilinearity in the area immediately around the church but it is not so extensive as in the case of some of the other minsters. An area to the east of the town is known as Newbury which Penn suggests may be of thirteenth-century date (Penn 1980, 68). Excavations to the south of the river (A on Fig 37) uncovered two ovens of middle-Saxon date in Chantry Fields. These may have been associated with the minster as they are thought not to have originated in an ordinary domestic context (Heaton 1992, 97-126). Alternatively they may indicate the presence of a royal site in the vicinity, though this seems less likely as the later royal site was to the east of the town at the confluence of another stream with the River Lodden.[6] At Sturminster Newton the relationship of minster to royal site is very similar (see below p 100). The development in the centre of Gillingham shows little sign of regular planning.

Bere Regis (Fig 38)

Bere Regis is situated to the north of the Milborne Brook at a point where the chalk meets the poorer heathlands around Poole harbour. The original focus of Bere Regis appears to have been the cross-roads to the north of the church. There is the suggestion of another north-south line within the town to the west of the main route, the northern part of which, Snow Hill Lane, has been proposed as a Roman road (Field 1992, 61, 63). There are two possible areas of market infill (a grant being made by King John): the area to the west of the Snow Hill Lane line; and the south-west corner of the cross-roads. In 1289 King Edward I made Bere a free borough.[7] Several areas of the town appear to have been planned and there are a group of very long thin plots stretching south from the main east-west road with its infilled market place to the brook, just to the west of the church, possibly the area of the borough. King John had a residence at Bere, the site of which is thought to have been on the site of the manor in the block of land to the east of the church (Pitfield 1978, 21). Most of the roads and boundaries in Bere are of north-south / east-west orientation. In the eastern part of the town two of the roads change course to comply with this orientation, perhaps implying that they are later than the rectilinear layout of the centre of Bere. The south-western corner of the church yard is curved but this appears to be the rounding of a corner rather than the remains of a curvilinear enclosure. All in all, the main part of Bere Regis has a strong rectilinear plan to which a borough appears to have been added in the thirteenth century.

Beaminster (Fig 39)

The town of Beaminster is situated at the focal point of the upper basin of the River Brit at the confluence of several streams. In 1298 William Ewet, prebendary of Sarum, was granted a market and fair in Beaminster and to the north of the church lies a rectangular block of development which has a large market at its north-east corner (Hutchins 2, 118). Development has been intense within the rectangular area to the north of the church and much subdivision of plots has taken place. There is little sign of regular planning in the central area of the town whereas there are some signs of regular elements along the roads in the east of the town. The church which is sited just above a stream, sits in a fairly large churchyard that was extended to the south-east in 1841 and the ground built up to the present level (Hine 1914, 84).

Cranborne (Fig 40)

The village of Cranborne straddles the River Crane with the church on the southern bank. Two streets run parallel to the river on either side, stretching eastwards from the church. A pit containing middle-Saxon occupation debris has been found on the north-eastern edge of Cranborne at Penny's Mead (Youngs et al 1988, 240). There is a market (recorded in 1330) to the north of the church and to its west lies the manor of Cranborne, the present structure dating from the time of King John (Penn 1980, 49; RCHM Dorset 5, 5). There were two manors in Cranborne, that of Cranborne Borough, and that of Cranborne Priory (thought to lie to the south of the church) (DPN 2, 206). Burgesses are mentioned in an Inquisition of 1314, but no charter survives and Penn has suggested that the status was probably a tenurial change rather than a new creation as no burgage plots were discernible (Penn 1980, 49, 52). There are areas of regular planning, however, and Penn's suggestion seems unlikely as boroughs were generally new creations designed to draw in new people in order to generate more income. Any signs of a minster precinct have been masked by the presence of the later monastery.

Sturminster Marshall (Figs 41, 42)

Sturminster Marshall lies on the south bank of the Stour at a point where a small stream enters the river. The main focus of roads in the village is the market area to the south-west of the church. The immediate vicinity of the church is sparsely developed, the main settlement being along the two streets that coalesce at the market. Hutchins described the market place as being 'disused beyond the memory of man' but noted that the shambles and some standings remained there.[8] Several blocks of development have a planned appearance especially along the High Street leading away from the market place. Excavations to the west of the church have shown that the already large churchyard extended westwards from its present site (Allen 1991, 170; SMR site no. 65, A-G). Church Dairy, the farm immediately to the east of the church, shown as the glebe of the impropriate rectory on the tithe map, may be the grange of the hospital of St Giles of Pont Audemer mentioned in 1324 (DRO, T/SML; DPN 2, 49). The vicarage was given to Eton College in 1457 with the confiscation of the land of the Alien Priories and its glebe then consisted of 140a. It is recorded in 1291 as being 130a plus 17a of pasture (Hutchins 3, 365). On the tithe map 122a

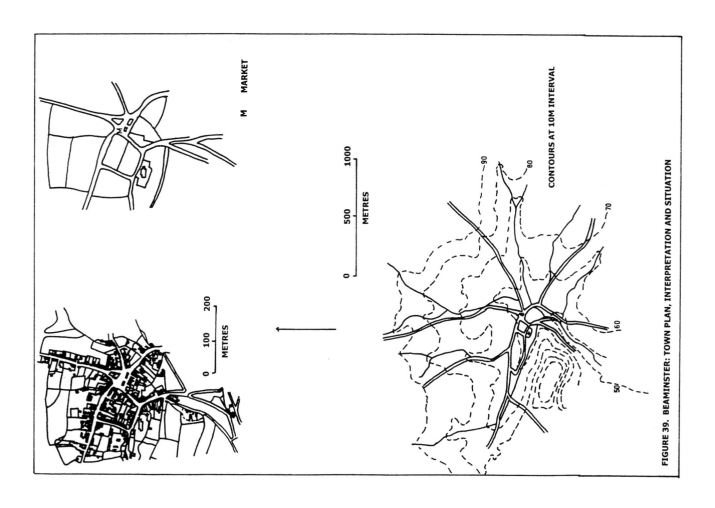

M   MARKET

CONTOURS AT 10M INTERVAL

FIGURE 39. BEAMINSTER: TOWN PLAN, INTERPRETATION AND SITUATION

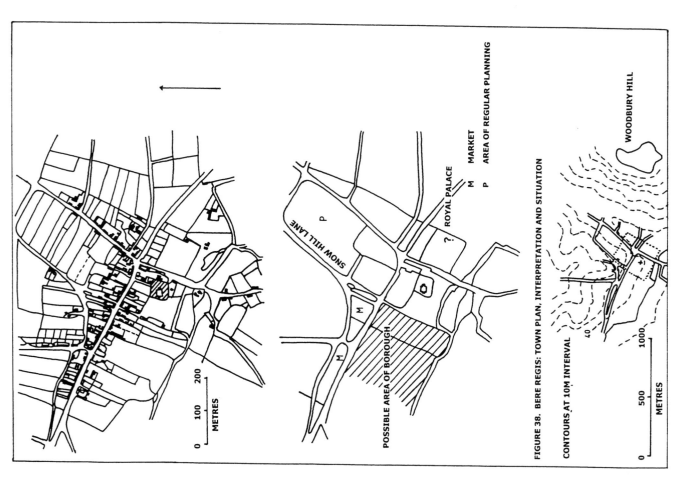

M   MARKET

P   AREA OF REGULAR PLANNING

ROYAL PALACE

SNOW HILL LANE

POSSIBLE AREA OF BOROUGH

WOODBURY HILL

FIGURE 38. BERE REGIS: TOWN PLAN, INTERPRETATION AND SITUATION

CONTOURS AT 10M INTERVAL

59

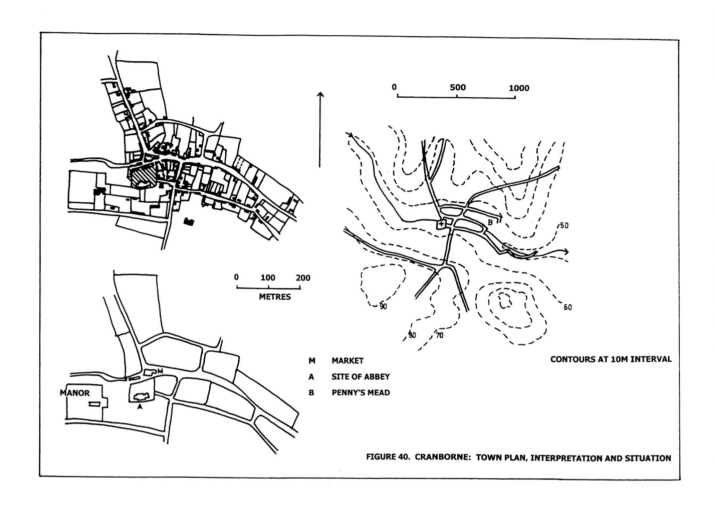

M   MARKET
A   SITE OF ABBEY
B   PENNY'S MEAD

CONTOURS AT 10M INTERVAL

FIGURE 40. CRANBORNE: TOWN PLAN, INTERPRETATION AND SITUATION

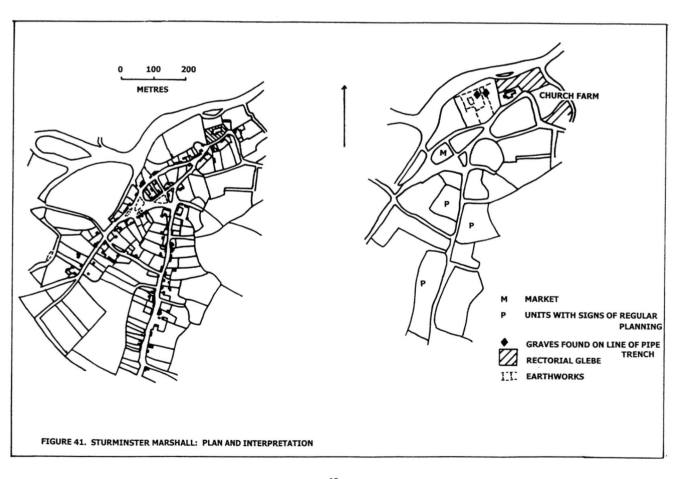

M   MARKET
P   UNITS WITH SIGNS OF REGULAR PLANNING
◆   GRAVES FOUND ON LINE OF PIPE TRENCH
▨   RECTORIAL GLEBE
⠿   EARTHWORKS

FIGURE 41. STURMINSTER MARSHALL: PLAN AND INTERPRETATION

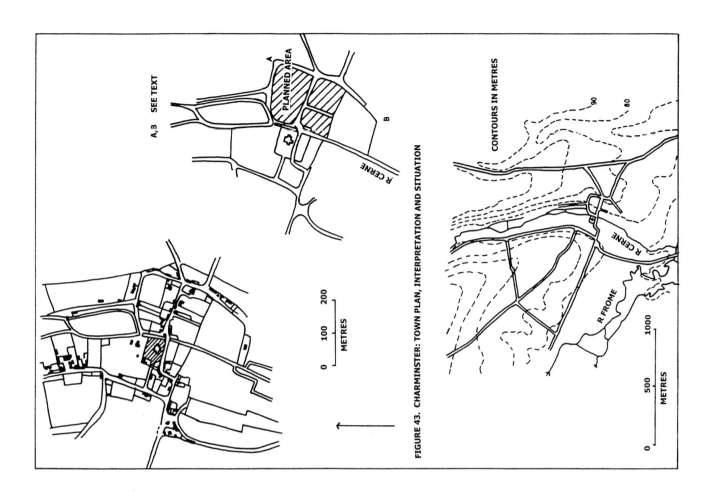

FIGURE 43. CHARMINSTER: TOWN PLAN, INTERPRETATION AND SITUATION

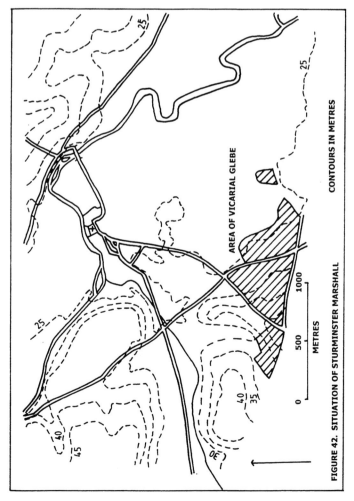

FIGURE 42. SITUATION OF STURMINSTER MARSHALL

61

3r 9p belong to the vicarage, and 7a 3r 4p to the impropriate rectory, Eton College. In contrast to the rectory glebe which clusters around the church, the glebe of the vicarage forms a large block to the south of Sturminster on the edge of the parish (DRO, T/SML). The ownership of land by the church in its immediate vicinity appears to have constrained development around the church, directing the expanding settlement along the road running south from the market area.

Charminster (Fig 43)

Situated to the north of the county town of Dorchester, Charminster straddles the river Cerne which joins the Frome about 800m south of the village. Its situation is similar to Sherborne and Wimborne in this respect. Charminster was a prebend of Salisbury comprising the land on the west bank of the river. On the east bank the parish is divided into strip settlements many of which had chapels dependent on Charminster. Charminster remained a small village well into the twentieth century with its settlement clustering to the east and west of the church on either side of the river. The eastern area has a planned appearance with a few tofts of similar size stretching to the north and south of the road. Their eastern edge comprises a length of lane (A-B on Fig 43), which gives the impression of having been an ancient boundary as two roads join it but do not cross it on the same alignment. To the west the settlement is more irregular. The bounds of the church yard appear to indicate that it was once a larger unit that extended to the south of the road that forms the present southern boundary. Within the immediate vicinity of the church the roads and boundaries all have north-south / east-west orientations.

Puddletown (Fig 44)

A large village about 7km north-east of Dorchester, Puddletown is sited on the southern bank of the river Piddle. To the north of the church lies the market place with central infill, and to its east is Ilsington House part of the manor of Ilsington which was possibly held by one of the clerks of the minster (see above p 17). In 1301 a market and fair were granted to the prior of Christchurch who held Puddletown manor (Hutchins 2, 614-15). The street and boundary pattern of Puddletown is very regular. The main east-west road appears to have been diverted through the market; the boundary line from A to B (Fig 44) suggests its original course. This would undoubtedly have been a ploy of the Prior following the grant of a market. The block of land to the north and south of the road proceeding westwards from A has a planned appearance and may well be another example of a planned unit added outside the minster precinct.

Yetminster (Fig 45)

Yetminster is a large village situated on the western bank of a tributary of the river Yeo. There were three prebends associated with Yetminster: Yetminster and Grimstone (part of Charminster); Yetminster Prima or Upbury; and Yetminster Secunda or Inferior. The main prebend appears to have been Yetminster and Grimstone, which belonged to the bishop of Sarum and to which the glebe lands and great tithes were attached. Upbury Farm (of fifteenth-century

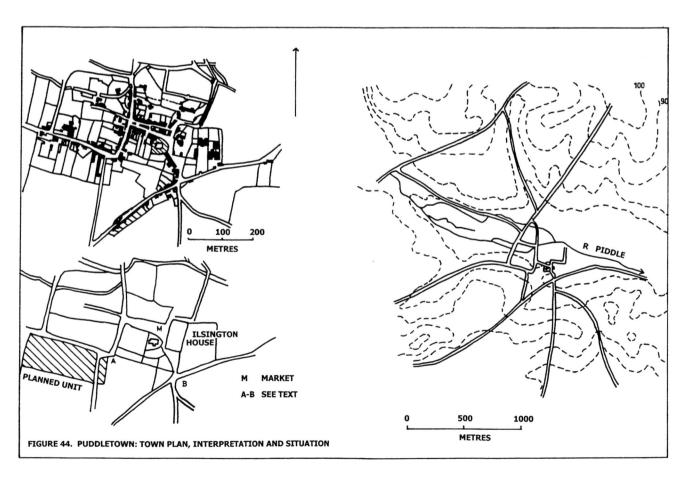

FIGURE 44. PUDDLETOWN: TOWN PLAN, INTERPRETATION AND SITUATION

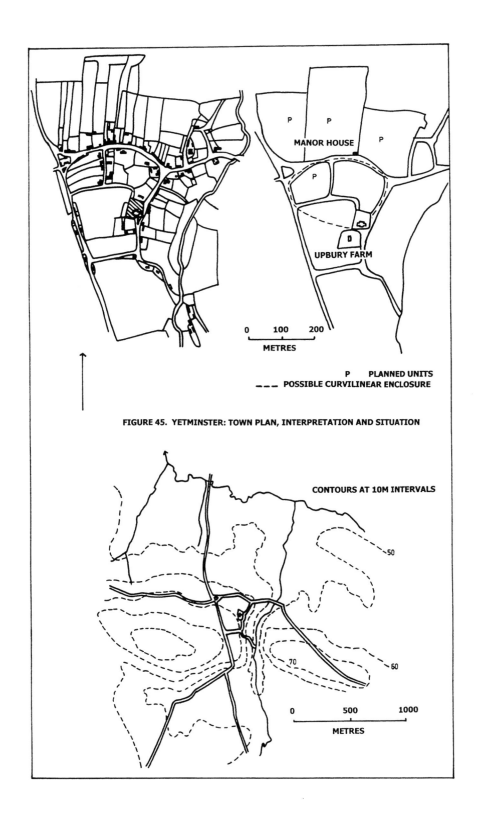

P   PLANNED UNITS
--- POSSIBLE CURVILINEAR ENCLOSURE

FIGURE 45. YETMINSTER: TOWN PLAN, INTERPRETATION AND SITUATION

CONTOURS AT 10M INTERVALS

build), lying just to the south-west of the church, was the focus of the second prebend and the *bury* element of the place-name may indicate a monastic settlement (see above p 53). In the reign of John, a fair was granted to the Dean of Sarum in Yetminster, and in 1300 the bishop was granted a fair and market there (Hutchins 4, 445, 447). The manor house to the north of the church, of early sixteenth-century date, may well have been associated with one of the other prebends. It lies within an area of planned appearance, development probably encouraged by one of the prebendaries. The curve in the roads in Yetminster may reflect an oval enclosure around the minster, though it does not sit centrally within it.

Burton Bradstock (Fig 46)

The village of Burton Bradstock lies on the river Bride at a point just over a kilometre inland from where it discharges into the sea. The site is sheltered from the sea by a narrow ridge the south edge of which forms a sea-cliff. Development within the village is confined to the northerly bank of the river beside which the church lies. What appears to be a market area lies to the west of the church at the junction of north-south and east-west routes, though no market is recorded. There are no obvious signs of planned development within the village. The southern-most branch of the stream follows a course that may have been canalized as has been suggested for the river at Cheddar (Blair 1996, 110).

Iwerne Minster (Fig 47)

Iwerne Minster is a large nucleated village at the source of the Iwerne brook. The pattern of roads in the village shows a large square unit within which the church sits, and at the south-western corner of which a market has developed. Bends in the roads at points A and B (Fig 47) may represent the edge of an enclosure around the church which possibly represents part of a once larger area of land attached to the church; in 1340, Iwerne church is recorded as having 100a of glebe (*Nonarum*, 43). The Shaftesbury Register records that Reinward the chaplain had 5 virgates of land (150 acres), 2 in Iwerne and 3 in Preston, the southern part of the parish of Iwerne (Hutchins 3, 537). None of the glebe lay in Preston at the time of the tithe survey when it was divided into two parts, the rectorial glebe totalling 72a 2r, and the vicarial 4a and 27 perches (DRO, T/IWM). The vicarial glebe lay in a block to the south of the church where the new vicarage was built in 1836. Hutchins records that there were the remains of an 'ancient monastic' building in the garden which was used in the construction of the vicarage (Hutchins 3, 555). Acton in 1895 says that the house was built on the site of the main fish pond serving the clergy house, so that the spring now rises in the cellar before flowing by drain into the lower fish pond. Acton also records that burials were found in the garden opposite the church in about 1855, and in the newly acquired ground forming a churchyard extension (Acton 1895, 44-47). Recently burials once again came to light in the same garden (Woodward 1994, 129-30). Some of the skeletons exposed were buried in a rather disorderly manner perhaps suggesting a plague pit, but the burials continued westwards in what appeared to be a more orderly fashion. This may constitute an early extension of the minster burial

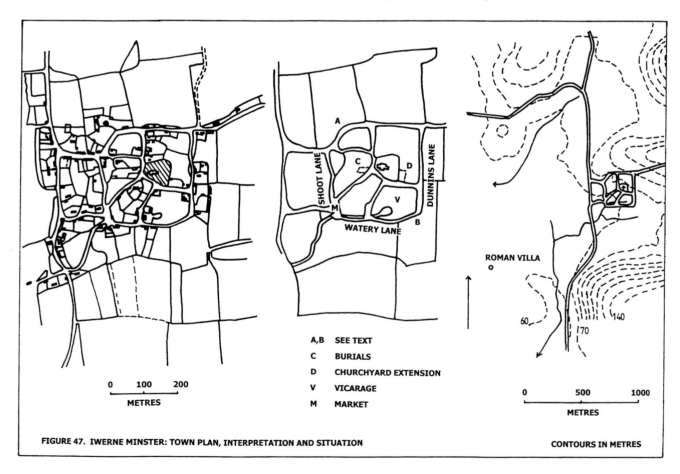

A,B   SEE TEXT
C   BURIALS
D   CHURCHYARD EXTENSION
V   VICARAGE
M   MARKET

ROMAN VILLA

FIGURE 47. IWERNE MINSTER: TOWN PLAN, INTERPRETATION AND SITUATION

CONTOURS IN METRES

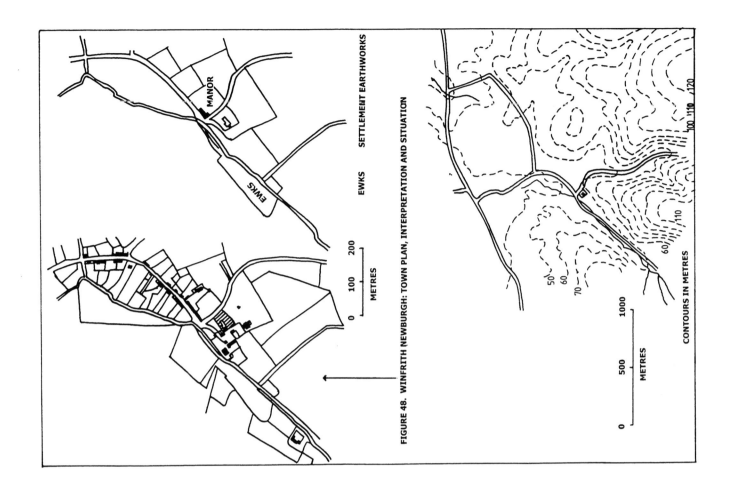

M MARKET
G GLEBE
CONTOURS AT 10M INTERVAL

EWKS   SETTLEMENT EARTHWORKS

FIGURE 48. WINFRITH NEWBURGH: TOWN PLAN, INTERPRETATION AND SITUATION

CONTOURS IN METRES

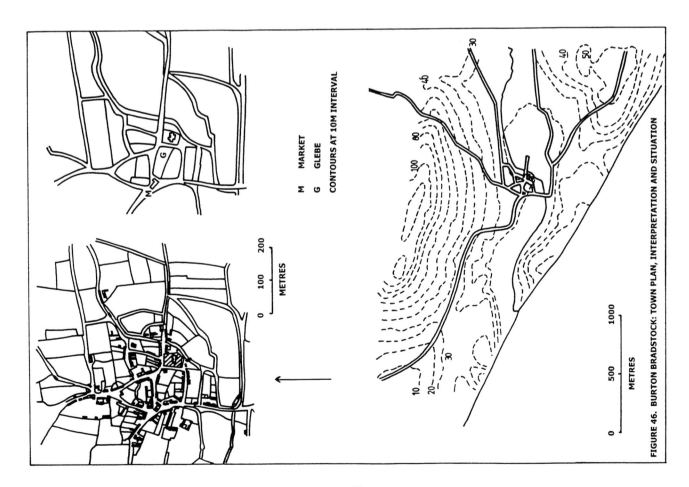

FIGURE 46. BURTON BRADSTOCK: TOWN PLAN, INTERPRETATION AND SITUATION

ground possibly associated with a chapel to the west of the minster though there is no evidence for one. The graveyard appears to have once been considerably larger than at present. Other than the blocks created by the roads, the village of Iwerne does not have any evidence for planned units. The rectilinear plan continues in field boundaries to the north and south of the village.

Winfrith Newburgh (Fig 48)

Winfrith Newburgh is situated near the south coast of Dorset on a small stream at the junction of the Chalk and Reading Beds. The church, which had one virgate of land in 1086, is sited at the end of a linear village with the rectory adjacent. To the north of the church lies Winfrith Fields Farm also known as the Manor House, built in the late 16th century (RCHM Dorset 2, 378). In 1222 when the patronage of the church was transferred to Sarum from Glastonbury Abbey, one third of the tithes, half the glebe and a house near the church were attached to the rectory: the rest was assigned to Glastonbury (Hutchins 1, 444). In the *Inquisitiones Nonarum*, one carucate of arable and 8 acres of pasture are described as being attached to the church, over four times the amount recorded in Domesday, but this can be accounted for by gifts of Robert de Newburgh of 80a of land 8a of meadow to Glastonbury Abbey (*Nonarum*, 53; Hutchins 1, 444). Because of the later donation of the Glastonbury lands to Bindon Abbey the glebe lands cannot be identified on the tithe map.

Plan attributes of the minster settlements: synthesis

Virtually all the minsters are sited besides rivers, many of them at confluences, and as has been shown above (Chapter 3), some sit at the hub of drainage basins. Where the sites of the royal vills associated with the minsters are known, most are at a discrete distance from the minsters. At Gillingham and Sturminster Newton (see pp 12, 100), the royal vills occupy similar sites to the minsters, but neither site has developed into a settlement. The royal site at Wimborne appears to have been at Kingston Lacy, well removed from the town. It is probable that within the *parochia* of Whitchurch Canonicorum, the royal vill was at Chideock, as this was the manorial name of the royal estate in Domesday Book. There is little evidence for the site of the royal vill at Sturminster Marshall, but it may have been at Charborough which was part of the *parochia* and in the hands of Harold forming the core of one of the rearranged hundreds (see above p 44). Again, neither Chideock nor Charborough developed as central places in the way that most of the minster settlements did.

Many of the minsters sit within areas of rectilinear planning with roads and boundaries aligned roughly north-south / east-west, following the general alignment of the churches (for a general comparison see Figs 49 and 50). This pattern is apparent also in the group of possible minsters at Fordington and Sturminster Newton (see below p 74). The rectilinear areas are in places bounded by fixation lines which indicate the former presence of a boundary of sufficient importance to act as a morphological frame, influencing the subsequent development of the settlements. The most plausible explanation for the boundary is that it

was the *vallum monasterii*, delineating the holy ground of the minster enclosures. Beyond these boundaries the rectilinear pattern breaks down: streets often change alignment; roads are less likely to be straight or oriented north-south / east-west; markets existed; regular suburbs or unplanned growth occurs; and focal points of roads align on the boundaries. The sudden change of alignment in King St, Wimborne was one of the factors that led Taylor to suggest that this line represented the wall surrounding the monastery reported by Rudolf of Fulda, *muris altis et firmis circumdata*, though the *vallum* of Cuthburh's monastery was probably originally in the form of a bank and ditch (Taylor 1967, 168-70; RCHM Dorset 5, 80). Bere Regis and Charminster also have roads (on their eastern sides) that behave in a similar fashion on leaving the rectilinear area. Roads converge at the edge of the rectilinear areas in the cases of Whitchurch, Sturminster Marshall, Charminster, Iwerne Minster, Puddletown and Burton Bradstock. Markets were sited at the edge of the enclosed area at Sturminster Marshall, Sturminster Newton, Shaftesbury, Bere Regis, Iwerne Minster, Burton Bradstock, and possibly also at Sherborne. Areas of 'extra-mural' growth occur in the form of planned units outside Sherborne, Wimborne, Puddletown, Sturminster Marshall and Bere Regis.

The main topographical characteristics of the minster settlements (not all of which are present in all cases) can be summarized as follows:
a) a waterside site, often at a confluence or in a bend in the river; occasionally sited at a spring
b) a central church within the rectilinear area
c) east-west / north-south alignment of roads and boundaries over a large area covering up to about 300m (e-w) by 400m (n-s)
d) the presence of a fixation line along what may have been a precinct enclosure
e) the presence of suburbs and / or a market outside the rectilinear area.

There are settlements among the definite minsters that do not have these characteristics. The precinct or enclosure is not apparent at Winfrith Newburgh, Yetminster, Gillingham, Cranborne or Beaminster. At Winfrith the church is aligned at a very peculiar angle, parallel to the stream, but there is no obvious differentiation in settlement pattern to indicate an enclosure. At Yetminster, and Gillingham there are signs of possible curvilinear enclosures. Cranborne displays the north-south / east-west alignment but the presence of the tenth-century monastic house complicates the picture and again there is no obvious enclosure. At Beaminster there is a strong curved line to the east of the church, in what is otherwise a fairly rectilinear plan.

The topography of the possible minster settlements

The plans of the possible minster settlements are analyzed below, but in less detail than those of the definite minsters. They are examined in groups determined by similar characteristics often brought about by similar histories such as the presence of an abbey or ownership by one. The plans of Milton Abbas, Abbotsbury and Cerne Abbas have all been influenced by the presence of their respective abbeys. The

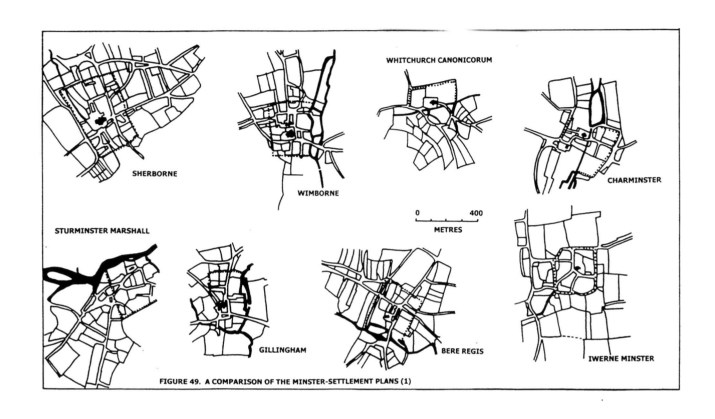

FIGURE 49. A COMPARISON OF THE MINSTER-SETTLEMENT PLANS (1)

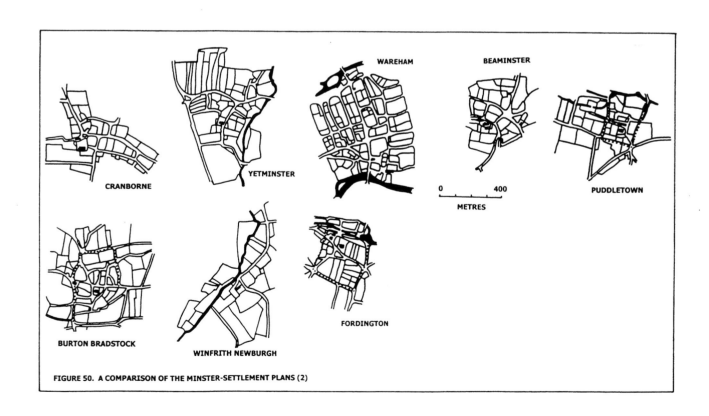

FIGURE 50. A COMPARISON OF THE MINSTER-SETTLEMENT PLANS (2)

small town which had grown up outside Milton Abbey gate was removed in the 18th century by the lord of the manor when he extended his park. The reconstruction of its plan (Fig 51) is based on Woodward's map of 1769x1771 and on the survey of earthworks by the RCHM (RCHM Dorset 3, 199). It is typical of many towns that owe their existence to an abbey: a market at the abbey gate with the tenements of the townspeople stretching away from the abbey. At Abbotsbury (Fig 51) the market is not immediately outside the Abbey precinct. The configuration of the roads suggests that West Street / Back Lane may have originally been the main east-west thoroughfare (Good 1966, 67-68). The abbey precinct possibly extended further north at some time incorporating the southern part of Rodden Row. To the west of the market place lies a very regular area of settlement known as the Furlongs, possibly a late-medieval extension of the town, its name indicating that it may have been laid out over part of the common fields (Penn 1980, 14). The town of Cerne Abbas (Fig 52) consists of a street leading away from the abbey gate towards an east-west street, Long St, which incorporates the market. Long St has a planned appearance with a back lane, and may date from the time of the market grant (see Appendix III). The plots to the west of the town along Acreman St appear to have been created from part of the common field as the northern plots have reversed 'S' shape boundaries (Taylor 1987, 82; Roberts 1987, 197-8). Corfe (Fig 53) is dominated by its castle, and the town has grown up at the gate in a similar fashion to those of the abbeys with several areas of planned units apparent, the southern-most of which appear to have been taken in from enclosed fields or *hawes*.

Shaftesbury (Fig 53), another abbey town, is a similar case, though the presence of the Anglo-Saxon burh complicates the picture. The market and business area of the town has grown up outside the abbey walls and the burh. Bridport (Fig 52) appears to have come into existence with the building of the burh and comprises a main central street, on which the church is situated, running down the spine of a peninsula of land at the confluence of two rivers. The main east-west road which cuts off the peninsula is thought to be a later addition to the plan (Penn 1980, 23-9).

Many of the possible-minster settlements have planned elements probably created by the monasteries to which they belonged. Sydling St Nicholas (Fig 54), a manor of Milton Abbey, has a very regulated plan with the church sitting to one side of a linear settlement parallel to the river.[9] The block of settlement running east from the church of Loders (Fig 54), bounded on the south by the river and on the north by a back lane appears to have been originally laid out as one unit. Loders Court immediately to the north of the church may have some fragmentary remains in its cellar of Loders Priory, the probable instigators of the planned element (RCHM Dorset 1, 139). Tarrant Monkton (Fig 55) belonged to Cranborne Abbey and, like Loders, is linear in form with a possible earlier nucleus around the church at its northern end. Earthworks on the east side of the High Street indicate that the village is shrunken. The village of Sixpenny Handley (Fig 55), a possession of Shaftesbury Abbey, is similar in form to both Loders and Tarrant Monkton. The line of the street is more sinuous but there are signs of

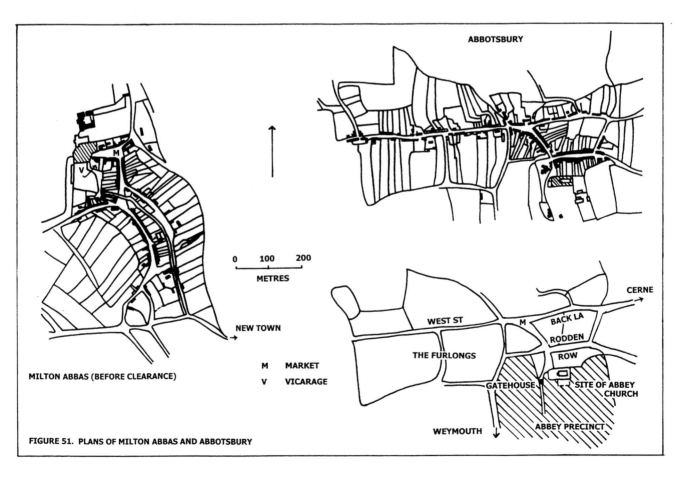

FIGURE 51. PLANS OF MILTON ABBAS AND ABBOTSBURY

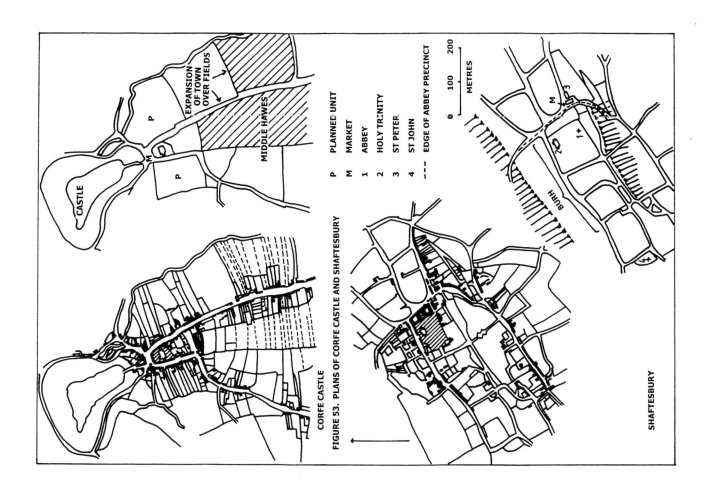

FIGURE 53. PLANS OF CORFE CASTLE AND SHAFTESBURY

CORFE CASTLE

SHAFTESBURY

CASTLE

EXPANSION OF TOWN OVER FIELDS

MIDDLE HAWES

BURH

P PLANNED UNIT
M MARKET
1 ABBEY
2 HOLY TRINITY
3 ST PETER
4 ST JOHN
--- EDGE OF ABBEY PRECINCT

0 100 200 METRES

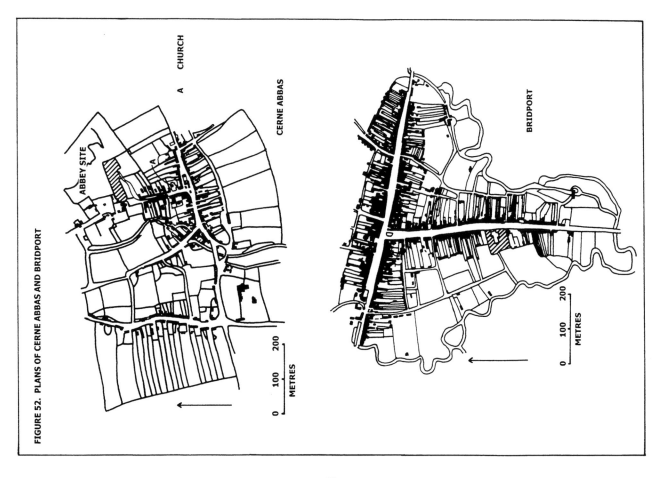

FIGURE 52. PLANS OF CERNE ABBAS AND BRIDPORT

ABBEY SITE

A CHURCH

CERNE ABBAS

BRIDPORT

0 100 200 METRES

0 100 200 METRES

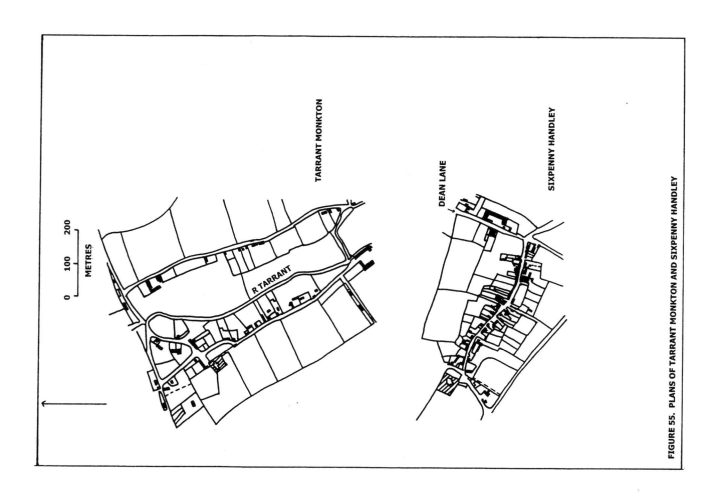

FIGURE 55. PLANS OF TARRANT MONKTON AND SIXPENNY HANDLEY

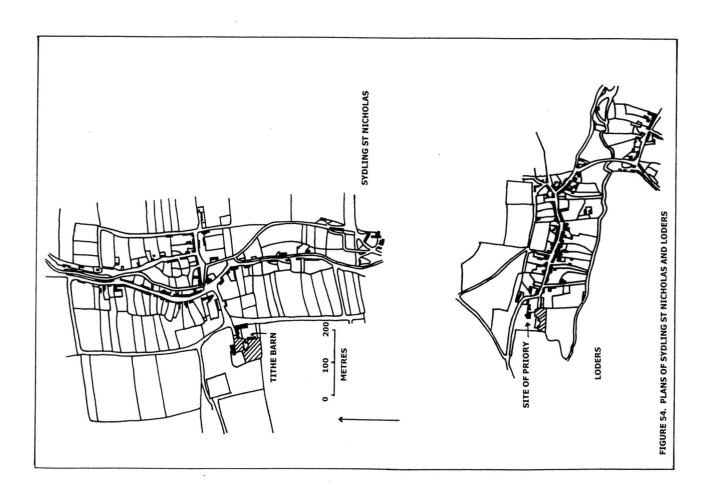

FIGURE 54. PLANS OF SYDLING ST NICHOLAS AND LODERS

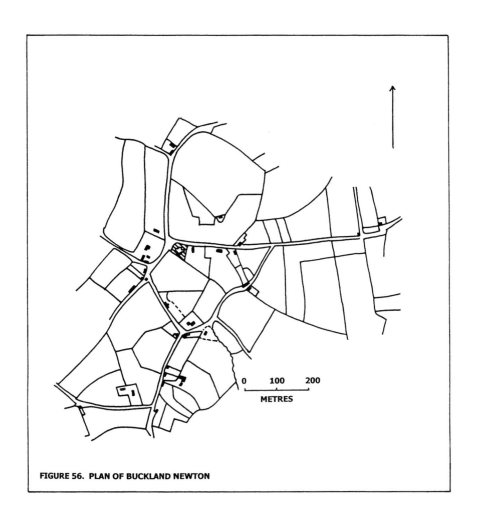

FIGURE 56. PLAN OF BUCKLAND NEWTON

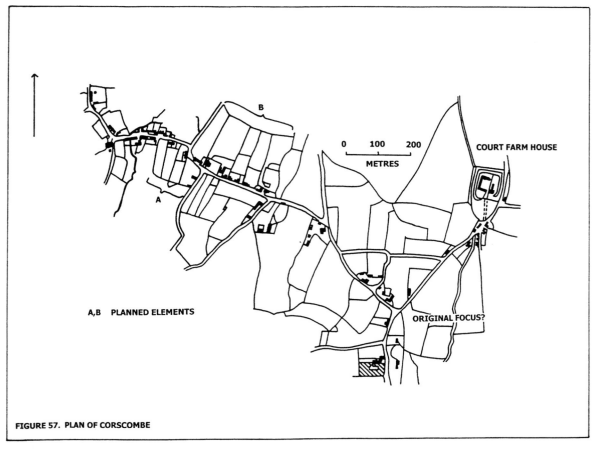

A,B   PLANNED ELEMENTS

COURT FARM HOUSE

ORIGINAL FOCUS?

FIGURE 57. PLAN OF CORSCOMBE

planning, probably of more than one phase. Medieval settlement remains have also been recorded at the end of the town to the west of the street running northwards from the crossroads (Sparey-Green 1988, 155-6). Regular planning is not associated with all the settlements in the possession of monastic houses. Buckland Newton (Fig 56), a Glastonbury manor, is a very irregular dispersed settlement. A fair was granted to the Abbey in 1240, and a fair and market some eighteen years later, but there is no obvious market-place. Corscombe (Fig 57), a possession of Sherborne Abbey, is a dispersed settlement with a polyfocal form. The early centre around the church has been deserted in favour of a planned element along the road to the west. To the north of the church lies Court Farm House, a moated manor house, originally the grange of Sherborne Abbey (RCHM Dorset 1, 106).

Neither Litton Cheney, Preston nor East Chaldon (Fig 58) were ecclesiastical possessions in 1086. At Chaldon, which was given to the Cistercian abbey of Bindon in 1292, the church sits within a rectangular enclosure, probably representing the glebe, outside of which the village stretches northwards to a possible green area (*CPR* 2, 475). Litton Cheney is more complicated. Its church sits at the highest point of the village beside a spring, on an east-west road. The village extends southwards at the western end of this road. To the east of the church there is another nucleus which is of less regular form. This area might be the site of the market granted to Ralph de Gorges in 1304 (Hutchins 2,

748). Preston, a possession of Salisbury from 1158, grew along an east-west route to the north of the church as far as the stream which flows south from Sutton Poyntz where there is a reputed Roman bridging point. A block of more regular tenements exists at the western end of the settlement.

Terrain can act restrictively on the pattern of settlement development and this is apparent at Powerstock, Netherbury and Portesham (Fig 59) which are situated in hilly landscapes. This is reflected in their plans with roads that are sinuous and are positioned in relation to the slope. Plan elements are much less in evidence and growth appears to be more organic.

Two of the settlements associated with the possible minsters are now dominated by large manor houses in parks. Canford village (Fig 60) consists of an estate village of Victorian date and no doubt any settlement that existed in the vicinity of the church was removed when the landscaped park was created in 1805, destroying evidence of the relationship between settlement and church. The church sits in a curved enclosure (Plate 9), but there is no difference in internal and external levels suggesting that the boundary may be part of landscaping changes. Stalbridge church and churchyard stand within the park of the Abbot of Sherborne and the town stretches away to the south (Fig 60). The market place (see Appendix III) has been narrowed through infilling. The planned element to its south known as The Ring is estate housing of early 19th century date.

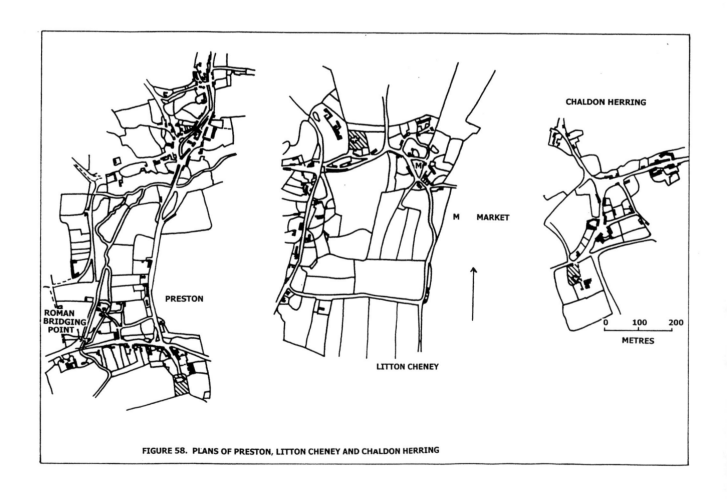

FIGURE 58. PLANS OF PRESTON, LITTON CHENEY AND CHALDON HERRING

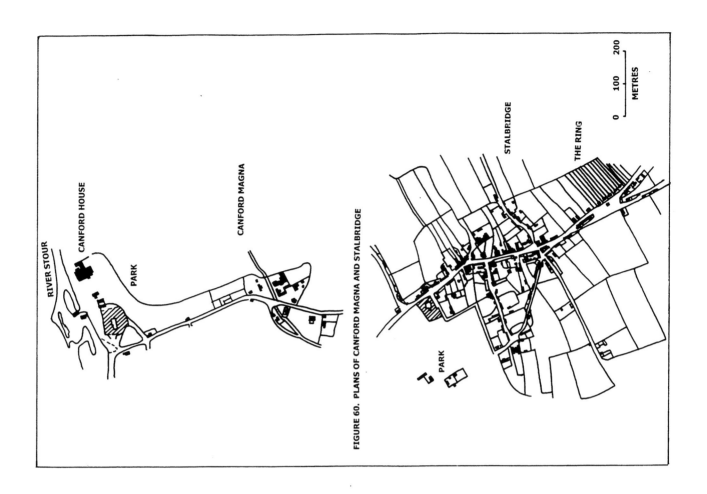

FIGURE 60. PLANS OF CANFORD MAGNA AND STALBRIDGE

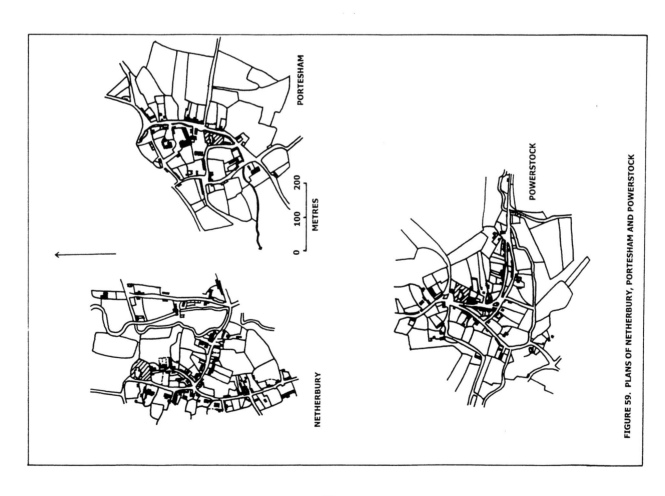

FIGURE 59. PLANS OF NETHERBURY, PORTESHAM AND POWERSTOCK

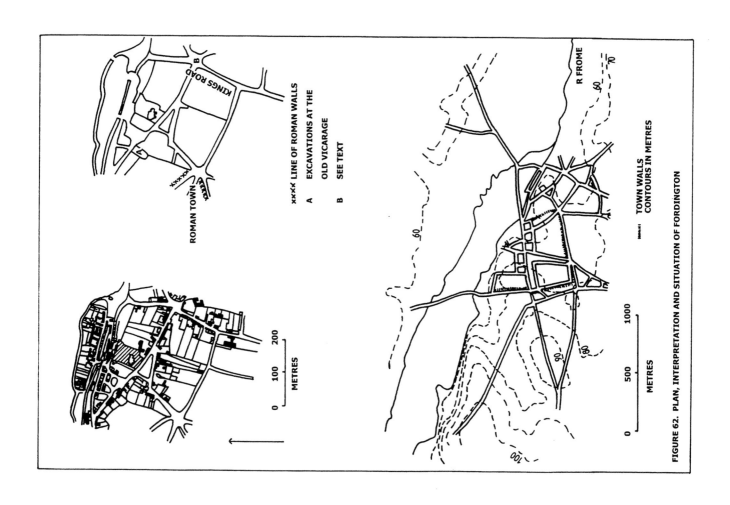

KINGS ROAD

ROMAN TOWN

xxxx   LINE OF ROMAN WALLS

A   EXCAVATIONS AT THE
      OLD VICARAGE

B   SEE TEXT

R FROME

TOWN WALLS
CONTOURS IN METRES

0   100   200

METRES

0   500   1000

METRES

FIGURE 62. PLAN, INTERPRETATION AND SITUATION OF FORDINGTON

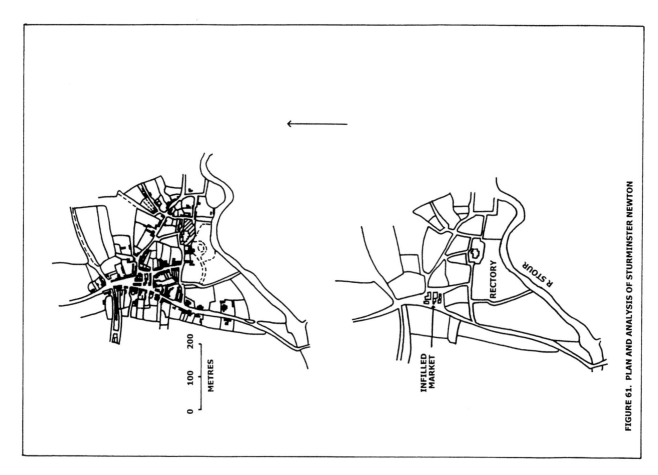

INFILLED
MARKET

RECTORY

R STOUR

0   100   200

METRES

FIGURE 61. PLAN AND ANALYSIS OF STURMINSTER NEWTON

74

In none of the possible-minster settlement plans examined so far, does the church exert the same degree of influence over its surroundings that is apparent in the settlement plans of the definite minsters. A small number of the settlements in this group, however, do bear some resemblance to the minster plans. At Sturminster Newton (Fig 61) the church and the rectory take up a sizeable portion of the town on the edge of the river which sweeps around Sturminster to give it a site similar to that of Wimborne Minster. At the edge of this block the town has developed around the market place. Fordington (Fig 62) has a quite distinct rectilinear layout angled at 45° to the Roman town. It is bounded on two sides by roads, on the third by property boundaries, the final side being formed by the river Frome. Fordington, as its name implies, grew up at an alternative crossing point of the river to that which leads into the town of Dorchester. The meeting point of roads, B on Fig 62, implies that King's Road is part of a fixation line, and that all the roads coming into Fordington have been directed to this particular point. Excavation at the Old Vicarage (A), showed a possible ditch across the plot in the area of the western boundary, which, unfortunately, was not excavated due to time constraints, but dates stratigraphically to between the Roman period and the fourteenth century (Startin 1981, 43-66).

Other settlements in the county with rectilinear plans

A brief examination of the town and village plans in the rest of Dorset produced an additional three villages with a strong rectilinear form, Milborne St Andrew, Bradford Abbas and Witchampton (see Fig 63). Milborne St Andrew, the mother-church to Dewlish, has been mentioned below p 95, as the possible site of a minster replaced by the later monastic foundation of Milton Abbas (*Nonarum*, 55; Hutchins 2, 602). Hutchins informed us that the parish of Milborne consisted of several manors, the main ones being Milborne St Andrew, Milborne Churcheston, Milborne Deveril and Milborne Stileham. He located the church in Churcheston (rather than St Andrew which he placed at the northern extremity of the parish). The existence of a separate manorial unit around the church may have resulted from its ownership by the College de Vaux, Salisbury, to whom it was given by its founder, Bishop Giles in the thirteenth century (Hutchins 2, 592). There is no record of the church being in episcopal hands in 1086, however, and prior to the Conquest the manor was held by John the Dane (*DB*, note 46,1). Bradford Abbas to the west of Sherborne has a very rectilinear plan immediately around the church and it has a small planned unit attached to the north of the rectilinear area.[10] The road that runs along the western edge of this enclosure is known as Westbury which might be a reflection of the area having been enclosed or even imply it was an early monastery as has been suggested above p 53. There is a possibility that Bradford may have originally had a minster (above p 33) as the church appears to have had chapels attached to it, and it did not fall within the peculiar controlled by the dean of Sarum whereas the rest of Sherborne's *parochia* did. A third village with a striking rectilinear enclosure preserved in the road and boundary pattern is Witchampton, to the north of Wimborne Minster. Whilst Witchampton has little to suggest that it had a high-

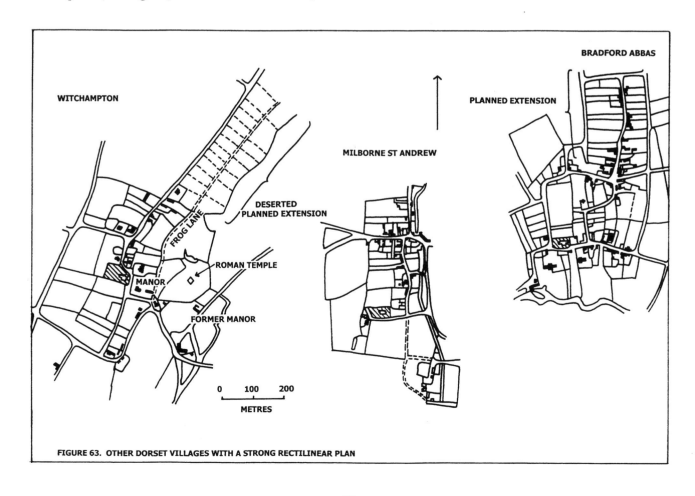

FIGURE 63. OTHER DORSET VILLAGES WITH A STRONG RECTILINEAR PLAN

status church, it did have a chapel attached at Edmondsham. The discovery of part of a set of whalebone chessmen from an earlier manor suggests that the site was high-status in the pre-Conquest period. The enclosure is sited beside the remains of a Romano-British temple which was discovered in the grounds of the old manor house (also outside the enclosure). The excavation of the temple site in the twenties produced a group of undated burials from above the Roman levels possibly suggesting a sub-Roman use of the site, which may also be implied in the *wicham* name (Gelling 1988, 67-74). The village has a planned (now deserted) extension from which Saxo-Norman pottery has been collected possibly indicating a pre-Conquest foundation for the plan unit (Hall 1993, 121-132).

The topography of the minster settlements: shape, function, dating and survival

That minsters settlements display a particular pattern of growth has already been recognized. Blair noted, ' 'minster towns' often show a distinctive topographical development' as at Thame, Lambourn and Cheddar. Three stages of growth might be expected: the minster precinct; organic late-Saxon growth around the edge, or along roads leading to the minster, and possibly a market place; and lastly, twelfth or thirteenth-century burgage plots (Blair 1988c, 36, 48-9; 1996, 110-12). The Dorset pattern suggests a slight modification of this model with infill of the minster precinct around the church, a process that probably started in the pre-Conquest period. The main apparent difference with the Dorset examples is their rectilinear form: the Dorset minster plans lack examples of the circular or sub-circular form (Appendix IV).[11] Blair's only examples of minster sites with rectilinear boundaries are those placed in Roman towns or fortifications; 'Except where Roman structures were reused, the typical enclosure was round or oval' (Blair 1992, 231). The predominance of strongly rectilinear areas surrounding the Dorset minsters suggests that the *vallum* of the minster precinct must have been rectilinear in form. The corners of some of the Dorset enclosures are rounded, such as at Iwerne Minster, Wimborne Minster and the north-east corner of Fordington. The degree of curvature suggests that it was only the corners that were rounded in the same manner as the ditches of Roman forts; weathering would make right-angles unlikely to survive in ditches, a fact understood by the Roman agrimensores.

Is a rectilinear plan form acceptable for the middle-Saxon period? Certainly by the 10th century rectilinear burhs were being created but Hassal and Hill suggested that the rectangular burh lacks an English prototype and they attributed the inspiration for its origin to the Franks (Hassal and Hill 1970, 188-95). However, recent excavations at Hamwic and at Hereford have shown two places of the early to middle eighth-century date with regular layouts of roads on a rectilinear plan (Morton 1992, 30; Whitehead 1982, 13-24; Shoesmith 1982, 88-94). Increasingly, archaeological reports also refer to rectangular enclosures in the early medieval period.[12] The evidence for a planned layout at Hereford dates to the second half of the 8th century and has been attributed to Offa. Whitehead suggested that 'a grid

pattern of streets and buildings was superimposed on the original crossroads settlement' (Shoesmith 1982, 91-92). Of Hamwic it has been said, 'virtually every feature or group of features found in Hamwic was aligned north-south, east-west' (Morton 1992, 30). The church of St Mary, probably a minster, sits within this area, though not centrally. The main streets were of a uniform width which Morton suggested implies a standardization of measurement, and possible use of surveying equipment. They were metalled individually, each street being completed in one go.[13] It would not be out of place, therefore, to have had similar rectilinear layouts around the minster settlements.

Grid forms can occur when there is centralized political control in colonial or quasi-colonial situations as long as the knowledge of the grid exists (Stanislawski 1946, 108). The West Saxons were taking over Dorset in the seventh/eighth centuries (see above p 2) when the minsters were established. They would have been aware of the grid form from deserted Roman towns, and also towns on the continent. It is probable that a knowledge of this form also existed from Roman literature in the *Corpus Agrimensorum*.[14] Aldhelm, the first West Saxon bishop of Sherborne, was, to quote Lapidge, 'perhaps the most widely learned man produced in Anglo-Saxon England' (Lapidge and Rosier 1985, 1). He had a wide knowledge of Latin poetry and literature, and had travelled abroad. He was strongly influential in Wessex, and was involved in drawing up the laws of Ine, the introduction of which states that the king and his advisors were gathered together to consider 'the salvation of our souls and the security of our Kingdom'. Religion and national security were viewed as two sides of the same coin, and Aldhelm's repeated allusions to monks and Christian people as, 'cohorts of legions', and the 'monastic army' and to the 'fortress of faith' in *De Virginitate*, suggest that he viewed the church as a latter-day Roman army (Lapidge and Herren 1979, 63, 68, 69, 131). Constructing a system of monastic houses or minsters with large rectilinear enclosures would be, therefore, not untenable.

The extent of these minster enclosures may at first seem on the large side but there are comparative enclosures elsewhere of this date and earlier. Continental examples are Solignac, which was reputed to have had an enclosure 1800m in circumference, and the later Carolingian monastery of St Riquier which was 500m across (James 1981, 40-41). Charles Thomas has pointed to earlier examples from the British Isles at Iona in Scotland and Clonmacnois in Ireland with 'valla enclosing large areas of approximately rectangular shape' (Thomas 1971, 27-32). The earliest monastic plan resembling the later orthodox layout was found at St Gall and is thought to date to the beginning of the ninth century. It has recently been suggested that this may have originally been Theodore's plan for St Augustine's, Canterbury, but the case was not argued convincingly (Horn and Born 1979; Noll 1982, 191-240). Even so, given Boniface's input into the Frankish reforms and his West Saxon origins, the inspiration for the St Gall plan may have been English.

The two questions of date of layout and likelihood of survival are linked. The dominance of this rectilinear plan form amongst the minster settlements in Dorset implies that it almost certainly formed part of their original layout and was perpetuated as a morphological frame for later urban development. It seems reasonable to suggest that the rectilinear plans were part of the original lay-out of the minster sites, as later replanning of sites on such a massive scale seems improbable. Their date, therefore, must be put at the time of the foundation of the minsters, at the end of the seventh and beginning of the eighth centuries. Conzen has argued for the stability of plans in an urban context, and Slater proposes that 'once they have been established, alterations in urban street alignments and property divisions are possible on a large scale only when a powerful ground landlord, extensive land clearance and a changed functional requirement, coincide in time' (Conzen 1960, 7; Slater 1984, 11-35 at 12). Whilst the early phase of the minsters could not be classed as urban, it is still difficult to imagine that such an exercise in replanning could occur at a later date, let alone a context for it. The 'landlord' or 'owner' and the function of the minster sites remained unaltered. Biddle notes that 'a planned layout can be eroded by gradual changes and even entirely lost, and that it could in the course of time be replaced by a later planned system laid out on new principles' (Biddle 1976, 19-32 at 20). This can be seen in the case of Roman walled towns. It is well-accepted that the present streets in former Roman towns usually bear little resemblance to the Roman layout. Normally, only the internal roads connecting the entrances to walled towns survive, due to the restrictions imposed by the entrances. In the case of Roman towns, the evidence points to desertion, and later re-colonization. There is no evidence for such desertion of the minster sites. Interruptions may have occurred during the Viking attacks, but these probably just formed a hiccup in the use of the site: obviously, all of the minsters identified in this study have continued in use as churches.

It is proposed that the *vallum monasterii* acted as a morphological frame around the minsters. In most cases the enclosed area has been encroached upon. In examples where the settlement has flourished, such as Sherborne and Wimborne, the enclosed area forms the most intensively developed part of the town. In others, such as Whitchurch Canonicorum and Sturminster Marshall, development is concentrated outside the rectilinear area which is not as well preserved as those instances were development has been more intensive. An undeveloped area around the minster would be more vulnerable to change than one within a town where the multiple interest of the residents would form a constraint on large-scale change. The lack of central development at Whitchurch and Sturminster may be due to the church as landlord not having taken up opportunities for commercial development (both were for quite long periods, owned by alien monasteries). The date of the encroachment of development into the enclosures cannot be ascertained. The disuse of the *vallum* must have coincided with a change in status of those serving the church. Wimborne changed from a double monastery to a collegiate church, probably at some time in the 10th century, and this might well have changed the nature of the site, allowing development for secular purposes to take place within the enclosure. Records show that the Dean of Wimborne controlled the main area of the town all of which lay within the enclosure. The Domesday account of Hinton Martell implies that Bishop Maurice held 8 burgesses in Wimborne and these may be an illustration of the commercialization of part of the former monastic precinct.

Conclusion

Analysis of the minster sites shows that there is little evidence for curvilinear enclosures in Dorset. Rather, the minsters are situated in areas of strong rectilinear planning aligned on the axis of the churches, possibly resulting from the presence of a *vallum monasterii*. Around these areas later suburbs have grown, and the enclosures have been infilled with settlement in many cases. It is striking that, as elsewhere, the settlements in Dorset that grew into central places were those of the minster sites (presumably because of the permanent nature of their settlement) rather than the royal vills (which were only intermittently occupied) and the incidence of markets (see Appendix III) shows that many were minster sites. The similarity of the settlement layouts and sites implies a uniformity of genesis: the establishment of minsters at certain key points in the landscape with large rectilinear precincts under their control. The existence of this plan form for Dorset minsters may support the argument that each kingdom was converted by a network of minsters within a generation of its conversion to Christianity as part of a deliberate royal and episcopal policy (Foot 1989, 117). It has been shown that a rectilinear layout for the minster enclosures would not be an inconsistent form in the Saxon repertoire in the late seventh / early eighth centuries despite the lack of evidence for rectilinear minster enclosures elsewhere in the country (Blair 1992). The search for curvilinear elements in the churchyard plans of the county (Appendix IV) shows that the *llan* form may not be completely absent but survives in a handful of lesser churches implying that in Dorset, at least, the Celtic church may have been suppressed and was certainly not used as the basis of the organization of the English church. The presence of such large rectangular areas around the minsters highlights the important role that archaeological investigation could play in some of the minster settlements where less development has taken place such as at Sturminster Marshall and Whitchurch Canonicorum. Such large areas may well have included provision of room for agricultural plots and corralling of beasts as has been suggested by Thomas for Clonmacnois and Iona (Thomas 1971, 30-31).

If the system was brought about by royal or episcopal authority its use must be expected in other parts of Wessex. Outside Dorset there are signs of such planning in parts of Somerset.[15] An examination of the counties to the north and east of Dorset may help to establish if the form was in use before the Saxon Conquest of Dorset, especially in Hampshire where Hase assigns the foundation of the minsters to the end of the seventh century. If a rectilinear plan continued in use as the Saxon Conquest continued westwards, its presence would help to distinguish newly founded minsters from any British Christian sites incorporated into the system.

---

[1]For example, the accuracy of the enlarged area of the town of Gillingham is very poor: T/GIL. Only 3 out of 270 surviving Dorset tithe maps were sufficiently accurate to be classed as 'first class maps': (Kain, Oliver and Baker 1991, 91,94).

[2]Barker's examples from outside Dorset, Lambourn, Charlbury and Thame, are much more convincing. All are much smaller enclosures directly comparable with *llan* forms in Cornwall, though at Thame the church does not stand within the enclosure (Barker 1982, 77-116, maps at 97).

[3] *DGPA*, 175. The main attribute lacking at Sherborne may have been town defences which were present at Old Sarum. This would also hold true for the other bishoprics moved at the same time: Lichfield to Chester; Selsey to Chichester; and the earlier move of Crediton to Exeter.

[4]For example, Congresbury: Gelling in Rahtz *et al*, 1992, 5; Burrow 1981, 50-51.

[5]It is not necessarily important that the present personal street names are not of any great antiquity. Personal names, as shown above for the Winterborne units, were likely to change with ownership, whereas the descriptive type names seem to be more stable.

[6]I owe this suggestion to James Bond.

[7]Not noted in Beresford and Finberg 1973; Hutchins 1, 140.

[8] A fair was granted in 1137:Hutchins 3, 336-67.

[9]The deserted village of Holworth on the south coast near Chaldon Herring, another of Milton's properties, also has a very regular plan which excavation suggests dates to the thirteenth century: Rahtz 1959, 130,133.

[10]The planned unit has been noted by Katherine Barker (1984, 17, 20).

[11]Analysis of the churchyards of the county was undertaken to see if this was confined to the minsters or if there was a general absence. None of the four curvilinear enclosures that may be British survivals was associated with a high-status church (see Appendix IV).

[12]   Brandon, Suffolk: *MA* 24, 232;   Great Linford, Buckinghamshire: *MA* 26, 173-4; Stonea Grange: *MA* 28, 210; Grove Priory, Leighton Buzzard: *MA 29*, 163; regularity of planning also occurs at Green Lane, Letchworth: *MA* 33, 196.

[13] This raises the interesting question, was Hamwic originally a monastic settlement? It might account for the lack of property boundaries, the egalitarian feeding and refuse-disposal habits of the occupants, and the large amounts of animal bone, perhaps resulting from the provision of skins for a scriptorium (Bourdillon 1988, 190).

[14]Though no copy is known to have existed in this country the earliest copy is thought to date from early sixth-century Italy and a copy was known to exist in Bobbio by 981. Bobbio was founded by the Irish monk Columbanus but it is not known if this work was brought with him (Dilke 1971, 128).

[15]See for example Milborne Port and Crewkerne (Aston and Leech 1977, 35-38, 92-5).

CHAPTER FIVE
CONCLUSION: THE IMPLICATIONS OF THE DORSET MINSTER SYSTEM

The widely accepted pattern of minster church serving a parochia based on a large royal or ecclesiastical estate is one that holds true for Dorset. The Dorset minsters possess characteristics in common with those that distinguish minsters in other parts of the country. Literary sources, and economic and physical characteristics, reveal a group of high-status churches within large *parochiae* in which they developed and maintained a measure of control over secondary or daughter churches. The better preserved minsters dominate large relict parishes (many of which remained intact until the nineteenth century) with groups of dependent chapels relying on the minsters for provision of clergy and burial. With the perspective gained from the examination of additional evidence of the relationship between *parochia*, royal demesne and hundred and the underlying geographical bases, along with the evidence accrued from the examination of minster-settlement morphology, it has been possible to arrive at a new model of Saxon Christian development in Dorset (Table 14). In Table 14, the final column attempts to associate the progress of Christianization and the foundation of the minster churches with key persons and events from the seventh to early tenth centuries arranged chronologically in the preceding columns.

The minster system in Dorset was instigated at royal hands as was found to be the case in Hampshire. Unlike Hampshire, however, where Hase has suggested that the parochial coverage of the minsters was almost complete, Dorset appears to have had only partial coverage in the seventh and eighth centuries. Hase suggested that all parts of Hampshire were within 8-10 miles (12-16 km) of a minster church and this is virtually true for Dorset but the Dorset minsters generally covered areas with a radius of about 4.5 miles (7km) leaving some parts of the county unprovided for (Hase 1975, 2; 1988, 45-66). One possible reason for the gaps might be that minsters did not survive in these places. However, the place-name evidence of the primary minster settlements shows a group of settlements with names sufficiently similar and almost exclusively confined to the minster settlements suggesting that this scenario is unlikely.[1] Failed primary minster sites should be apparent from the place-names, unless of course, these too have been lost. The minster provision in Dorset, therefore, appears to have been less extensive in the first instance than that suggested for Hampshire but there is evidence of later supplementation of the system. The characteristics that point to minster status are not confined solely to the early Saxon or primary minsters, however: other churches in the county possess sufficient of these characteristics to suggest that their origins were not as daughter churches to one of the minsters. An examination of additional features such as place-names and ownership suggests that the remaining high-status churches divide into two types; those associated with Alfredian reorganization, and those serving large monastic estates. These high status churches served some of the areas not covered by the minsters.

The group of the high-status churches linked with the Alfredian burhs were probably created after Alfred's defeat of Guthrum in 878. Shaftesbury, Wareham and Bridport appear to have been founded on the boundaries of adjoining *parochiae* or royal estates. At Wareham and Bridport the boundaries are formed by rivers and it was these vulnerable areas between territories which provided entry points for the Viking attacks, and were singled out by Alfred for defensive settlements (Smyth 1995, 31). Whilst Wareham was already in possession of a minster church before the burh defences were built, the pattern of parishes suggests that another two churches were established at that time and Wareham's *parochiae* rearranged to provide for them. Haslam suggested a similar pattern of development in eastern London and he proposed that the founding of new ecclesiastical institutions was 'an integral part of Alfred's burghal policy' (Haslam 1988b, 35-43, quote at 38). The churches of Shaftesbury and Bridport, both of which were probably Alfredian minsters, likewise seem to have been given parts of the *parochiae* of the neighbouring minsters. The second group of high-status churches apparent in the county are those serving large estates owned by monasteries, examples of which are Corscombe, Buckland Newton and Handley, owned by Sherborne, Glastonbury and Shaftesbury abbeys, respectively. Essentially many of the characteristics displayed by these churches are the same as those of the primary minsters but the lack of primary place-names and coherent geographical units discourages the idea that these were simply less successful primary minsters. Instead they appear to have been founded by the monasteries to serve their isolated estates possibly as early as the eighth century.[2] Costen's work on Glastonbury Abbey suggests that the acquisition of the majority of its estates post-dates the refounding of the abbey by Dunstan in the tenth century. It seems probable, therefore, that some of this group of high-status churches are of a later foundation date than the older, royal minsters, possibly dating to as late as the tenth century in some instances. Even if the two were founded contemporaneously, the royal minsters were superior in wealth and size of *parochia*.[3] The three different types of high status church identified by this research may well exist in neighbouring counties, and a comparison of the pattern with that of Somerset might be particularly revealing with regard to illuminating the progress of Saxon Christianity in the south-west.

The majority of Dorset minsters were founded at the centre of the large royal estates that formed the 'night's farms' at Domesday (though some such as Sturminster Marshall had been alienated by that time). The exceptions were the minsters that were sited at the centre of the core estates of the episcopal see of Sherborne. These episcopal estates, given with the foundation of the bishopric were of an equivalent size to the royal estates. Evidence suggests that the land units given to support the minsters, however, were on a completely different scale - small fragmented areas of the large royal holdings. The place-names of some of the later parishes, or manors in some cases, indicate that the minsters were endowed with small areas of land often on the periphery of the royal demesne such as Hinton Martell, Hinton Parva, and Hampreston in the case of Wimborne

Table 14. Model of Saxon Christian development in Dorset

DATE	KING	BISHOP	EVENTS	MODEL / INTERPRETATION
611	CYNEGILS			Sparse presence of British Christianity, 3 possible origins: a) Roman continuity b) 5th/6th century Welsh influence c) Continental influence
626			Battle: Cynegils v Penda at Cirencester	
634			Birinus (from Gaul) preaches to the West Saxons	Introduction of West Saxons in Upper Thames basin, Hampshire, Wiltshire and Berkshire, to Roman Christianity by Birinus (called the 'Roman bishop' in the ASC).
635		BIRINUS	Cynegils baptized at Dorchester on Thames. Dorchester is given as the episcopal seat.	West Saxon conversion to Christianity begins.
642	CENWALH		Cenwalh baptized	Dorset is conquered by the West Saxons in this period. They press westwards following defeat along their northern borders with Mercia.
646				
648			Minster at Winchester founded	Large geographically-based areas of royal demesne are established in Dorset and Somerset taking their names from the rivers.
c650		AGILBERT		Christianity becomes the main religion for the Saxons – pagan burials are very scarce in Dorset and the south-west.
652			Battle: Cenwalh v ?Mercia at Bradford on Avon	
658			Battle: Cenwalh v Welsh at Penselwood – the Welsh are driven as far as the R Parrett	The bishopric is moved by Cenwalh from Dorchester to Winchester because of the insecurity of Dorchester on Thames.
660		WINE	Agilbert leaves to be bishop of Paris	
661			Battle: Cenwalh v ?? at *Posentesbyrg*	
663			Synod of Whitby	The Roman faction defeats the Celtic faction at the Synod of Whitby.
664			Colman with his companions went to his native land	Those wishing to remain Celtic monks leave England for western Ireland. Suppression of the Celtic church.
668			Arrival of Archbishop Theodore at Canterbury	Initiation of regular synods and councils following the Roman tradition.
670		LEUTHERE	Arrival of Hadrian	Establishment of the Canterbury school.
672			Council of Hertford	Aldhelm, abbot of Malmesbury, spends 2 years at Canterbury.
673	SEAXBURH			Following the council of Hertford Aldhelm writes to King Geraint to condemn Celtic church customs.
674	AESCWINE			
675			Battle: Aescwine v Wulfhere of Mercia	
676	CENTWINE	HAEDDI		
680			Synod of Hatfield	Theodore calls synod in order to 'amend the doctrines of the Christian faith'.
682			Centwine drove Britons to sea	
685/6	CADWALLA			
688	INE		Cadwalla goes to Rome where he is baptized and dies	
690			Archbishop Theodore dies	
703		DANIEL		

DATE	KING	BISHOPS		EVENTS	MODEL / INTERPRETATION
704/5	INE (cont)	DANIEL	ALDHELM	Division of the diocese of Wessex into Winchester and Selwood	Foundation of the diocese of Selwood with the see established at Sherborne. The possible British Christian foundation of *Lanprobi* is suppressed and its endowments go to form the lands of the new bishopric.
709			FORTHERE		
710				Battle: Ine and Nunna v Geraint	Ine continues to push westwards into Devon.
715				Battle: Ine v Ceolred at Adam's Grave	Mercia attacks the northern borders of Wessex.
722				Queen Aethelburh destroys Taunton and Ealdberht is banished / Battle: Ine v South Saxons	Taunton was a minster site and may well have been taken by Ealdberht in a similar fashion to Aethelwold seizing Wimborne in 900.
726	AETHELHEARD			Ine abdicates to Rome	As time passes, British Christian sites are absorbed into the Roman church rather than being resited.
733				Athelbald captures Somerton	
737			HEREWALD	Bishop Forthere and Queen Frithugyth journey to Rome	
740	CUTHRED				
743			AETHELMOD	Cuthred & Athelbald v the Welsh	
786	BEORHTRIC		DENEFRITH	First Viking incursion at Portland in Dorset	
800	EGBERT		WIGBEORHT	Battle:The Wiltshire men defeated the Hwicce	
813			EALHSTAN	Egbert raided Cornwall from east to west	Beginnings of Saxon control of Cornwall.
823				Battle: Britons against Devon men at Galford, W Devon	
871	ALFRED		ATHELHEAH		Alfred creates burhs at Bridport, Shaftesbury and Wareham, vulnerable places between royal estates, and increases the number of churches to serve these new creations.
876				Vikings camp in Wareham	
878			WULFSIGE	Alfred defeats Guthrum at Edington	
891			ASSER		From 891 Alfred starts granting land to, and exchanging land with, his *comes* and *dux* as part of his defence policy. Preston is acquired. As the royal estates become more fragmented, proprietary churches are established on the new land units of the thegns
899	EDWARD				
909				Diocese divided : Sherborne, Crediton and Wells	
961				Dunstan is made Archbishop of Canterbury	Following Dunstan's reformation more land accrues to the monasteries and further high-status churches emerge serving these large estates. Failing minsters are reformed as new enclosed monasteries.

Minster. It has to be unrealistic to suppose that all minsters were given large amounts of land because the logical conclusion of such a practise would entail too great a diminution of royal land.

Cambridge and Rollason saw the fragmentation of the system of *parochiae* as the result of aristocrats usurping royal authority (Cambridge and Rollason 1995, 99-101). However, the fragmentation of large royal estates was brought about by the gift of land units to the aristocracy which in turn led to the usurpation of *ecclesiastical* authority as the lords of the new estates created churches for their own use and to serve the estate occupants. This desire to provide a local church for their dependants on the estate shows them emulating royal policy: the king had provided churches to serve his large multiple royal estates. In the south of the *parochia* of the episcopal seat at Sherborne, the lords of the enfranchised manors founded their own churches with the permission of the bishop but the incentive to do so was theirs and the chapels remained firmly in the grip of the minster church at Sherborne until the nineteenth century. The founding of churches was very definitely linked to the ownership of the estate: a response brought about for the sake of the convenience of the communicants not as the result of pastoral intervention by the bishop. The pattern of fragmentation of the Wimborne estate is reflected in the hundredal arrangement.

The question of whether pastoral care existed in seventh/eighth century England has recently been raised again by Cambridge and Rollason who argued that the characteristics by which we identify minsters only became associated with them in the post-Viking period and that many of the minsters referred to in contemporary literature were enclosed monasteries with no duty of pastoral care. If this were the case we might expect to be able to distinguish between minsters such as Wimborne which was recorded as a double monastery between c700 and c.950, and Sherborne, the seat of the bishop, and therefore, presumably, involved in pastoral care in its *parochia* from the outset. The Dorset evidence shows no noticeable difference, however, between the development of these two *parochiae*. The same pattern of foundation of manorial churches is apparent in both suggesting that the pastoral care undertaken was common to both. Furthermore, whilst Cambridge and Rollason disagree that pastoral care was the norm for pre-Viking *monasteria*, they concede that '...it is likely that the reputable *monasteria* at least would have undertaken pastoral care in the strict sense for the inhabitants of their own estates' (Cambridge and Rollason 1995, 94). It hardly seems plausible to suggest, however, that the minsters would serve their own estates and not those of their royal founders in whose midst they were situated. Aldhelm, the first bishop of Sherborne, noted on two separate occasions whilst he was abbot of Malmesbury, that he had been 'weighed down with the burden of pastoral care'.[4] As abbot of Malmesbury he founded churches at Malmesbury, Bruton, Bradford on Avon, Wareham and on the river Frome, all of which would probably have been staffed by monks or clerics from Malmesbury (Lapidge and Rosier 1985, 8, 36). That missionary work, of which pastoral care has to be an integral

part, was seen as part of the ethos of monastic life at that time seems incontrovertible and must surely have formed the model on which Boniface, a product of the West Saxon system, went on to convert Germany.

The minster *parochiae* of Dorset are based on the royal estates of the county which comprise areas of strong geographical delineation. These well-defined units are often centred on river basins, or parts thereof, their boundaries being formed by the surrounding watersheds. Everything within this catchment area gravitates down towards the central place with its minster and in many cases a market in the middle ages. The division of the *parochiae* into parish units, which is essentially a reflection of the fragmentation of the royal estates, was also to a lesser degree, influenced by the physical environment as the units all required access to water supply, arable, pasture, meadow and waste. The boundaries of these units are less likely to follow geographical features, however. It is impossible to tell at present if the system of royal estates reflects an earlier one of Roman villa estates, a situation which will undoubtedly prevail until a much fuller picture of the Roman settlement pattern within the county is available. Whilst the origins of the royal estates remain obscure, they can be seen as the foundation of the later hundredal system. Minster *parochiae* have been shown to relate to hundreds in many areas of the country and it has been suggested in this study that the relationship is incidental in that the *parochiae* and the hundreds are both based on the royal estates. The relationship between *parochiae* and hundreds is not immediately apparent in Dorset as the hundreds mutated with the pre-Conquest introduction of a tenurial element into the hundredal system whilst the minster *parochiae* mutated as their daughter-churches gained independence and diminished their original coverage.

One of the main points to emerge from this study is the impact of Romanization on the West Saxon church following the appointment of Archbishop Theodore. The Saxons started pressing into Dorset probably from about 650 onwards by which time the upper echelons of West Saxon society were newly converted to Christianity as a consequence of the missionary activity of bishop Birinus in 634. With the arrival of Theodore and Hadrian at Canterbury (668/9), a period of consolidation of Roman allegiance began following hard on the heels of the Roman victory at Whitby in 663. Hadrian's specific remit from Pope Vitalian was to make sure that Theodore adhered to the Roman tradition (though by all accounts this was probably unnecessary as Theodore had played a major role in the Lateran Council of 649 which condemned monothelite heresy and he was consulted by a later pope, Agatho, on the issue) (Bischoff and Lapidge 1994, 70-81). At the synod of Hatfield in 679 Theodore stated his total support for the *acta* of the 649 Lateran Council painting a picture of an archbishop intent upon developing Christianity along orthodox lines, coming as he did from the wellspring of Roman influence. Aldhelm, Abbot of Malmesbury and later Bishop of Selwood, spent some time in the monastic school of Theodore and Hadrian at Canterbury, possibly the years 670-672, his study terminating in his attendance of the council of Hertford (September 672), where he was commissioned to write to the British concerning their unorthodox customs. Aldhelm's high-handed tone suggests that the British Christianity which the West Saxons found in the south-west was unacceptable. We are given a taste of this disapproval in Aldhelm's epistle to King Geraint: the British clergy wore the wrong tonsure, after the fashion of the heretic Simon, 'and the ten books of Clement give witness to what sort and how great was the deception of necromancy that he fraudulently devised against the blessed Peter'; they calculated Easter wrongly; and when suffered to meet with members of the English church, insisted that they fast for forty days before they would meet them, imitating 'the heretics, who liked to call themselves *cathari*' (Lapidge and Herren 1979, 155-60). All in all, Aldhelm's view of the members of the British church was that they were heretical, but all this could be instantly made right if they would follow the teachings of St Peter and adhere to the Roman tradition. It was in an atmosphere saturated with the necessity to conform to Roman orthodoxy that the West Saxons consolidated their holdings in Dorset.

This study found little supportive evidence for the British Christian continuity suggested for Dorset. The primary layer of Saxon minsters did not simply fill in the gaps in an already existing church structure put in place by the renewed expansion of the British church in the south-west in the late fifth to sixth centuries from Wales (Ralegh Radford 1962, 33; Hase 1994, 51). There is little evidence that the influx of Welsh monasticism extended very far inland from the Somerset and north Devon coasts, probably not reaching as far south as Dorset. Additionally, Pearce has questioned the date of the Celtic dedications attributing them to the 11th century, though they may reflect earlier traditions of Celtic foundation (Pearce 1973, 104-7). Thomas suggested Dorset as one of the few areas where Christianity may have survived from the Roman period, but Snyder's recent database of sub-Roman sites reveals that only two Dorset sites have any evidence of continuity, Poundbury and Maiden Castle. The sub-Roman Poundbury settlement was situated on the main Roman cemetery of Dorchester which contained possible Christian burials but the settlement shows no signs of Christian continuity and appears to have been brought abruptly to an end with the Saxon invasion (Thomas 1985, 268-71, 352; Snyder 1996, 22-23). The examination of the oft-quoted relationship between villas and minster sites in Dorset shows that there are few if any definite examples. More minor churches are associated with Roman remains than minsters indicating that the incidence is probably as a result of continuity of estate centre rather than reuse of villas as monasteries. Yet whilst such continuity, or the later reuse of villa sites is far from being proven, three Dorset minster sites have a modicum more evidence of a British Christian predecessor: Sherborne, Shaftesbury and Wareham. Of these, Wareham with its engraved memorial stones is the best attested, but its southerly aspect suggests that it may have been influenced from Brittany rather than Wales. The raised curvilinear churchyards at Gussage St Michael (Plate 10), Toller Porcorum, Kinson, and Church Knowle may signify areas of British Christian survival but these are all minor churches which may in any event turn out to be of later foundation.

The distinctive pattern of phased growth at minster sites drawn to our attention by Blair at Thame and Lambourn, and recently at Cheddar, has been identified earlier in this thesis in many of the Dorset minster settlements (Blair 1988c, 49; 1996, 97-121). The point of divergence of the Dorset minster settlement plans from those in many other parts of the country is in the high degree of rectilinear planning which comes as something of a surprise after the emphasis that has been placed on curvilinear enclosures. Rectilinear planning associated with early monasteries has not gone entirely unnoticed in the past, however. Thomas observed that 'some at least of the sixth-century foundations possessed *valla* enclosing large areas of approximately rectangular shape', citing as examples Clonmacnois and Iona, and suggesting that Glastonbury may also belong to this group. Thomas noted that the only parallel form was the legionary marching camp. The possibility of this having been used as a blueprint has been looked at in Chapter Four but whilst one copy of the *Corpus Agrimensorum* was scripted in Italy in the seventh century there is no direct evidence that it would have been known to Theodore and Hadrian or their pupil Aldhelm (see above, p 76). Thomas went on to suggest that the rectilinear form might have derived instead from Egypt, the Levant, Greece or North Africa (Thomas 1971, 29-32). The monasteries of Clonmacnois and Iona are unlikely to have been the model for the Dorset minsters though they are earlier than them, but Thomas's other suggested origins of form can still be usefully examined as precursors. Two of the countries suggested by Thomas, Greece and North Africa, are of particular interest here, being the homelands of Archbishop Theodore and Abbot Hadrian respectively. Thomas talks of the 'oriental concept of the monastery as a veritable fortress of the soldiers of God', a theme that runs constantly through Aldhelm's works (Thomas 1971, 32). It seems possible, therefore, that as both Theodore and Hadrian were living in eastern monasteries in Rome before their secondment to Britain, the concept of rectilinear planning may well have established in Dorset through their influence on Aldhelm.

Various facets of the Dorset evidence suggest a suppression of the British church: the confiscation of land from British monasteries; the resiting of churches; and the domination of possible British sites by Saxon minsters. Sherborne may have been provided with the lands of a British monastery, *Lanprobi*, and it was certainly resited. All the churches with curvilinear enclosures possibly denoting British origins are minor churches or chapelries of the minsters. One much cited example of possible continuity from pre-Saxon times, the church in Knowlton Rings, was a chapel of Horton. Concrete examples of the discontinuity between the British and English church exist outside Dorset at such sites as Uley. Uley had been a religious hilltop site since at least the Iron Age, and the pagan/Roman area was taken over as a Christian site probably in the 5th century. The cessation of use of the site is put in the eighth century or beyond when a new church was sited at the foot of the hill (Woodward and Leach 1993, 327). Ine is reputed to have founded the churches of Glastonbury and Wells, both of which have

Rahtz notes that whilst the characteristic imported dark age Mediterranean wares have been found in association with the site on Glastonbury Tor which he interprets as a British monastery, none of the pottery has yet been found on the present abbey site: 'No finds or other datable material have been recovered which would show that the Abbey site way developed as a monastery before the seventh century' (Rahtz 1993, pp 54, 59, 99). The abbey site may therefore, have been newly laid out in a rectilinear form by Ine. Was this a part of the suppression of the British church and the foundation of a new Roman system linked with the establishment of a new ruling class? Further west in Somerset particularly along the coast and beyond the river Parrett, there may have been more integration of the two churches evinced by the possible survival of dedications to British saints and an increase in the circular or sub-circular form of churchyard possibly resulting from a more lenient attitude adopted on the demise of Aldhelm in 709, or the acceptance of the Roman ideal by the conquered British churches. It is proposed here that this study has revealed the first topographical signs of the suppression of the British church following the Synod of Whitby and the reinforcement of the subjection of the English church to Rome.

The identification of a distinctive pattern of town morphology brought about by the form of the early minsters in Dorset provides a model of town / village development against which future work in the county can be measured and which should be borne in mind when work is undertaken at any of these sites. In addition to elucidating the development of settlements within Dorset, an examination of the distribution of the rectilinear planning associated with the royal minsters of Dorset in neighbouring counties may well provide a vital clue in the determination of the progression of Saxon infiltration into the West Country.

---

[1]The only place with a suitable place-name but no high-status church is Frampton which is in an ideal position to have served the upper reaches of the Frome (see Fig 77).

[2]Corscombe is recorded as a gift of Cuthred (740x56) in Faustina A ii (O'Donovan 1988, xxviii,xli).

[3] Monasteries often appropriated most of the wealth from churches on their estates thus stopping them from becoming as wealthy as the minsters.

[4] In the prose version of *De Virginitate* and in his *Epistola ad Acircium* (Lapidge and Rosier 1985, 8).

APPENDICES

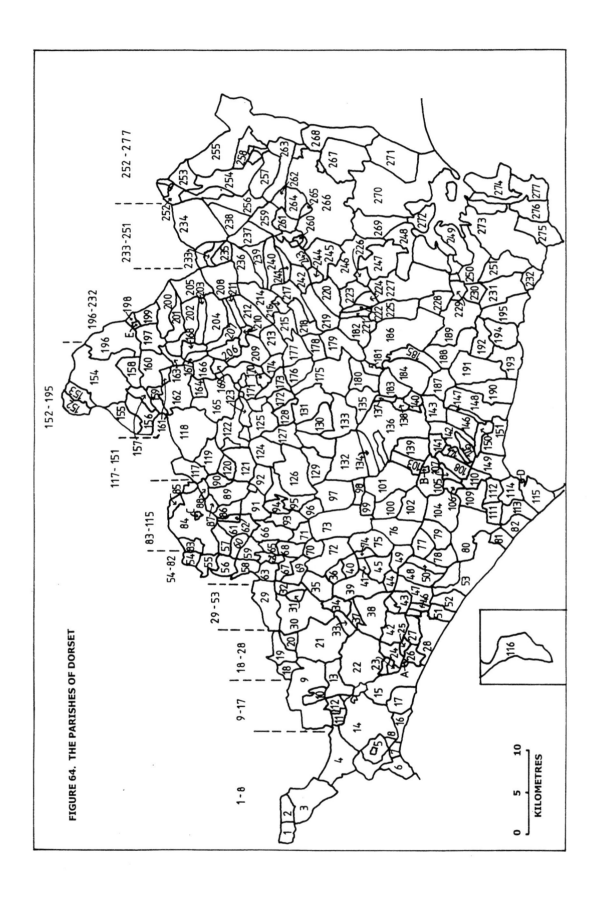

FIGURE 64. THE PARISHES OF DORSET

Parishes in numerical order

1 Crawley	63 Melbury Osmund	122 Lydlinch	181 Milborne Stileham
2 Wambrook	64 Stockwood	123 Fifehead Neville	182 Winterborne
3 Chardstock	65 Chetnole	124 Pulham	Kingston
4 Hawkchurch	66 Leigh	125 Hazelbury Bryan	183 Tolpuddle
5 Wootton Fitzpaine	67 Melbury Sampford	126 Buckland Newton	184 Affpuddle
6 Lyme Regis	68 Melbury Bubb	127 Mappowder	185 Turner's Puddle
7 Charmouth	69 Evershot	128 Stoke Wake	186 Bere Regis
8 Catherston Leweston	70 Frome St Quintin	129 Alton Pancras	187 Moreton
9 Broadwindsor	71 Batcombe	130 Melcombe Horsey	188 Wool
10 Burstock	72 Cattistock	131 Hilton	189 East Stoke
11 Bettiscombe	73 Sydling St Nicholas	132 Piddletrenthide	190 Chaldon Herring
12 Pilsdon	74 Frome Vauchurch	133 Cheselbourne	191 Winfrith Newburgh
13 Stoke Abbott	75 Maiden Newton	134 Piddlehinton	192 Coombe Keynes
14 Whitchurch	76 Frampton	135 Dewlish	193 West Lulworth
Canonicorum	77 Winterbourne Abbas	136 Puddletown	194 East Lulworth
15 Symondsbury	78 Little Bredy	137 Burleston	195 Tyneham
16 Stanton St Garbriel	79 Winterbourne	138 Athelhampton	196 Motcombe
17 Chideock	Steepleton	139 Stinsford	197 Shaftesbury St James
18 Mosterton	80 Portesham	140 Tincleton	198 Shaftesbury Holy
19 South Perrott	81 Langton Herring	141 West Stafford	Trinity
20 Cheddington	82 Fleet	142 West Knighton	199 Cann
21 Beaminster	83 Nether Compton	143 Woodsford	200 Melbury Abbas
22 Netherbury	84 Sherbonre	144 Whitcombe	201 Compton Abbas
23 Allington	85 Oborne	145 Broadmayne	202 Fontmell Magna
24 Bradpole	86 Longburton	146 Warmwell	203 Sutton Waldron
25 Walditch	87 North Wootton	147 Watercombe	204 Iwerne Minster
26 Bothenhampton	88 Haydon	148 Owermoigne	205 Ashmore
27 Shipton Gorge	89 Folke	149 Preston	206 Child Okeford
28 Burton Bradstock	90 Caundle Marsh	150 Poxwell	207 Iwerne Courtney
29 Halstock	91 Holnest	151 Osmington	208 Tarrant Gunville
30 Corscombe	92 Wootton Glanville	152 Bourton	209 Shillingstone
31 West Chelborough	93 Hilfield	153 Silton	210 Hanford
32 East Chelborough	94 Hermitage	154 Gillingham	211 Iwerne Steepleton
33 Mapperton	95 Minterne Magna	155 Buckhorn Weston	212 Stourpaine
34 Hooke	96 Up Cerne	156 Kington Magma	213 Durweston
35 Rampisham	97 Cerne Abbas	157 West Stour	214 Pimperne
36 Wraxall	98 Nether Cerne	158 East Stour	215 Bryanston
37 North Poorton	99 Godmanstone	159 Fifehead Magdalene	216 Blandford
38 Powerstock	100 Stratton	160 Stour Provost	217 Langton Long
39 Toller Porcorum	101 Charminster	161 Todber	Blandford
40 Chilfrome	102 Bradford Peverell	162 Marnhull	218 Blandford St Mary
41 Toller Fratrum	103 Frome Whitfield	163 Margaret Marsh	219 Charlton Marshall
42 Loders	104 Winterborne St	164 Hinton St Mary	220 Spetisbury
43 Askerswell	Martin	165 Sturminster Newton	221 Anderson
44 Compton Abbas	105 Fordington	166 Manston	222 Winterborne Tomson
45 Wynford Eagle	106 Winterborne	167 West Orchard	223 Almer
46 Chilcombe	Monkton	168 East Orchard	224 Winterborne Zelstone
47 Litton Cheney	107 Winterborne	169 Hammoon	225 Bloxworth
48 Long Bredy	Herringston	170 Belchalwell	226 Charborough
49 Compton Valance	108 Winterborne Came	171 Okeford Fitzpaine	227 Morden
50 Kingston Russell	109 Upway	172 Woolland	228 Wareham St Martin
51 Swyre	110 Bincombe	173 Ibberton	229 Wareham Lady St
52 Puncknowle	111 Buckland Ripers	174 Turnworth	Mary
53 Abbotsbury	112 Broadway	175 Milton Abbas	230 East Holme
54 Over Compton	113 Chickerell	176 Winterborne	231 Steeple
55 Bradford Abbas	114 Radipole	Houghton	232 Kimmeridge
56 Clifton Maybank	115 Wyke Regis	177 Winterborne	233 Farnham
57 Thornford	116 Portland	Stickland	234 Handley
58 Ryme Intrinseca	117 Purse Caundle	178 Winterborne	235 Chettle
59 Yetminster	118 Stalbridge	Clenston	236 Tarrant Hinton
60 Beer Hackett	119 Stourton Caundle	179 Winterborne	237 Long Crichel
61 Lillington	120 Bishop's Caundle	Whitechurch	238 Gussage St Michael
62 Leweston	121 Holwell	180 Milborne St Andrew	239 Tarrant Launceston

240 Tarrant Monkton
241 Tarrant Rawston
242 Tarrant Keyneston
243 Tarrant Rushton
244 Tarrant Crawford
245 Shapwick
246 Sturminster Marshall
247 Lytchett Matravers
248 Lytchett Minster
249 Arne
250 Wareham Holy
　　Trinity
251 Church Knowle

252 Woodyates East and
　　West
253 Pentridge
254 Wimborne St Giles
255 Cranborne
256 Gussage All Saints
257 Woodlands
258 Edmondsham
259 More Crichel
260 East Hemsworth
261 Witchampton
262 Chalbury
263 Horton

264 Hinton Martell
265 Hinton Parva
266 Wimborne Minster
267 Hampreston
268 West Parley
269 Corfe Mullen
270 Canford Magna
271 Kinson
272 Hamworthy
273 Corfe Castle
274 Studland
275 Worth Matravers
276 Langton Matravers

277 Swanage

A Bridport
B Dorchester
C Castleton
D Melcombe Regis
E Shaftesbury St Peter

Parishes in alphabetical order

APPENDIX II
Gazetteer of Minsters not included in text of Chapter 2

The minsters have been divided into the following categories:
M1 – Primary minster
M2 – High status church in ecclesiastical ownership
M3 – Alfredian minster

Beaminster – M1? and *Netherbury* – M2 (Fig 65)

Beaminster is mentioned in a list of benefactions to Gloucester Abbey, compiled 1382x1412.[1] Professor Finberg dated the list to the 9th century, and suggested that the 120 hide gift of land at Beaminster and Portland had formed part of the property of Osric's sister, Cyneburh, the first abbess of St Peter's, Gloucester at some time between 677 and 757 (Finberg 1964, 156 and 1972, 160-165). By 1001x1002 Beaminster belonged to the bishop of Sherborne when Bishop Wulfsige is recorded as having died in his manor of *Bega Monasterium* (O'Donovan 1988, lvii). Despite this strong literary indication of minster status, which is also implied in the place-name, the church next enters the records as a chapel of Netherbury, another of the bishop's holdings.[2] In one of the two fourteenth century lists of Sherborne's endowments, Faustina Aii, Netherbury is cited as the gift of Aethelwulf (839x858). Beaminster is not mentioned in either list but the hidage suggests that it was probably included in the grant of Netherbury, implying that it was considered as parcel of that manor from before the Conquest.[3] Netherbury itself displays some minster church characteristics, with Mapperton and Melplash recorded as chapels in addition to Beaminster (Hutchins 2, 115-6). Place-name evidence and the Gloucester Abbey list suggest that Beaminster was an early minster site even though later records show Netherbury to be the dominant church. It may be that the system was rearranged following the gift of land to the bishopric, possibly when the two manors were divided into prebends.[4]

Bridport – M3 (Fig 66)

Bridport is now accepted as the burghal hidage fort of Bredy (Keen 1984, 234). Its church, dedicated to St Mary, was held in 1086 by St Wandrille. Keen notes that there is no evidence for settlement at Bridport prior to the establishment of the burh, and the church has little in the way of a *parochia* (Keen 1984, 234). The burh straddles the edge of two fairly well-preserved *parochiae*, Whitchurch and Burton Bradstock, and it seems probable that its lands originally formed part of Burton Bradstock. The place-name, Bridport, means 'harbour or port belonging to Bredy'. Whilst Mills identifies this as Long Bredy, the logical choice would seem to be Burton Bradstock, the caput of the royal estate lying just to the east of Bridport, which takes its name from the river Bride on which it stands (Mills 1986, 43,48). Bridport church, was, therefore, probably contemporary with the creation of the burh.

Buckland Newton – M2 (Fig 67)

Buckland Newton together with Plush, was acquired by Glastonbury at some time after 941 when it had been granted by King Edmund to a religious woman, Elfleda.[5] The church was fairly wealthy with chapels at Plush and Duntish (Hutchins 3, 694, 710; IPM 1, 1904, 181). The ownership of these estates by Glastonbury probably created a situation where Buckland took on the characteristics of a minster through serving the subsidiary estates. It would be superfluous for Glastonbury to supply two clerics to serve two nearby units of land when the job could be accomplished by one. As noted above (p 25) the place-name Buckland is not suggestive of an early minster founded at the centre of a royal estate.

Burton Bradstock – M1 (Fig 66)

The wealthy church of Burton Bradstock belonged to St Wandrille's in 1086 (see above Table 9)(Hutchins 2, 280). The church of St Mary had at least five chapels: St Martin in Shipton Gorge, which paid 4s a year in acknowledgement of the right to bury in Burton; Sturthill had a chapel of St Luke, which paid 6s 8d to the mother-church for burial there; the chapel at Bonvil's Bredy, now Bredy Farm, which made a failed attempt at independence in about 1320; and two chapels existed in the vicinity of St Mary's church, St Laurence and St Catherine (*Dorset Records* H3, De Banco Rolls 1316-1321,no. 233.11, 616). On the tithe map, Burton had a detached area of land around St Lukes Farm (DRO, T/BBK). The manor of Burton Bradstock was, moreover, ancient royal demesne in 1086.

Canford Magna – M1 (Fig 68)

Canford was a wealthy church with a well-defined *parochia* (*Taxatio*, 178). In 1086, the manor was held by Edward of Salisbury, sheriff of Wiltshire. The church was subsequently given to Bradenstoke priory by Walter, son of Edward, the founder of the priory. There is a reference to a group of clergy holding the church in a late 12th-century charter (*Monasticon* 6, 338). Canford church had chapels at Poole, Kinson, and Longfleet. There is also evidence for an oratory in the manor of Canford, the chaplain being supported by land and rent in Canford to the value of 5 marks (*CPR* 2, 1893, 136).

Cerne Abbas – M2 (Fig 67)

There is little evidence for a minster at Cerne. Leland states that three monks were living in Cerne before the 10th-century foundation: *ante novam fundationem Cernelii tantum est trium monachorum coenobiolum, ubi nunc est parochialis ecclesia de Cernel* (Leland 1774, 67). William of Malmesbury attributes the original foundation to St Augustine, after whom the holy well at the edge of the monastic enclosure is named, but this is unlikely. Tradition also states that St Edwold, brother to St Edmund the Martyr, led a hermit's life beside a spring in the vicinity, his relics being translated to Cerne by Ailmer.[6] Cerne does not behave as a mother-church and the churches that pay pensions or portions to the abbey in 1291 are all properties of the abbey. If there was a minster at Cerne it must have ceased to function long before the abbey's foundation in the 10th century, though it is quite possible that the site had attracted hermits before then.

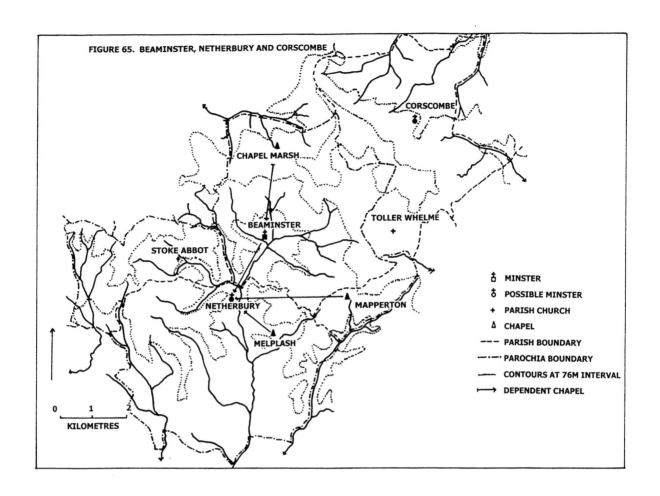

FIGURE 65. BEAMINSTER, NETHERBURY AND CORSCOMBE

CORSCOMBE

CHAPEL MARSH

BEAMINSTER

TOLLER WHELME

STOKE ABBOT

NETHERBURY

MAPPERTON

MELPLASH

⚰ MINSTER
♁ POSSIBLE MINSTER
+ PARISH CHURCH
△ CHAPEL
--- PARISH BOUNDARY
-·-·- PAROCHIA BOUNDARY
—— CONTOURS AT 76M INTERVAL
⟶ DEPENDENT CHAPEL

0   1   2
KILOMETRES

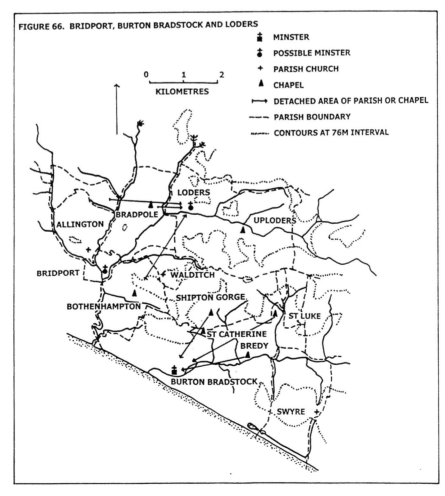

FIGURE 66. BRIDPORT, BURTON BRADSTOCK AND LODERS

⚰ MINSTER
♁ POSSIBLE MINSTER
+ PARISH CHURCH
▲ CHAPEL
⟼ DETACHED AREA OF PARISH OR CHAPEL
--- PARISH BOUNDARY
~~~ CONTOURS AT 76M INTERVAL

0   1   2
KILOMETRES

LODERS

BRADPOLE

UPLODERS

ALLINGTON

BRIDPORT

WALDITCH

BOTHENHAMPTON

SHIPTON GORGE

ST LUKE

ST CATHERINE

BREDY

BURTON BRADSTOCK

SWYRE

91

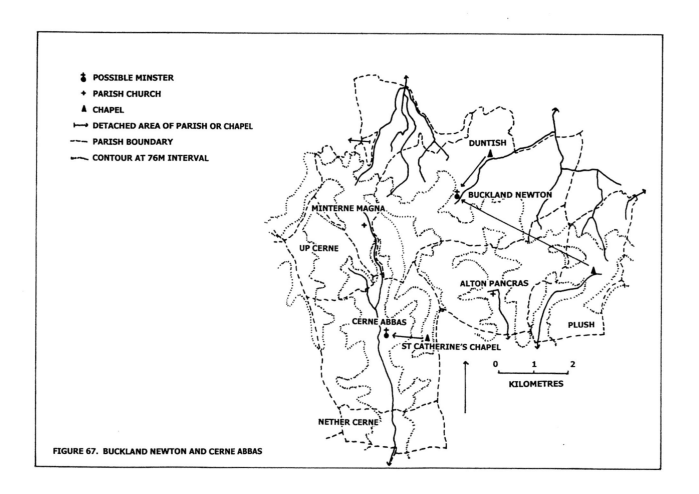

POSSIBLE MINSTER
PARISH CHURCH
CHAPEL
DETACHED AREA OF PARISH OR CHAPEL
PARISH BOUNDARY
CONTOUR AT 76M INTERVAL

DUNTISH

BUCKLAND NEWTON

MINTERNE MAGNA

UP CERNE

ALTON PANCRAS

PLUSH

CERNE ABBAS

ST CATHERINE'S CHAPEL

0 1 2
KILOMETRES

NETHER CERNE

FIGURE 67. BUCKLAND NEWTON AND CERNE ABBAS

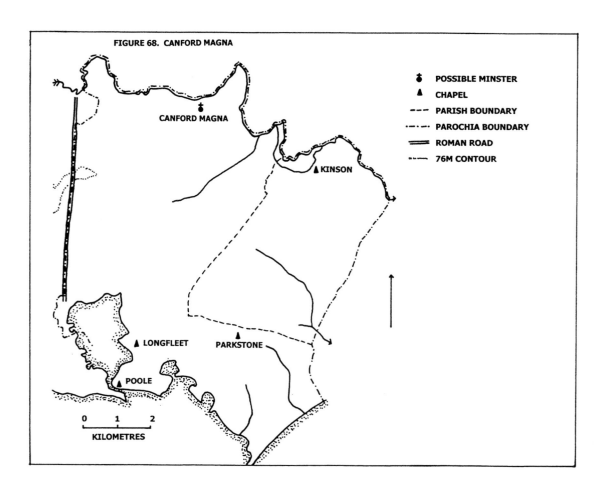

FIGURE 68. CANFORD MAGNA

POSSIBLE MINSTER
CHAPEL
PARISH BOUNDARY
PAROCHIA BOUNDARY
ROMAN ROAD
76M CONTOUR

CANFORD MAGNA

KINSON

LONGFLEET

PARKSTONE

POOLE

0 1 2
KILOMETRES

Chaldon Herring – M2 (Fig 69)

At Domesday, Chaldon church was held by Bolle the priest along with the churches of Puddletown and Fleet; all three were manors that had belonged to Earl Harold. A chapel existed at Grange Farm, but was part of the Cistercian Abbey of Bindon founded in 1172, before which the patronage of Chaldon Herring was in private hands (Hutchins 1, 343; Calthrop 1908, 82). West Chaldon, originally a separate parish, was united to Chaldon Herring in 1446 due to the reduction of that vill to a single farmstead (Hutchins 1, 344). The main characteristic suggesting high status in this case is the separate ownership of church and manor in 1086. Whilst Chaldon had been in Harold's hands, it was not as important a manor as Puddletown and the payment of a pension by Chaldon to Preston suggests that it was a manorial church rather than a minster (*RJC*, 11). The parish lies adjacent to Winfrith Newburgh and may well have been donated from that royal manor to become part of the earldom of Wessex.

Charminster – M1 (Fig 70)

Charminster was undoubtedly a minster church, though not recorded as such. After the endowment of the bishopric of Salisbury it formed a prebend of the cathedral jointly with Bere Regis church (see p 15).[7] Charminster had three chapels, Pulson, Stratton and Forston, and Frome Whitfield may have been a fourth as it was supplied with chrism from Charminster (*RJC*, 10; Hutchins 2, 417; Osmund, 255). In addition there was an oratory at Wolveton (Hutchins 2, 547). Other indications of minster status are the church plan, which appears to have been cruciform, and the place-name

suggests that it was a primary settlement, probably donated to the bishopric from royal demesne (RCHM Dorset 3, 60).

Corfe – M2 (Fig 71)

Corfe church was a possession of Shaftesbury Abbey and was probably acquired with the manor as the gift of King Edred in 948.[8] It was presumably in royal ownership before that date as the murder of Edward the Martyr at Corfe passage indicates a royal residence, possibly on the site of the present castle (ASC, 123; RCHM Dorset 2, 57). The church of St Edward had a chapel at Kingston. In addition, a 'free' chapel existed at Afflington and the king had a chapel in Corfe Castle, both of which appear to have been oratories. The chapel at Kingston was initially proposed as the site of a minster by Keen but Hinton has recently rejected it in favour of Corfe, which has several minster characteristics (Keen 1984, 213; Hinton 1994, 11). The parish of Corfe is large, stretching from the south coast across Purbeck to the shores of Poole harbour thereby severing the remaining parishes of Studland, Swanage, Worth Matravers and Langton Matravers, presenting the possibility that they may have initially depended on Corfe.

Corscombe – M2 (Fig 65)

Corscombe belonged to Sherborne Abbey and is recorded as the gift of Cuthred (740-56) though only 11th-century charters survive (O'Donovan 1988, xli, 51-58). Whilst Corscombe parish is fairly large, the church did not have dependent chapelries and its place-name indicates that it was not a primary settlement. The church was probably founded after the donation of the estate to the bishop.

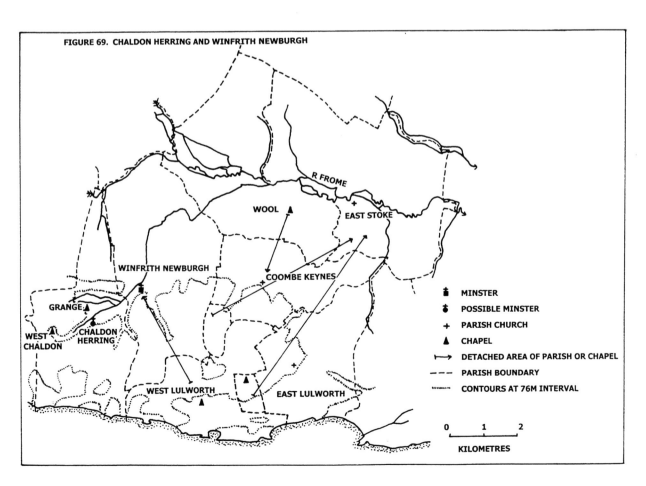

FIGURE 69. CHALDON HERRING AND WINFRITH NEWBURGH

R FROME

WOOL

EAST STOKE

WINFRITH NEWBURGH

COOMBE KEYNES

GRANGE

WEST CHALDON

CHALDON HERRING

WEST LULWORTH

EAST LULWORTH

MINSTER

POSSIBLE MINSTER

PARISH CHURCH

CHAPEL

DETACHED AREA OF PARISH OR CHAPEL

PARISH BOUNDARY

CONTOURS AT 76M INTERVAL

0   1   2

KILOMETRES

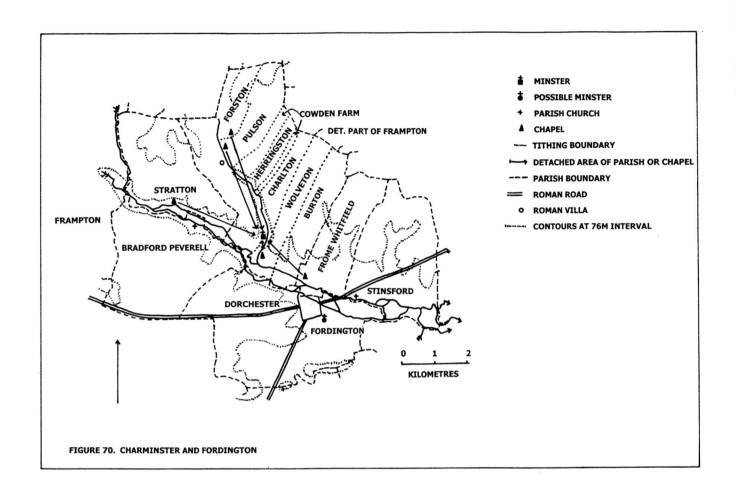

FIGURE 70. CHARMINSTER AND FORDINGTON

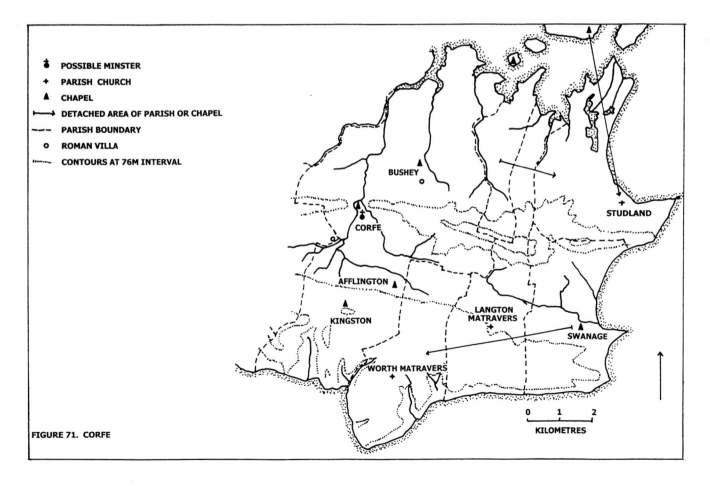

FIGURE 71. CORFE

Cranborne – M1 (Fig 72)

Despite the complications of the history of the church of St Mary's at Cranborne brought about by the foundation of a monastery there *c*980, the church has sufficient characteristics to point to it having been a primary minster. A record of the foundation of Cranborne preserved in the Chronicle of Tewkesbury, states that it was founded by Aylward Sneaw (supposed grandfather of the pre-Conquest holder Beortric), on his Cranborne demesne. Dugdale noted that there was a belief that the church may have succeeded a group of secular canons but that he found no evidence for it (*Monasticon* 4, 465-8). By Domesday Cranborne was one of the least well-endowed of the Dorset abbeys with only 21 hides in the county and a further 21 hides in Wiltshire. The church of Cranborne, however, had a high value with chapels at Upwimborne, Alderholt, and Boveridge, and a further two, one in the earl's court and one in the cemetery (Hutchins 3, 394).[9] In 1291 five churches paid pensions to Cranborne, Sturminster Newton, Dewlish, Edmondsham, Tarrant Gunville and Wimborne All Saints, most of which probably resulted from donations by Fitz Hamon and his knights when Cranborne became a cell of Tewkesbury (*Taxatio*, 178,179; Hutchins 3, 382). Wimborne Abbas, however, belonged to Cranborne before the Conquest and was served by the vicar: it was probably part of the original *parochia*. Edmondsham may have been another dependency though one of its two churches was a chapel of Witchampton and served from there. A carved cross fragment, thought to be 9th century, was found in a pond 150 yds north-east of the Cranborne church (RCHM Dorset 5, 5). It has been suggested that the stone, which may have come from an early religious building, predates the foundation of the later abbey (RCHM Dorset 5, xxxvii). Pottery associated with a large pit in Penny's Mead 500m east of church suggests middle-Saxon settlement in the vicinity.[10] In addition to the physical and economic evidence, the place-name, being a river-name, indicates that this was a primary settlement.

Fordington – M1/M3? (Fig 70)

Fordington has been proposed as a minster church by Keen (Keen 1984, 233). Factors in its favour are its ecclesiastical ownership; its position on a royal estate; the size and wealth of the church; and a possible chapel of *La Maudelyne* (though this may have been inside the church). The real problem with Fordington as a minster is that it has no discernible *parochia* and, in addition, its place-name is not primary. The church may have assumed more importance with the establishment of Dorchester as a burh though the rectilinear layout around the church might also suggest that it was a primary minster.

Litton Cheney – M1? (Fig 73)

The church of Litton Cheney had chapels at Ashley and North Eggardon, both of which were set in detached areas of parish (DRO, T/LIC; Hutchins 2, 751, 754). A third chapel, valued at £10 in 1316, apparently an oratory, existed in the hamlet of Coombe.[11] It has not been possible to identify Litton Cheney at DB, but Thorn suggests that it may either lie in the group of king's manors including Burton Bradstock and Shipton, or have been the unidentified land of Hugh Boscherbert (*DB*, notes 1,2 and 53m2). Litton Cheney may represent an example of a minster church at the centre of a depleted royal estate. However, its place-name suggests a later formation than the minsters of the main royal estates (p 26), and it might just be an early estate church gaining minster characteristics through manorial ownership.

Loders – M2? (Fig 66)

A cell of Monteburgh was founded at Loders following the gift of the church and manor to that abbey by Richard de Redvers who had acquired it from Henry I (*CDF* 1, 313, 314; *Monasticon* 6, 1097). A chapel at Bradpole, gift of William de Morville, appears to have been attached to Loders after its donation to Monteburgh whereas the chapel of Bothenhampton was part of the original gift of Loders and may have depended on Loders before the transfer (Guilloreau 1908, 23, 27). Another chapel existed at Dottery, a small hamlet at the southern extremity of Netherbury parish. Hutchins notes that there was a chapel in Uploders, possibly dedicated to St Peter (Hutchins 2, 310). It cannot be certain if Loders was an early minster or if the characteristics were assumed after its donation to Monteburgh.

Milton Abbas – M2 (Fig 74)

Milton Abbas was the head manor of the monastery of Milton founded by Athelstan in 933/4 as a community of clerks, replaced by monks in 964 by Edgar. The main endowment of the abbey was 26 hides of land at Milborne, 24 hides of which the Abbey still held in 1086 (Traskey 1978, 7). *Mideltune* is not a topographical name, suggesting that the Abbey did not replace an earlier minster on the same site. To its south, however, lies Milborne St Andrew named from the river which gave its name to the land unit from which Milton was endowed. The church at Milborne St Andrew enters the records in the hands of Bishop Roger of Salisbury as a donation to the College de Vaux (Hutchins 2, 602). The settlement of Milborne St Andrew was otherwise known as Milborne Churcheston and the church of Dewlish is often cited as a dependent chapel (*Dorset Records* 5, 102; Hutchins 2, 592, 602). It seems unlikely that Milton was a minster before its foundation by Athelstan, but it may have replaced a defunct minster at Milborne St Andrew. Payments to the Abbey in 1291 reflect the possessions of the abbey rather than an earlier *parochia*.

Powerstock – M1? (Fig 73)

Powerstock church had five chapels: West Milton, Wytherstone, Hooke, Stapelford, and North Poorton (*RSG*, 236; Hutchins 2, 170, 183). Whilst at Domesday it was in lay hands it is recorded among the possessions of Sherborne in Faustina A ii as a gift of Egbert (O'Donovan 1988, xlii). In 1157 Roger of Arundel granted the church to the Abbey of Monteburgh in Normandy, his decision probably influenced by the presence of the neighbouring priory at Loders (*Sarum*, 26). In 1213 it was given by Monteburgh Abbey to the church of Sarum. A reference of 1157 in the bishop's registers refers to more than one

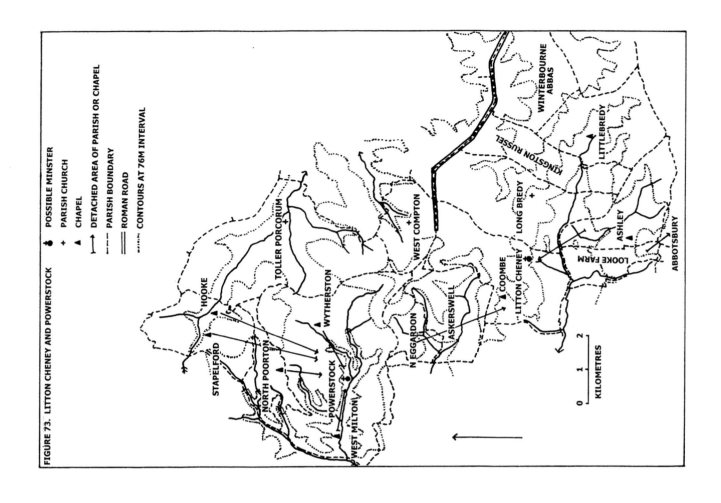

FIGURE 73. LITTON CHENEY AND POWERSTOCK

POSSIBLE MINSTER
PARISH CHURCH
CHAPEL
DETACHED AREA OF PARISH OR CHAPEL
PARISH BOUNDARY
ROMAN ROAD
CONTOURS AT 76M INTERVAL

STAPELFORD
HOOKE
TOLLER PORCORUM
NORTH POORTON
WEST MILTON
POWERSTOCK
WYTHERSTON
N EGGARDON
ASKERSWELL
WEST COMPTON
COOMBE
LITTON CHENEY
LONG BREDY
KINGSTON RUSSEL
WINTERBOURNE ABBAS
LITTLEBREDY
ASHLEY
LOOKE FARM
ABBOTSBURY

0   1   2
KILOMETRES

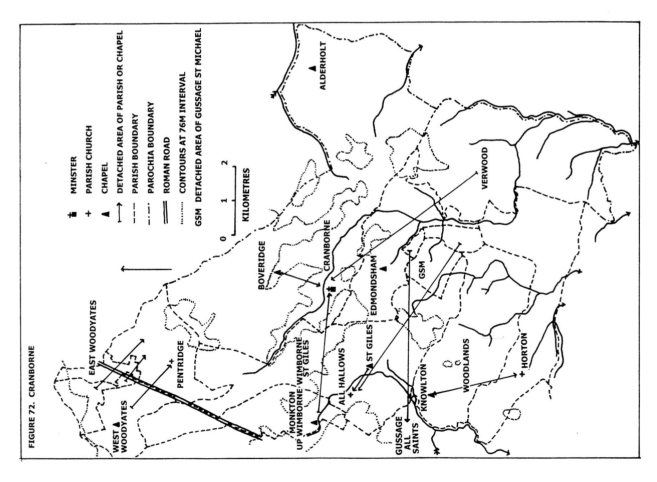

FIGURE 72. CRANBORNE

MINSTER
PARISH CHURCH
CHAPEL
DETACHED AREA OF PARISH OR CHAPEL
PARISH BOUNDARY
PAROCHIA BOUNDARY
ROMAN ROAD
CONTOURS AT 76M INTERVAL
GSM   DETACHED AREA OF GUSSAGE ST MICHAEL

0   1   2
KILOMETRES

WEST WOODYATES
EAST WOODYATES
PENTRIDGE
MONKTON UP WIMBORNE
WIMBORNE ST GILES
ALL HALLOWS
ST GILES
GUSSAGE ALL SAINTS
KNOWLTON
WOODLANDS
HORTON
BOVERIDGE
CRANBORNE
EDMONDSHAM
GSM
VERWOOD
ALDERHOLT

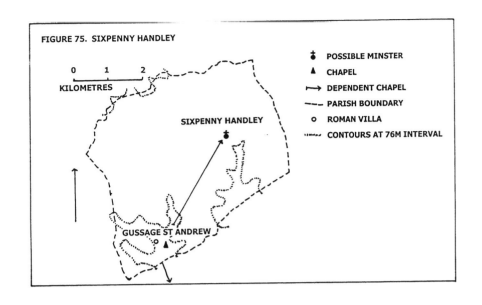

FIGURE 75. SIXPENNY HANDLEY

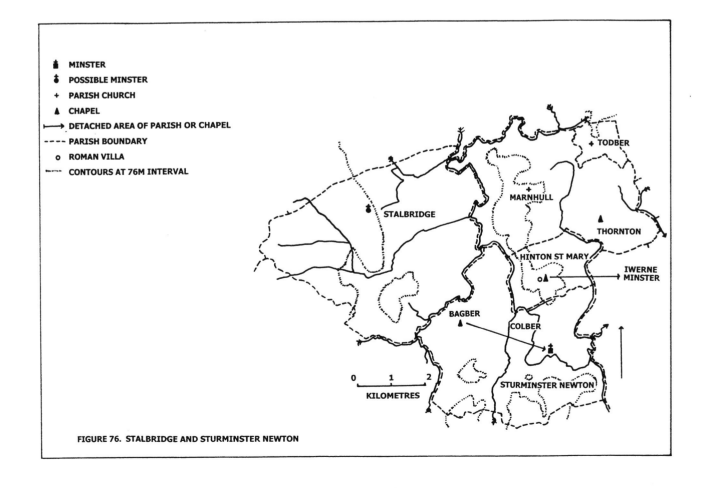

FIGURE 76. STALBRIDGE AND STURMINSTER NEWTON

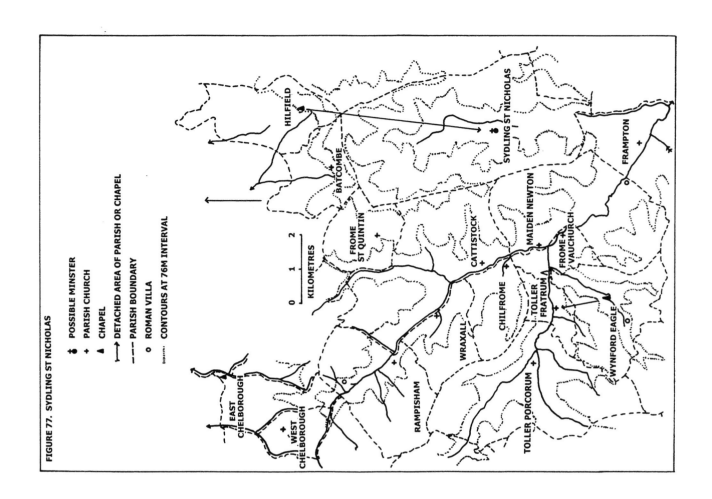

FIGURE 77. SYDLING ST NICHOLAS

✚ POSSIBLE MINSTER

+ PARISH CHURCH

▲ CHAPEL

⟶ DETACHED AREA OF PARISH OR CHAPEL

--- PARISH BOUNDARY

o ROMAN VILLA

······· CONTOURS AT 76M INTERVAL

KILOMETRES
0 1 2

HILFIELD

BATCOMBE

FROME
ST QUINTIN

CATTISTOCK

WRAXALL

CHILFROME

SYDLING ST NICHOLAS

MAIDEN NEWTON

TOLLER
FRATRUM

FROME
VAUCHURCH

FRAMPTON

WYNFORD EAGLE

TOLLER PORCORUM

RAMPISHAM

EAST
CHELBOROUGH

WEST
CHELBOROUGH

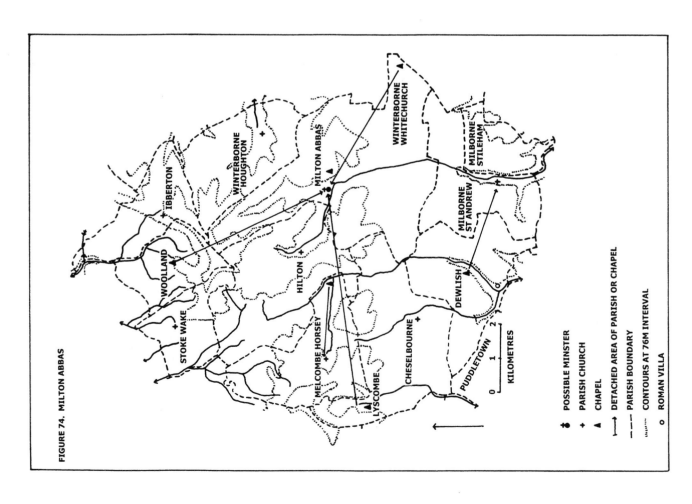

FIGURE 74. MILTON ABBAS

IBBERTON

WINTERBORNE
HOUGHTON

WOOLLAND

STOKE WAKE

HILTON

MILTON ABBAS

WINTERBORNE
WHITECHURCH

MILBORNE
STILEHAM

MILBORNE
ST ANDREW

DEWLISH

MELCOMBE
HORSEY

LYSCOMBE

CHESELBOURNE

PUDDLETOWN

KILOMETRES
0 1 2

✚ POSSIBLE MINSTER

+ PARISH CHURCH

▲ CHAPEL

⟶ DETACHED AREA OF PARISH OR CHAPEL

--- PARISH BOUNDARY

······· CONTOURS AT 76M INTERVAL

o ROMAN VILLA

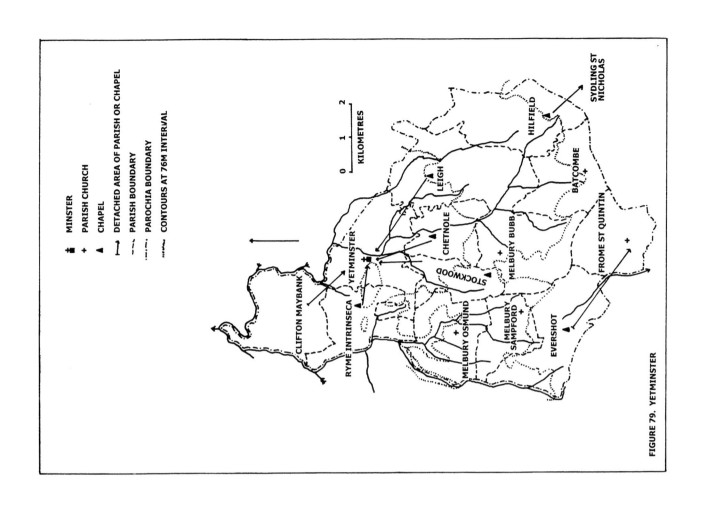

Legend (Figure 79)

- ⊞ MINSTER
- + PARISH CHURCH
- ▲ CHAPEL
- ↑ DETACHED AREA OF PARISH OR CHAPEL
- – – PARISH BOUNDARY
- –··– PAROCHIA BOUNDARY
- ······ CONTOURS AT 76M INTERVAL

KILOMETRES
0   1   2

Labels on map: CLIFTON MAYBANK, RYME INTRINSECA, YETMINSTER, CHETNOLE, LEIGH, HILFIELD, STOCKWOOD, MELBURY BUBB, BATCOMBE, MELBURY OSMUND, MELBURY SAMPFORD, EVERSHOT, FROME ST QUINTIN, SYDLING ST NICHOLAS

FIGURE 79. YETMINSTER

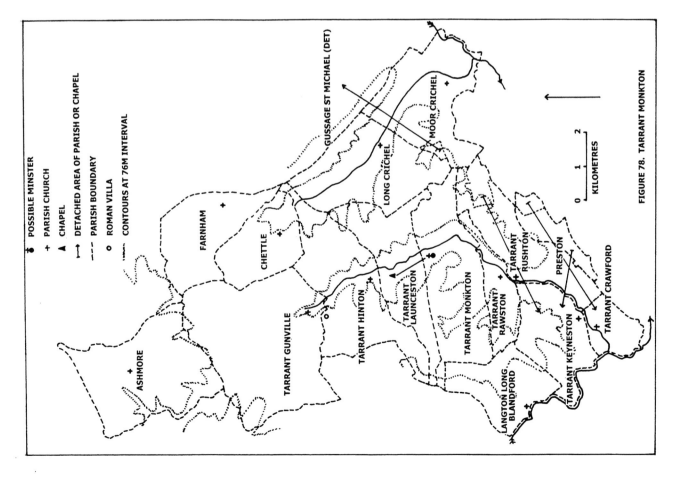

Legend (Figure 78)

- ⊞ POSSIBLE MINSTER
- + PARISH CHURCH
- ▲ CHAPEL
- ↑ DETACHED AREA OF PARISH OR CHAPEL
- – – PARISH BOUNDARY
- ○ ROMAN VILLA
- ······ CONTOURS AT 76M INTERVAL

KILOMETRES
0   1   2

Labels on map: ASHMORE, FARNHAM, CHETTLE, TARRANT GUNVILLE, GUSSAGE ST MICHAEL (DET), LONG CRICHEL, MOOR CRICHEL, TARRANT HINTON, TARRANT LAUNCESTON, TARRANT MONKTON, TARRANT RAWSTON, TARRANT RUSHTON, PRESTON, TARRANT KEYNESTON, TARRANT CRAWFORD, LANGTON LONG BLANDFORD

FIGURE 78. TARRANT MONKTON

clergyman at Powerstock; *Almerus sacerdos ....cum suis doubus clericis, Herveo et Huluricico* (*Sarum*, 27). This may indicate that there was a community of clerks present here as has been suggested for Canford Magna.

Shaftesbury M3 (Fig 10)

The status of the church at Shaftesbury is entirely obscured by the existence of the abbey. Most of the churches in the town were under the patronage of the Abbess though whether through the conventual church having been a minster or by gift is uncertain (the church of St James was a gift, granted to the abbess by Robert Bingham, bishop of Salisbury) (Hutchins 3, 57). Ownership of houses within the burh is divided between the king and the abbess in 1086 and the fact that Cnut died in Shaftesbury suggests that the king had a royal residence within the burh. Shaftesbury's marginal position between two *parochiae* and its status as a burh suggest that its church was an Alfredian foundation.

Sixpenny Handley - M2 (Fig 75)

Before being annexed to Iwerne Minster in 1327 Handley church had been a separate parish, one of the prebends of Shaftesbury Abbey. The Abbey registers record half a hide of land attached to the church and there was a chapel at Gussage St Andrew (Hutchins 3, 541, 544). Whilst the church controlled a large parish, most of it was part of Shaftesbury Abbey estates.

Stalbridge M2 (Fig 76)

From at least the 10th century, Stalbridge belonged to the monastery of Sherborne. The two fourteenth century lists of donors cite Aethelbert (860-866) as benefactor but no charter survives to confirm this (O'Donovan 1988, xlii). Stalbridge church was at the centre of a large monastic estate and it did not develop chapelries. The abbot of Sherborne had a park at Stalbridge and the church's income was appropriated to the monastery. This is probably another example of a monastic estate church taking on minster characteristics.

Sturminster Newton - M1?(Fig 76)

Sturminster Newton had been granted to Glastonbury Abbey in 968 by King Edgar, barring a small area of land called Colber, which was still part of the royal demesne in 1086 and may have been the caput of the former royal estate.[12] Colber lay in a bend of the river Stour opposite the site of the town of Sturminster. The church of Sturminster had a chapel at Bagber in 1340 (*Nonarum*, 59). There is no evidence for the minster suffix of the place-name earlier that the Conquest but its site, royal associations and place-name all indicate that it was probably the site of a minster church.

Sydling St Nicholas - M2 (Fig 77)

Sydling St Nicholas was one of the chief manors of Milton Abbey. The 1311 confirmation of the possessions of Milton Abbey included Hilfield, La Halvehide and the church of Sydling and chapels of Hilfield and Upsydling in the manor of Sydling (*CPR* 1, 389-90). The ruinous chapel of Upsydling was situated near the mansion house of the Hardy's (Hutchins 4, 503). The minster characteristics possessed by Sydling, namely its high value and its chapels, could all be accounted for by its monastic ownership. Nearly all the churches of Milton were appropriated to the abbey and appear to have been served from there.

Tarrant Monkton - M2 (Fig 78)

Tarrant Monkton manor and church belonged to the abbey of Cranborne. The manor of Tarrant was probably originally parcel of Aylward Sneaw's lands, the founder of the Abbey. The manor of Tarrrant Launceston, a chapel, was still in the hands of his grandson Beortric, prior to the Conquest (*DB*, 21,1). Tarrant Monkton church was wealthy in 1291(£20) but there is not enough evidence to suggest that it was definitely a minster, though there may well have been one in the Tarrant valley.

Winfrith Newburgh - M1? (Fig 69)

The church of St Peter (now St Christopher) at Winfrith was identified as a possible minster by Blair on Domesday evidence, but Hinton felt that it might have been created shortly before the Conquest when the royal demesne was rearranged (Blair 1985, 108; Hinton 1987, 52). The manor was held by King Edward and remained in royal hands until it was given to Robert Newburgh by Henry I (Hutchins 1, 436). The church was valuable but paid a pension to the priory of Wareham, leading Hinton to suggest that it may once have been dependent on Lady St Mary. The pension may alternatively have been the result of a gift of tithes to the abbey of Lyre which held the church of Lady St Mary.[13] The parish of Winfrith is large with a chapel at West Lulworth and gives its name to the hundred.

Yetminster - M1(Fig 79)

Yetminster, a possession of the bishop of Sherborne, does not occur in records before DB. The place-name combines the personal name *Eata*, possibly the founder, with the *minster* suffix (Fagersten 1978, 227-8). Yetminster church had four chapels; Chetnole, Leigh, Ryme Intrinseca, and Clifton Maybank (*Osmund*, 198-200; *Taxatio*, 182; *Nonarum*, 51). The inhabitants of Chetnole and Clifton Maybank buried their dead at Yetminster whilst those of Ryme had gained the right to bury and baptize by 1631 but the dues were still to go to the mother-church (Hutchins 4, 431, 450, 494). Stockwood was grouped with Yetminster's chapels in Dean Chandler's register suggesting that it may have originally belonged in this *parochia*, though by 1331 it was a member of the liberty of Sutton Poyntz (Hutchins 4, 442). The church at Yetminster can be included in the definite minsters and at least part of its *parochia* reconstructed.

[1] S. 1782.

[2] By 1291 Beaminster is part of a prebend in which Netherbury is the dominant place: *Taxatio*, 181; Hutchins 2, 134.

[3] O'Donovan 1988, xlii: O'Donovan notes that in Faustina A.ii, '36 hides' is written by Netherbury and a place called *Ethelbaldingham* (possibly Beaminster), but that it is unclear if the hidage refers to Netherbury or to the estates of Chard, Halstock and Yetminster. As the hidage of Beaminster and Netherbury totals 36 in DB, whereas the hidage of Chard 8, Yetminster 15 and Halstock (which is not mentioned may be included in Corscombe's 10 hides), falls short of the 36 required Netherbury seems more likely.

[4] Netherbury comprised three prebends and Beaminster two: Hutchins 2, 105,140.

[5] S. 474, seen as authentic.

[6] A possible site for his hermitage was at St Edwold's church in Stockwood to the north of Cerne.

[7] Because of the connection between the two churches, Pitfield suggested that Charminster was the church named as Dorchester held by Brictward with Bere Regis in *DB*.: Pitfield 1981, 6-8. This seems unlikely as the manor of Charminster was held by the Bishop of Sherborne at DB, and only those churches which were held separately from manors are recorded in Dorset Domesday. The Dorchester church mentioned was, therefore, much more likely to have been Fordington.

[8] S.534; DCM, E A Fry, *Dorset Records F1, Coram Rege Rolls 1273-1294*, no.56.8, 63-65,

[9] Alderholt chapel was demolished in 1690 but had been sited in Chappel Hays, called Blounts in Hutchins time. St Aldhelm's church at Boveridge was mentioned in 1595: *DPN* 2, 213.

[10] Dorset County SMR, Cranborne, site no.56.

[11] DCM, E A Fry, *De Banco Rolls* Vol. H3, 449.

[12] S.764; seen as authentic.

[13] Wareham received a portion from Shapwick church which represented tithes given by Robert Earl of Leicester (see above p11).

APPENDIX III : Markets in the county of Dorset

Minsters are categorized as: M1 – Primary minster; M2 – High status ecclesiastical church; M3 – Alfredian creation

TOWN	MINSTER	BURH	MARKET	BOROUGH
Bridport	M3	In burghal hidage		
Shaftesbury	M3	In burghal hidage		
Wareham	M1 & M3	In burghal hidage		
Dorchester	-	Burh at DB		
?Wimborne Minster	M1	?bugages at DB	1218	1326
Sturminster Marshall	M1	-	1137	-
Sherborne	M1	-	1146	1227/8
Cerne Abbas	-	-	1154x89	-
Bere Regis	M1	-	1215,1229, 1267	1284
Blandford Forum	-	-	1217/18	1244
Melcombe Regis	-	-	1217, 1280	1268
Handley	M2	-	1218	-
Sturminster Newton	?M1	-	1218/19	-
Maiden Newton	-	-	1221,1242	-
Tarrant Gunville	-	-	1233	-
Fleet	-	-	1244	-
Corfe Castle	?M2	-	1248	1268
Poole	-	-	-	c1284
Weymouth	-	-	1248	1252
Winterborne Whitechurch	-	-	1248	-
Wyke Regis	-	-	1248	-
Lyme Regis	-	-	1249/50	-
Milton Abbas	?	-	1252	-
Buckland Newton	M3	-	1258	-
Iwerne Courtney	-	-	1261	-
Dewlish	-	-	1264	-
Whitchurch Canonicorum	M1	-	-	1265
Shapwick	-	-	1267	1289
Winterborne St Martin	-	-	1267	-
Puddletown	M1	-	1270	-
Hilton	-	-	1272	-
Hinton Martell	-	-	1272	-
Abbotsbury	?M1/2	-	1274/5	-
Beaminster	M1	-	1274/5, 1285	-
Charmouth	-	-	1278	1320
Wool	-	-	1280	-
Okeford Fitzpaine	-	-	1282	-
Kingston Russel	-	-	1284	-
Newton (Purbeck)	-	-	1286	1286
Kington Magna	-	-	1286	-
Stalbridge	M2	-	1286	-
Evershot	-	-	1286	-
Ryme Intrinseca	-	-	1298	-
Yetminster	M1	-	1300	-
Puddletown	M1	-	1301	-
Litton Cheney	?M1	-	1304	-
East Hemsworth	-	-	1304	-
Cranborne	M1	-	-	1314
Child Okeford	-	-	1327	-
Buckhorn Weston	-	-	1333	-
Witchampton	-	-	1347	-
Frampton	-	-	1351	-
Fordington	?M1/3	-	1355	-
Castleton	-	-	-	1538

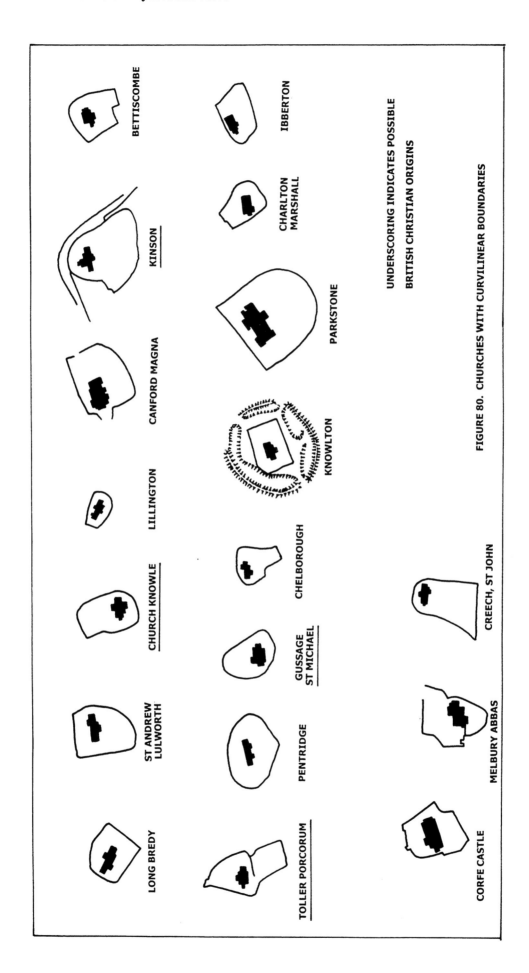

BETTISCOMBE

IBBERTON

KINSON

CHARLTON MARSHALL

PARKSTONE

CANFORD MAGNA

KNOWLTON

LILLINGTON

CHELBOROUGH

CHURCH KNOWLE

GUSSAGE ST MICHAEL

CREECH, ST JOHN

ST ANDREW LULWORTH

PENTRIDGE

MELBURY ABBAS

LONG BREDY

TOLLER PORCORUM

CORFE CASTLE

UNDERSCORING INDICATES POSSIBLE BRITISH CHRISTIAN ORIGINS

FIGURE 80. CHURCHES WITH CURVILINEAR BOUNDARIES

Plate 1. The twin towers of Wimborne Minster seen above the town which lies just off the floodplain at the confluence of the rivers Allen and Stour

Plate 2. Winterborne Tomson church – one of the chapels of the minster at Bere Regis

Plate 3.

The crossing of Wimborne Minster showing the narrower opening of the south transept

Plate 4. The possible Saxon flooring under the nave of Wimborne Minster

Plate 5. The shrine of St Wite ,Whitchurch Canonicorum, in the north transept of the church

Plate 6. Lady St Mary church, Wareham, situated within the Saxon burh, just above the River Frome

Plate 7.
Wareham St Martin perched
above the gate in the north wall

Plate 8. The proprietary church of Wootton Fitzpaine with the manor house behind on the right

Plate 9. The curving boundary of Canford Magna which possibly results from landscaping within Canford Park

Plate 10. Gussage St Michael churchyard – a candidate for a British Christian enclosure?

BIBLIOGRAPHY

Manuscript Sources

Dorset County Museum, Dorchester:
  C D Drew Index - card index of medieval references to Dorset places arranged by parish, currently in the Turret Room.
  E A Fry's transcipts of 'Dorset Records', in the library.

Dorset Record Office, maps:
  Abbotsbury: Inclosure 68; T/ABB
  Beaminster, T/BE
  Bere Regis: Photocopies 2/17, 2/23; D1/KL8; T/BER
  Bettiscombe, T/BET
  Bishop's Caundle, T/BCD
  Bradford Abbas, T/BRA
  Bridport, DC/BTB:R2, T/BT
  Buckland Newton, T/BCN
  Burton Bradstock, T/BBK
  Canford Magna, T/CAM
  Caundle Marsh, T/CDM
  Cerne Abbas, D/PIT:P6; T/CEA
  Chaldon Herring, T/CHH
  Charminster, Photocopy 1/9; T/CMR
  Corfe Castle, T/COC
  Corscombe, T/COR
  Cranborne: Photocopies 311-12; 17c map of manor from terrier of Cranborne; T/CRA
  Folke: T/FOL
  Fordington: Photocopy 402;T/FOR
  Gillingham: T/GIL
  Holnest: T/HON
  Iwerne Minster: PE/IWM/M12,3; T/IWM
  Litton Cheney: Inclosure 12; T/LIC
  Loders: T/LOD
  Milborne St Andrew: T/MIA
  Milton Abbas: D311/1:D1/NL1A; D919/5; Photocopy 67.
  Netherbury: T/NBY
  Portesham: T/POR
  Powerstock: T/POW
  Preston: D/WLC:P22; T/PRE
  Puddletown: T/PUD
  Shaftesbury: T/SY (SJ)
  Sherborne: T/SH; 1850 Almshouse Property
  Sixpenny Handley: T/SIX
  Stalbridge: T/STG
  Sturminster Marshall: T/SML
  Sturminster Newton: T/SN
  Sydling St Nicholas: Photocopy 370; T/SSN
  Tarrant Monkton: T/TTM
  Wareham: D/RWR/EI8; D1/10,367; T/WA (HT); T/WA (SM); T/WA (BV)
  Whitchurch Canonicorum: D/SBS 10-11; T/WCC
  Wimborne Minster: T/WM
  Winfrith Newburgh: D/WLC/E19; T/WFN
  Witchampton: Photocopy 346; Photocopy 1/37; T/WIT
  Wootton Fitzpaine: T/WFP
  Yetminster:T/YET

Printed Sources

Aldhelm: The Prose, M Lapidge and M Herren (1979).

Aldhelm: The Poetic Works, M Lapidge and J L Rosier (1985).

Alfred the Great: Asser's Life of King Alfred and Other Contemporary Sources, S Keynes and M Lapidge (1983).

The Anglo-Saxon Chronicle, M J Swanton, trans. and ed., (1996).

Bede: A History of the English Church and People, L Sherley-Price, trans and ed., (2nd end, 1968).

Calendar of Documents Preserved in France Illustrative of the History of Great Britain and Ireland, J H Round, ed., (1899).

Calendar of Inquisitions Post Mortem and Other Analogous Documents Preserved in the Public Record Office

Calendar of the Liberate Rolls Preserved in the Public Record Office Henry III AD1245-1251

Calendar of Papal Letters 1-14,HMSO (1894-61)

Calender of Patent Rolls preserved in the Public Record Office, HMSO (1901- in progress).

Cartulaire de Loders (Dorset) Prieuré dépendant de l'abbaye de Montebourg, L Guilloreau, ed., (1908).

Charters and Documents Illustrating the History of the Cathedral City and Diocese of Salisbury in the Twelfth and Thirteenth Centuries, W R Jones and W D Macray, eds, (1891).

Councils and Synods, with other Documents relating to the English Church I: AD 871-1204, D Whitelock, M Brett, and C N L Brooke, eds, (1981).

A Descriptive Catalogue of Ancient Deeds in the Public Record Office 1-6, HMSO (1890-1915)

Domesday Book: Dorset, F Thorn and C Thorn, eds (1983).

Dorset Records: Full Abstracts of the Feet of Fines Relating to the County of Dorset, remaining in the Public Record Office, London, from their commencement in the reign of Richard I, E A Fry and G S Fry, eds, (1896).

The Early History of Glastonbury: an Edition, Translation and Study of William of Malmesbury's De Antiquitate Glastonie Ecclesiei, J Scott, trans and ed., (1981).

English Historical Documents 1: 500-1042, D Whitelock, ed., (1955).

J Leland, *De Rebus Britannicus Collectanea* 4, (1774).

Monasticon Anglicanum: A New Edition, J Caley, H Ellis, and B Bandinel, eds, (1817-30).

Nonarum Inquisitiones in Curia Scaccarii. Temp. Regis Edwardi III, G Vanderzee, ed., Record Commission (1807).

The Register of John Chandler 1404-17, T C B Timmins, ed., (1984).

Registrum Simonis de Gandavo Diocesis Saresbiriensis AD 1297-1315, C T Flowers and M C B Dawes, eds, (1934).

J Scott, 1981, *The Early History of Glastonbury: an Edition, Translation and Study of William of Malmesbury's De Antiquitate Glastonie Ecclesie*

Taxatio Ecclesiastica Angliae et Walliae, Auctoritate P. Nicholai IV, circa *AD 1291,* J Caley, ed., Record Commission (1834)

*Vetus Registrum Sarisberiense alias dictum Registrum S. Osmundi Episcopi,*W R Jones, ed., (1883).

William of Malmesbury, *De Gestis Pontificum Anglorum*, Rolls Series 52 (1870).

Secondary Works

J Acton, 1895, 'Iwerne Church', *PDNHAS* 16, pp.44-7.

T Allen, 1991, 'Sturminster Marshall', *PDNHAS* 113, p.170.

F Arnold-Foster, 1899, *Studies in Church Dedications or England's Patron Saints*.

M Aston, 1985, *Interpreting the Landscape: Landscape Archaeology in Local Studies*.

M Aston et al., 1989-1995, *The Shapwick Project*, Reports 1-6.

M Aston and R Leech, 1977, *Historic Towns in Somerset: Archaeology and Planning*.

M Aston, D Austin and C Dyer, eds, 1989, *The Rural Settlements of Medieval England: Studies Dedicated to Maurice Beresford and John Hurst*.

M A Aston and C Lewis, 1994, *The Medieval Landscape of Wessex*.

D Baker, ed., 1979, *The Church in Town and Countryside*.

A Ballard and J Tait, 1923, *British Borough Charters 1216-1307*.

K Barker, 1977, 'The origins of Sherborne: a preliminary report', *PDNHAS* 99, pp.127-8.

K Barker, 1982, 'The early history of Sherborne', in S M Pearce, *The Early Church in Western Britain and Ireland*, pp.77-116.

K Barker, 1984, 'Sherborne in Dorset: An early ecclesiastical settlement and its estate', in *Anglo-Saxon Studies in Archaeology and History* 3, pp.1-33.

K Barker, 1988, 'Aelric the Mass-priest and the Anglo-Saxon estates of Cerne Abbey', in K Barker, ed., *The Cerne Abbey Millenium Lectures*, pp.27-42.

K Barker and R Kain, 1991, *Maps and History in South-West England*.

M W Barley, ed., 1976, *The Plans and Topography of Medieval Towns in England and Wales*, CBA Research Report 14.

M Beresford and H P R Finberg, 1973, *English Medieval Boroughs: a Handlist*.

W Stuart Best, 1955, 'Evidence for a British Origin for Sherborne', *SDNQ*, pp.189-90.

J H Bettey, 1987, *Church and Parish: A Guide for Local Historians*.

M Biddle, 1976, 'The evolution of towns: planned towns before 1066' in M W Barley, ed., *The Plans and Topography of Medieval Towns in England and Wales*, CBA Research Report 14, pp.19-32.

B Bischoff and M Lapidge, 1994, *The Biblical Commentaries from the Canterbury School of Theodore and Hadrian*.

J Blair, 1985, 'Secular minster churches in Domesday Book', in P H Sawyer, ed., *Domesday Book: A Reassessment*, pp. 104-42.

J Blair, 1988a, 'Introduction: from minster to parish church', in J Blair, ed., *Minsters and Parish Churches: The Local Church in Transition 950-1200*.

J Blair, ed., 1988b, *Minsters and Parish Churches: The Local Church in Transition 950-1200*.

J Blair, 1988c, 'Minster churches in the landscape', in D Hooke, ed., *Anglo-Saxon Settlements*, pp.35-58.

J Blair, 1991, *Early Medieval Surrey: Landholding, Church and Settlement Before 1300*.

J Blair, 1992, 'Anglo-Saxon minsters: a topographical review', in J Blair and R Sharpe, eds, *Pastoral Care Before the Parish*, pp.226-66.

J Blair, 1994, *Anglo-Saxon Oxfordshire*.

J Blair, 1995, 'Debate: Ecclesiastical organization and pastoral care in Anglo-Saxon England', *EME* 4.2, pp.193-212.

J Blair, 1996, 'Palaces or minsters? Northampton and Cheddar reconsidered', *ASE* 25, pp.97-121.

J Blair, and R Sharpe, eds, 1992, *Pastoral Care Before the Parish*.

C J Bond, 1977, 'The topography of Pershore' in C J Bond and A M Hunt, 'Recent archaeological work in Pershore', *VEHSRP* 6, pp.2-38.

C J Bond and A M Hunt, 1977, 'Recent archaeological work in Pershore', *VEHSPR* 6, pp.1-76.

J Bourdillon, 1988, 'Countryside and town: the animal resources of Saxon Southampton' in D Hooke, ed., *Anglo-Saxon Settlements*, pp.177-195.

R V H Burne, 1969, 'Church dedications in Dorset', *PDNHAS* 90, pp.269-281.

I Burrow, 1981, *Hillfort and Hilltop Settlement in Somerset in the First to Eighth Centuries AD*, BAR British Series 81.

M M C Calthrop, 'Ecclesiastical History' in VCH *Dorset* 2 pp.1-90.

E Cambridge and D Rollason, 1995, 'Debate: The pastoral organization of the Anglo-Saxon church: a review of the "Minster Hypothesis"', *EME* 4.1, pp.87-104.

J Campbell, 1979a, 'The church in Anglo-Saxon towns', in D Baker, ed., *The Church in Town and Countryside*, pp.119-135.

J Campbell, 1979b, 'Bede's words for places' in P H Sawyer, ed., *Names, Words and Graves:Early Medieval Settlement*, pp.34-54.

H B Clarke, and H Brennan, eds, 1981, *Columbanus and Merovingian Monasticism*.

M Clayton, 1990, *The Cult of the Virgin Mary in Anglo-Saxon England*.

R Coates, 1989, *The Place-Names of Hampshire*.

D Coe, and J W Hawkes, 1992, 'Excavations at 29 High Street, Wimborne Minster, Dorset, 1990', *PDNHAS* 114, pp.135-44.

J Coker, 1732, *A Survey of Dorsetshire*.

G Constable, 1984, *Monastic Tithes From Their Origins to the Twelfth Century*.

M R G Conzen, 1960, 'Alnwick, Northumberland: A study in town plan analysis', *Institute of British Geographers* 27.

M Costen, 1992a, *The Origins of Somerset*.

M Costen, 1992b, 'Dunstan, Glastonbury and the economy of Somerset in the tenth century', in N Ramsay, M Sparks, and T Tatton-Brown, eds, *St Dunstan: His Life, TImes and Cult*, pp.25-44.

P H Coulstock, 1993, *The Collegiate Church of Wimborne Minster*, Studies in the History of Medieval Religion 5.

B Cox, 1976, 'The place-names of the earliest English records', *JEPNS* 8, pp.12-66.

P W Cox, 1992, 'Excavations at the former site of the Wimborne Model Town, 1991', *PDNHAS* 114, pp.145-50.

J H Denton, 1970, *English Royal Free Chapels, 1100-1300: A Constitutional Study*.

O A W Dilke, 1971, *The Roman Land Surveyors: An Introduction to the Agrimensores*.

C Druitt, 1898, 'The church of St Candida and St Cross at Whitchurch Canonicorum', *PDNHAS* 19, pp.145-9.

R W Dunning and R J E Bush, 1978, 'Crewkerne' in R W Dunning, ed, *VCH Somerset 4*, pp.4-38.

N Edwards and A Lane, 1992, *The Early Church in Wales and the West*.

E Ekwall, 1960, 4th edn, *The Concise Oxford Dictionary of English Place-Names*.

A Everitt, 1977, 'River and wold, reflections on the historical origin of regions and pays', *JHG* 3, pp.1-19.

A Everitt, 1986, *Continuity and Colonization: The Evolution of Kentish Settlement*.

R W Eyton, 1878, *A Key to Domesday, showing the Method and Exactitude of its Mensuration, and the precise Meaning of its More Usual Formulae: Analysis and Digest of the Dorset Survey*.

A Fagersten, 1978, *The Place-Names of Dorset*.

D H Farmer, 1978, *Oxford Dictionary of Saints*.

N H Field, 1972, 'The Leaze, Wimborne: An excavation in a deserted medieval quarter of the town', *PDNHAS* 99, pp.49-62.

N H Field, 1992, *Dorset and the Second Legion*.

H P R Finberg, 1955, *Roman and Saxon Withington: A Study in Continuity*, Department of English Local History Occasional Paper No. 8.

H P R Finberg, 1964a, *Lucerna*.

H P R Finberg, 1964b, *The Early Charters of Wessex*.

H P R Finberg, 1972, *The Early Charters of the West Midlands*.

R Fleming, 1985, 'Monastic lands and England's defence in the Viking age', *EHR* 100, pp. 247-265.

S R I Foot, 1989, 'Anglo-Saxon minsters AD597-*ca*900: the religious life in England before the Benedictine Reform', unpubl. Ph.D. thesis, Cambridge.

S R I Foot, 1992, 'Anglo-Saxon minsters: a review of terminology' in J. Blair and R. Sharpe, eds, *Pastoral Care Before the Parish*, pp.212-225.

J Fowler, 1951, *Mediaeval Sherborne*.

H S A Fox, 1970 'The boundary of Uplyme', *TDA* 102, pp.35-47.

M J Franklin, 1986, 'Identification of minsters in the Midlands', in *Anglo-Norman Studies 7*, pp.69-88.

E A Fry, 1915, 'The Augmentation Books: 1650-1660 in Lambeth Palace', *PDNHAS* 36, pp.48-105.

M Gelling, 1978, *Signposts to the Past: Place-Names and the History of England*.

M Gelling in P Rahtz, A Woodward, I Burrow, A Everton, L Watts, P Leach, S Hirch, P Fowler, K Gardner, 1992, *Cadbury Congresbury 1968-73: A Late/Post Roman Hilltop Settlement in Somerset*.

C Gerrard, 1987, 'Trade and settlement in medieval Somerset', unpubl. Ph.D. thesis, University of Bristol.

J H P Gibb, 1975, 'The Anglo-Saxon cathedral at Sherborne', *ArchJ* 132, pp.71-110.

R Good, 1966, *Old Roads of Dorset*.

A H Graham, 1984, 'Wimborne Minster, Dorset -excavations in the town centre, 1983', *PDNHAS* 106, pp.74-86.

R Graham, 1929, 'English Ecclesiastical Studies*, Chapter 11, 'The taxation of Pope Nicholas IV, pp.271-301.

M Green, 1990, 'A Roman building in Gussage St Andrew', *PDNHAS* 112, p.117.

D Hall, 1988, 'The late Saxon countryside: villages and their fields' in D Hooke, ed., *Anglo-Saxon Settlements*, pp.99-122.

T Hall, 1990, 'Excavations at the parish church of All Saints, Chalbury, Dorset, 1989', *PDNHAS* 112, pp.43-50.

T Hall, 1993, 'Witchampton: village origins', *PDNHAS* 115, pp.121-132.

T Hall and A Sims, 1984, 'Observations at Mill Lane, Wimborne', *PDNHAS* 106, p.123.

F E Harmer, 1989, 2nd edn, *Anglo-Saxon Writs*.

P H Hase, 1975, 'The development of the parish in Hampshire, particularly in the eleventh and twelfth centuries', unpubl. Ph.D. thesis, University of Cambridge.

P H Hase, 1988, 'The mother churches of Hampshire', in J. Blair, ed., *Minsters and Parish Churches: The Local Church in Transition 950-1200*, pp.45-66.

P H Hase, 1994, 'The church in the Wessex heartlands', in M A Aston and C Lewis, eds, *The Medieval Landscape of Wessex*, pp.47-81.

J Haslam, 1984, *Anglo-Saxon Towns in Southern England*.

J Haslam, 1988a, 'The Anlgo-Saxon burh at *Wigingamere*', *Landscape History* 10, pp.25-36.

J Haslam, 1988b, 'Parishes, churches, wards and gates in eastern London' in J Blair, ed., *Minsters and Parish Churches: The Local Church in Transition 950-1200*, pp.35-43.

J M Hassal and D Hill, 1970, 'Pont De L'Arche: Frankish influence on the West Saxon burh?', *ArchJ* 127, pp.188-195.

M J Heaton, 1992, 'Two Mid-Saxon grain-driers and later medieval features at Chantry Fields, Gillingham, Dorset', *PDNHAS* 114, pp.97-126.

D Hill, 1981, *An Atlas of Anglo-Saxon England*.

R Hine, 1914, *The History of Beaminster*.

R Hingley, 1989, *Rural Settlement in Roman Britain*.

D A Hinton, 1977, 'Excavations at Wareham, 1974-5', *PDNHAS* 99, pp.42-83.

D A Hinton, 1987, 'Minsters and royal estates in south-east Dorset', *PDNHAS* 109, pp.50-54.

D A Hinton, 1992, 'The inscribed stones in Lady St Mary Church, Wareham', *PDNHAS* 114, p.260.

D A Hinton, 1994, 'Some Anglo-Saxon charters and estates in South-East Dorset', *PDNHAS* 116, pp.11-20.

D Hooke, 1988, 'Regional variation in southern and central England in the Anglo-Saxon period and its relationship to land units and settlements', in D Hooke, ed., *Anglo-Saxon Settlements*, pp.123-151.

D Hooke, ed., 1988, *Anglo-Saxon Settlements*.

W Horn and E Born, 1979, *The Plan of St Gall: A Study of the Architecture and Economy of, and Life in, a Paradigmatic Carolingian Monastery*.

W G Hoskins, 1952, 'The making of the agrarian landscape', in W G Hoskins and H P R Finberg , *Devonshire Studies*, pp.289-333.

W G Hoskins and H P R Finberg , 1952, *Devonshire Studies*.

W Hudson, 1908, 'The "Norwich Taxation" of 1254, so far as it relates to the Diocese of Norwich', Norfolk Archaeology 17, pp.46-157.

J Hutchins, 3rd edn 1861-70, *History and Antiquities of Dorset* 1-4.

E James, 1981, 'Archaeology and the Merovingian monastery', in H B Clarke and H Brennan, eds, *Columbanus and Merovingian Monasticism*, pp.33-55.

G R J Jones, 1979, 'Multiple estates and early settlement' in P H Sawyer, ed., *English Medieval Settlement*, pp.9-34.

R Kain, R Oliver and J Baker, 1991, 'The tithe surveys of south-west England', in K Barker and R Kain, *Maps and History in South-West England*, pp.89-118.

L J Keen, 1983, 'Archaeological recording in churches', *PDNHAS* 105, p.152.

L J Keen, 1984, 'The towns of Dorset', in J Haslam, ed., *Anglo-Saxon Towns in Southern England*, pp.203-247.

L J Keen, 1991, 'A ninth-century mount from Bowleaze Cove, Weymouth', *PDNHAS* 113, p.184.

B R Kemp, 1968, 'The churches of Berkeley Hernesse', *TBGAS* 87, pp.96-110.

S Keynes, 1989, 'The lost cartulary of Abbotsbury Abbey', *ASE* 18, pp.207-243.

M K Lawson, 1993, *Cnut: The Danes in England in the Early Eleventh Century*.

E Levien, 1872, 'Wareham and its religious houses', *JBAA* 28, pp.154-170 and 244-258.

R N Lucas, 1993, *The Romano-British Villa at Halstock, Dorset: Excavations 1967-1985*.

A D Mills, 1977-89, *The Place-Names of Dorset 1-3*, EPNS, 52,53,59/60.

A D Mills, 1986, *Dorset Place-Names: Their Origins and Meanings*.

G S Minchin, 1908, 'Table of Population' in W Page, ed., *VCH Dorset* 2, pp. 264-273.

R Morris, 1989, *Churches in the Landscape*.

R Morris and J Roxan, 1980, 'Churches on Roman buildings', in W J Rodwell, ed., *Temples, Churches and Religion: Recent Research in Roman Britain* BAR 77, pp.175-203.

A D Morton, 1992, *Excavations at Hamwic, Volume 1, Excavations 1946-83, excluding Six Dials and Melbourne St*, CBA Research Report 84.

E Murphy, 1991, 'Anglo-Saxon Abbey Shaftesbury - Bectun's base or Alfred's foundation?', *PDNHAS* 113, pp.23-32.

G Noll, 1982, 'The origin of the so-called plan of St Gall', *Journal of Medieval History* 8, 191-240.

M A O'Donovan, 1988, *Anglo-Saxon Charters III: Charters of Sherborne*.

E Okasha, 1993, *Corpus of Early Christian Inscribed Stones of South-West Britain*.

N Orme, 1991, 'From the beginnings to 1050', in N. Orme, ed., *Unity and Variety: A History of the Church in Devon and Cornwall*, pp. 1-22.

N Orme, ed., 1991, *Unity and Variety: A History of the Church in Devon and Cornwall*.

D M Owen, 1971, *Church and Society in Medieval Lincolnshire*.

D M Owen, 1975, 'Medieval chapels in Lincolnshire', *LHA* 10, pp.15-23.

O J Padel, 1988, *Cornish Place-Name Elements*, EPNS 56/57.

W Page, 1908, ed., *VCH Dorset* 2.

W Page, 1915, 'Some remarks on the churches of the Domesday Survey', *Archaeologia* 66, pp.61-102.

S M Pearce, 1973, 'The dating of some Celtic dedications and hagiographical traditions in South Western Britain', *The Devonshire Association* 105, pp.95-120.

S M Pearce, 1978, *The Kingdom of Dumnonia: Studies in History and Tradition in South-Western Britain AD 350-1150*.

S M Pearce, 1982, 'Estates and church sites in Dorset and Gloucestershire: the emergence of a Christian society', in, S M Pearce, ed., *The Early Church in Western Britain and Ireland: Studies Presented to C A Ralegh Radford* BAR British Series 102, pp.117-138.

S M Pearce, ed., 1982, *The Early Church in Western Britain and Ireland: Studies Presented to C A Ralegh Radford*.

K J Penn, 1980, *Historic Towns in Dorset*.

C Phythian-Adams, 1993, 'Introduction: an agenda for English Local History', in C Phythian-Adams, *Societies, Cultures and Kinship, 1580-1850: Cultural Provinces and English Local History*, pp.1-23.

C Phythian-Adams, 1993, *Societies, Cultures and Kinship, 1580-1850: Cultural Provinces and English Local History*.

F P Pitfield, 1981, *Dorset Churches A-D*.

F P Pitfield, 1978, *Bere Regis*.

F P Pitfield, 1985, *Purbeck Parish Churches*.

A Preston-Jones, 1992, 'Decoding Cornish churchyards' in N Edwards and A Lane *The Early Church in Wales and the West*, pp.104-124.

R B Pugh, ed., 1968, *VCH Dorset* 3.

P Rahtz, 1959, 'Holworth, Medieval Village Excavation 1958', *PDNHAS* 81, pp.127-147.

P Rahtz, A Woodward, I Burrow, A Everton, L Watts, P Leach, S Hirch, P Fowler, K Gardner, 1992, *Cadbury Congresbury 1968-73: A Late/Post Roman Hilltop Settlement in Somerset*.

C A Ralegh Radford, 1962, 'The church in Somerset down to 1100', *Proceedings of the Somerset Archaeology and Natural History Society* 106, pp.28-45.

N Ramsay, M Sparks, and T Tatton-Brown, eds, 1992, *St Dunstan: His Life, Times and Cult*.

RCHM, 1959, 'Wareham West Walls', *MA* 3, pp.120-138.

RCHM, 1952-1976, *Dorset* 1-5.

O J Reichel, 1939, 'The church and the hundreds in Devon', *TDA* 71, pp.331-42.

M Richardson, 1996, 'Parish boundaries, minster *parochiae*, and parish fragmentation in Leicestershire: new methods of boundary analysis', unpubl. MA dissertation, University of Leicester.

S J Ridyard, 1988, *The Royal Saints of Anglo-Saxon England: A Study of West Saxon and East-Anglian Cults*.

B K Roberts, 1985, 'Village patterns and forms: some models for discussion' in D Hooke, ed., *Medieval Villages:A Review of Current Work*, OUCA Monograph 5, pp.7-25.

B K Roberts, 1987, *The Making of the English Village*.

B K Roberts, 1989, 'Nucleation and dispersion: distribution maps as a research tool' in M Aston, D Austin and C Dyer, eds, *The Rural Settlements of Medieval England: Studies Dedicated to Maurice Beresford and John Hurst*, pp.59-75.

W Rodwell, 1993, *The Origins and Early Development of Witham, Essex: A Study in Settlement and Fortification, Prehistoric to Medieval*, Oxbow Monograph 26.

P H Sawyer, ed., 1968, *Anglo-Saxon Charters: An Annotated List and Bibliography*.

P H Sawyer, ed., 1979, *English Medieval Settlement*.

P H Sawyer, ed., 1985, *Domesday Book: A Reassessment*.

J Sheppard, 1976, 'Medieval village planning in Northern England: some evidence from Yorkshire', *JHG* 2, pp.3-20

R Shoesmith, 1982, *Hereford City Excavations: Excavations On And Close To The Defences*, Vol. 2, CBA Research Report 46

T R Slater, 1984, 'The topography and planning of medieval Lichfield: a critique', *TSSAHS* 26, pp.11-35.

T R Slater, 1990, 'The English medieval new towns with composite plans: evidence from the Midlands', in T R Slater, ed., *The Built Form of Western Cities*, pp.60-82.

T R Slater, ed., 1990, *The Built Form of Western Cities*.

A H Smith, 1956, *English Place-Name Elements* 1, EPNS 25.

A Smyth, 1995, *King Alfred the Great*.

C Sparey-Green, 1988, 'Excavations at the Town Farm House site, Sixpenny Handley, Dorset, 1988', *PDNHAS* 110, pp. 155-6.

G Squibb, Sept. 1984, 'The foundation of Cerne Abbey', *SDNQ*, pp.373-376.

P A Stafford, 1980, 'The "Farm of one night" and the organization of King Edward's Estates in Domesday', *EHR* 2nd Series 33, pp.491-502.

D Stanislawski, 1946, 'The origin and spread of the grid-pattern town', *Geographical Review* 36, pp.105-120.

D W A Startin, 1981, 'Excavations at the Old Vicarage, Fordington, Dorchester', *PDNHAS* 103, pp.43-66.

F Stenton, 3rd edn, 1971, *Anglo-Saxon England*.

M G Stuart, 1892, 'The proceedings of the Dorset Natural History and Antiquarian Field Club during the season 1890-91', *PDNHAS* 12.

H Sumner, 1924, 'Roman Britain in 1924', *JRS* 14.

C H Talbot, 1959, 'The life of St Wulsin of Sherborne by Goscelin', *Revue Bénédictine* 69, pp.68-85.

C C Taylor, 1967, 'Wimborne Minster', *PDNHAS* 89, pp.168-170.

C C Taylor, 1970, *The Making of the English Landscape: Dorset*.

C C Taylor, 1977, 'Polyfocal settlement and the English Village', *MA* 21, pp.189-93.

C C Taylor, 1983, *Village and Farmstead: A History of Rural Settlement in England*.

C C Taylor, 1987, *Fields in the Landscape*.

H M Taylor and J Taylor, 1965, *Anglo-Saxon Architecture* 2.

H M Taylor, 1978, *Anglo-Saxon Architecture* 3.

A Thacker, 1992, 'Monks, preaching and pastoral care in early Anglo-Saxon England', in J Blair and R Sharpe, eds, *Pastoral Care Before the Parish*, pp. 137-170.

C Thomas, 1971, *The Early Christian Archaeology of North Britain*.

C Thomas, 1985, 2nd edn, *Christianity in Roman Britain to AD500*.

F Thorn, 1991, 'Hundreds and wapentakes', in A Williams and G H Martin, eds, *The Dorset Domesday: Introduction and Translation*, pp.27-44.

C Thornton, 1988, 'The demesne of Rimpton, 938 to 1412; a study in economic development', unpubl. Ph. D thesis, University of Leicester.

J P Traskey, 1978, *Milton Abbey: A Dorset Monastery in the Middle Ages*.

D A Whitehead, 1982, 'The historical background to the city defences', in R Shoesmith, *Hereford City Excavations: Excavations On And Close To The Defences*, Vol. 2, CBA Research Report 46, pp.13-24.

A Williams, 1968, 'Domesday Survey', in R B Pugh, ed., *VCH, Dorset* 3.

A Williams and G H Martin, eds, 1991, *The Dorset Domesday*.

A Winchester, 1990, *Discovering Parish Boundaries*.

A Woodward and P Leach, 1993, *The Uley Shrines: Excavation of a ritual complex on West Hill, Uley, Gloucesterhire 1977-9*.

P J Woodward, 1983, 'Wimborne Minster, Dorset - Excavations in the town centre 1975-80', *PDNHAS* 105, pp.57-74.

P J Woodward, 1994, 'Dorset Archaeology', *PDNHAS* 116, p.130.

D Woolner and A Woolner, 1962, 'The antecedents of Whitchurch Canonicorum, Dorset', *PDNHAS* 83, p.83.

S Youngs, J Clark, D Gaimster and T Barry, 1988, 'Medieval Britain and Ireland in 1987', *MA* 32.

B Yorke, 1990, *Kings and Kingdoms of Early Anglo-Saxon England*.

B Yorke, 1995, *Wessex in the Early Middle Ages*.

INDEX

115

Shapwick Grange (Dev) 31
Shene Priory 15
Sherborne 2, 4, 11, 13, 15, 20, 21,
24, 25, 29, 31, 33, 35, 37, 38, 41,
45, 47, 49, 53, 62, 66, 75, 76, 77,
78, 82, 83, 90
Sherborne Abbey 40, 72, 79, 93, 95,
100
Shilvinghampton 20
Shipton Gorge 90, 95
Sigferth 8
Silton 15
Sir Richard de Mandevil 13
Sixpenny Handley 19, 24, 40, 68,
79, 100
Sixpenny hundred 44
Solignac 76
Somerset 8, 26, 28, 77, 79
South Perrott 45
Spetisbury 17
Stafford 19
Stalbridge 40, 72, 100
Stanborough 35,
Stanton St Gabriel 13, 31, 38
Stapleford 95
Stigand 17, 44, 47
Stockwood 11, 13, 19, 100
Stratton 93
Street (Som) 29
Studland 20, 21, 93
Sturminster Marshall 4, 17, 25, 28,
41, 44, 47, 58, 62, 66, 77, 79
Sturminster Newton 19, 58, 66, 75,
95, 100
Sturthill 90
Surrey 47
Sutton Poyntz 19, 25, 47, 72, 100
Sutton Waldon 35
Swanage 20, 93
Sydling St Nicholas 40, 68, 100
Symondsbury 20, 31, 38
Synod of Hatfield 82
Synod of Whitby 2, 82

Tarrant Crawford 20, 24
Tarrant Gunville 95
Tarrant Launceston 100
Tarrant Monkton 68, 100
Tatton 20
Tawton (Dev) 25
Tewkesbury Abbey 95
Thame (Oxon) 76, 78, 83
Theodore 2, 11, 76, 82, 83
Thornford 11, 33, 37
Thornton 17
Toller Porcorum 41, 83
Torrington (Dev) 25
Trent 33
Turner's Puddle 15

Uley (Gloucs) 83
Upbury 62
Uploders 95
Uplyme (Dev) 31, 33

Upsydling 100
Upwimborne 95

Waddon 20
Wales 83
Wareham 2, 4, 11, 13, 15, 28, 30,
31, 35, 41, 44, 47, 56, 79, 82, 83,
100, 101
Watchet 29
Waterston 17
Wells 13, 84
Wellwood 45
Wessex 1, 2
West Chaldon 93
West Lulworth 100
West Milton 95
West Parley 82
West Stour 15
Whitchurch Canonicorum 4, 13, 20,
24, 25, 26, 28, 31, 33, 38, 40, 41,
44, 49, 53, 56, 66, 77
Whitcombe 19
William 38
William of Malmesbury 15, 90
Wiltshire 5, 8, 26, 95
Wimborne All Saints 95
Wimborne Minster 2, 4, 8, 11, 20,
21, 24, 25, 26, 29, 41, 45, 47, 50,
53, 66, 62, 66, 75, 76, 77, 79, 82
Winfrith Newburgh 28, 66, 93, 100
Winterborne Abbas 44
Winterborne Farrindon 19
Winterborne Kingston 15, 17, 38
Winterborne Monkton 19
Winterborne Tomson 15, 38
Witchampton 24, 47, 75, 95
Withington (Gloucs) 1, 24
Wolveton 93
Woodbury 15
Wootton Abbas 48
Wootton Fitzpaine 13, 31, 49
Worgret 35
Worth Matravers 20, 93
Wrington (Som) 24
Wulfsige, bishop 11, 13, 90
Wyke Farm 37
Wytherstone 95
Yetminster 13, 19, 25, 40, 45, 66,
62, 64, 100, 101